# SOLDIERS AND STATESMEN

# SOLDIERS AND STATESMEN

## REFLECTIONS ON LEADERSHIP

## John S. D. Eisenhower

UNIVERSITY OF MISSOURI PRESS    COLUMBIA AND LONDON

5  4  3  2  1     16  15  14  13  12

Cataloging-in-Publication data available from the Library of Congress.
ISBN 978-0-8262-1970-1

∞™ This paper meets the requirements of the
American National Standard for Permanence of Paper
for Printed Library Materials, Z39.48, 1984.

Designer: Kristie Lee
Typesetter: K. Lee Design & Graphics
Printer and binder: Thomson-Shore, Inc.
Typefaces: Palatino and Impact

# To Fred Ladd

# Contents

## The Western European Theater, including the Mediterranean

Map by Chris Robinson

## Tunisia–Last Phases

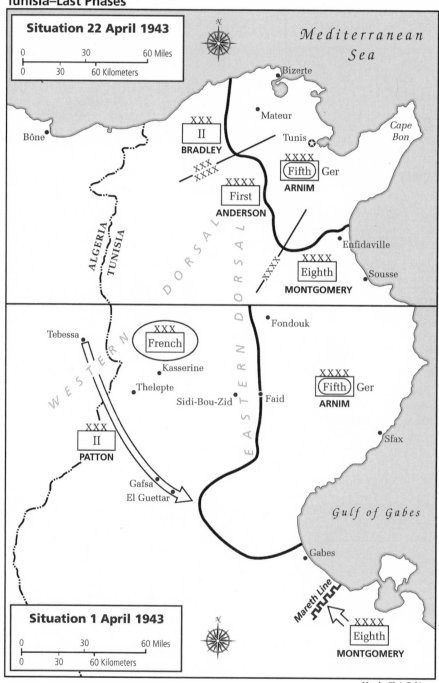

**Situation 22 April 1943**

0   30   60 Miles
0   30   60 Kilometers

*Mediterranean Sea*

Bizerte

Bône

Mateur

Tunis

*Cape Bon*

XXX
II
**BRADLEY**

XXX
XXXX

XXXX
Fifth   Ger
**ARNIM**

XXXX
First
**ANDERSON**

ALGERIA
TUNISIA

*DORSAL*

*DORSAL*

XXXX

Enfidaville

XXXX
Eighth
**MONTGOMERY**

Sousse

**Situation 1 April 1943**

Tebessa

XXX
French

Kasserine

Thelepte

Sidi-Bou-Zid   Faid

Fondouk

*EASTERN DORSAL*

*WESTERN*

XXXX
Fifth   Ger
**ARNIM**

Sfax

XXX
II
**PATTON**

Gafsa
El Guettar

*Gulf of Gabes*

Gabes

Mareth Line

XXXX
Eighth
**MONTGOMERY**

0   30   60 Miles
0   30   60 Kilometers

Map by Chris Robinson

x

## Landings in Sicily and Italy, 1943

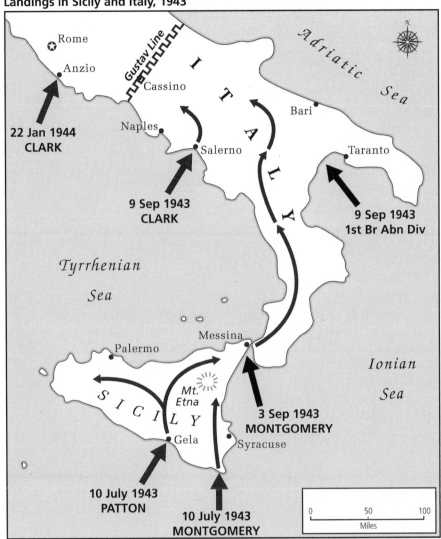

Rome

Anzio

Gustav Line

Cassino

**22 Jan 1944
CLARK**

Naples

Salerno

**9 Sep 1943
CLARK**

*Adriatic Sea*

*I T A L Y*

Bari

Taranto

**9 Sep 1943
1st Br Abn Div**

*Tyrrhenian Sea*

Palermo

Messina

*Ionian Sea*

Mt. Etna

*S I C I L Y*

Gela

Syracuse

**3 Sep 1943
MONTGOMERY**

**10 July 1943
PATTON**

**10 July 1943
MONTGOMERY**

| 0 | 50 | 100 |
|---|---|---|

Miles

*Map by Chris Robinson*

## Pre – D-Day Allied Plan for the Final Offensive in Germany

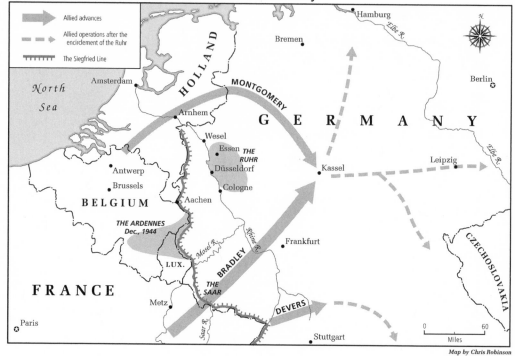

Map by Chris Robinson

# Breakout in Normandy, August 1944

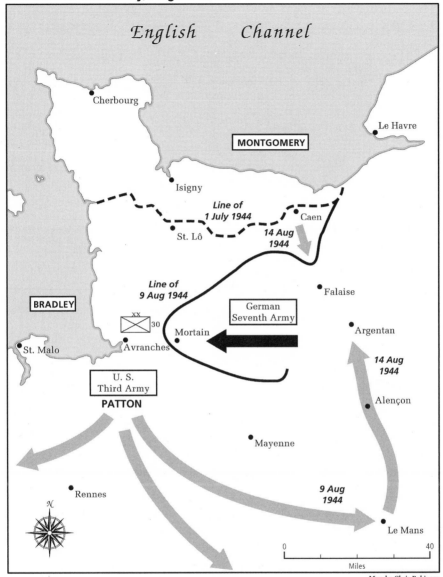

Map by Chris Robinson

## MacArthur's Landings, 1944

C H I N A

OKINAWA

IWO JIMA

FORMOSA

*Pacific Ocean*

Hong Kong

**NIMITZ**
XXXXX
**MACARTHUR**

HAINAN

LUZON

*South*

*China*

MARIANA ISLANDS

**PHILIPPINES**

**INDOCHINA**

Manila

MINDORO

GUAM

*Sea*

**20 Oct.
(Leyte)**

**15 Dec.**

MINDANAO

**15 Sep.**

CAROLINE ISLANDS

**MALAYA**

**30 Jul.**

**17 May**

**22 Apr.**

**2 Jan.**

Singapore

BORNEO

CELEBES

NEW GUINEA

NEW
BRITAIN

*D U T C H   E A S T   I N D I E S*

SUMATRA

JAVA

Port
Moresby

TIMOR

XXXXX
SWP

*Coral
Sea*

*Indian Ocean*

**A U S T R A L I A**

0          400          800
Miles

Map by Chris Robinson

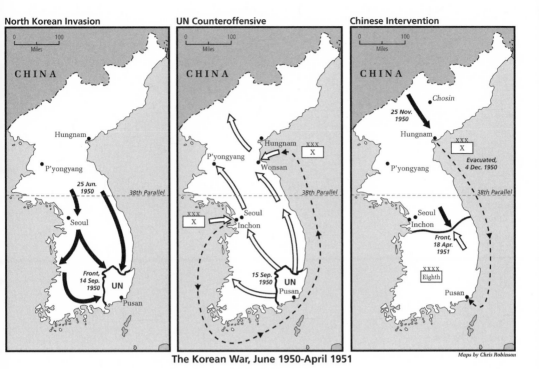

**North Korean Invasion**

CHINA

Hungnam

P'yongyang

*38th Parallel*

*25 Jun. 1950*

Seoul

*Front, 14 Sep. 1950*

UN

Pusan

**UN Counteroffensive**

CHINA

Hungnam

P'yongyang

Wonsan

XXX
X

*38th Parallel*

XXX
X

Seoul
Inchon

*15 Sep. 1950*

UN

Pusan

**Chinese Intervention**

CHINA

Chosin

*25 Nov. 1950*

Hungnam

XXX
X

*Evacuated, 4 Dec. 1950*

P'yongyang

*38th Parallel*

Seoul
Inchon

*Front, 18 Apr. 1951*

XXXX
Eighth

Pusan

**The Korean War, June 1950-April 1951**

*Maps by Chris Robinson*

# Acknowledgments

As with all my books for nearly twenty years, I have relied on Mrs. Dorothy W. (Dodie) Yentz to keep the manuscript in an orderly condition, to prepare it for final submission, and to perform a myriad of other functions. We are truly partners in the enterprise.

My wife, Joanne, as always, took time out from her own book to provide suggestions and encouragement. She practically took over the procurement of photographs, assisted greatly by Jeff Bridgers, of the Prints and Photographs Division of the Library of Congress.

Friends have also helped, especially Professor Louis D. Rubin Jr., of Chapel Hill, North Carolina, who provides editorial comments on request and above all encouragement. And Mitchell Yockelson, of the National Archives, assists with all my work and provided photographs from that source.

Stacy Meuli, of the Eisenhower Library, helped in procuring photographs.

My thanks also go to my expert topographer Chris Robinson, for his competence and patience.

Kara Lesinski and Sylvia Graham, of the Association of Graduates, West Point, provided invaluable obituaries for deceased members of the Military Academy.

I am also indebted (in alphabetical order) to John H. (Jack) Cushman, Dorothy Daniel, David Driscoll, Robert Ferrell, Judy Haddaway, Daniel D. Holt, Beverly Jarrett, June Koch, Gerard F. McCauley, and Robert and Cecelia Nobel.

It would have been a lonely chore indeed without the privilege of sharing the experience with all of them.

# Author's Note

In the course of a long career writing on political-military subjects, I have become convinced that many readers have too often labored under false assumptions in dealing with the Second World War and the years immediately following. Most Americans have, for example, bought into British prime minister Winston Churchill's calculated image as being "half-American" in his sentiments rather than "all British," as he really was. Another example has been a tendency to underestimate, even deride, the contributions of General Mark W. Clark, whom I regard, despite his glaring faults, as one of the great figures of the war. To add a third example, the eventual break that occurred between Harry Truman and Dwight Eisenhower has left the impression with many people that the relationship was sour from the beginning. Such was far from the case.

Admittedly, none of these issues is earthshaking. The Second World War was won, and Truman and Eisenhower together helped ensure that we survived the cold war that followed. Nevertheless, I have developed an itch to set the record straight, at least as I saw it. From time to time, therefore, I have taken a moment out from other activities to write a few essays to put my views on paper. As I went on, my subject list expanded to include descriptions of men who I believed deserve more recognition than they have received. Hence this small book.

My viewpoint is admittedly subjective. Though much of my material has been drawn from my writings, my viewpoint has been influenced by many long and informal conversations with my father, Dwight D. Eisenhower. And I personally met nearly all the men described in these pages. When I first started out, I tried to leave myself completely out of the picture. I soon discovered, however, that doing so would be impossible. I could never, for example, have described Churchill's frustration at Whitehall during the storm of June 1944 without explaining how I came to be there.

I first came into the privileged position of observer in early June 1944, just after the Allied landings in Normandy. On orders from General George C. Marshall, Army Chief of Staff, I sailed that same day from the New York Port of Embarkation aboard the British liner *Queen Mary*, then in use as an American troopship. A week later the *Queen Mary* docked in Scotland, and I joined my father in London. Our visit extended a little more than two weeks, at the end of which I returned to Fort Benning to attend the Infantry School. Then, a year later, with the European war over, my father took me with him as a temporary aide on some very informative trips. More than ten years later I served in the White House as a junior officer. Personal experiences, then, have contributed mightily to the views I express in these pages.

There is no rhyme or reason for the order in which these essays are arranged. I chose to spare myself the responsibility of devising an order of merit. The same haphazard sequence applies to the appendix, "Home Movies," in which I indulge myself by presenting irreverent vignettes of a military life, most of which I found amusing.

As I went through several drafts of the manuscript, I began to realize, to my surprise, what a critical influence George Marshall exerted on nearly every subject of this book. Churchill, though often at odds with Marshall, once called him "the noblest Roman of them all." Harry Truman idolized him. Mark Clark, Terry Allen, Omar Bradley, Matthew Ridgway, and to some extent George Patton were his protégés. Of my subjects, Marshall's only critic—a severe one—was Douglas MacArthur, who never ceased to believe, throughout the war, that Marshall was secretly conspiring against him. I did not attempt to include an essay of Marshall, however; the job would be too big.

As with any antiquated storyteller, I owe the reader the disclaimer that, to quote British diplomat Sir Alfred Duff Cooper, "Old Men Forget." There will be places where my memory will be faulty. I only hope that they are not too extensive.

# SOLDIERS AND STATESMEN

Prime Minister Winston S. Churchill (Library of Congress)

# 1

# Churchill, a Formidable Ally

There is only one thing worse than fighting with allies, and that is fighting without them

—Winston Churchill

Prime Minister Winston Churchill, behind his desk in the British War Office at Whitehall, London, was in a foul mood. The date was June 20, 1944, two weeks after the Allies had landed in Normandy, on June 6. Outside his window the worst storm in fifty years was raging over Great Britain and the English Channel, a storm so violent that it could conceivably destroy the Anglo-American OVERLORD beachheads on the coast of Normandy. The fruits of years of preparation were in greater peril that day than they had been on the better-remembered D-day itself.

In Churchill's office, for a short visit, was my father, General Dwight D. Eisenhower, with me present as an aide. Dad and I had been planning to visit OMAHA Beach, in Normandy, the day before. Now we found ourselves marooned in Dad's "Telegraph Cottage" south of London, incapable of taking any action whatsoever. Frustrated at his enforced isolation, Dad decided to drive up to London to see Prime Minister Winston Churchill.

After minimal greetings, all three of us sat down at the large table in Churchill's office and said little except for Churchill's fretting over the situation. He slouched in his chair, glaring at the floor. "They have no right," he growled, "to give us weather like this!" So sure was he of the rightness of the Allied cause that he took this storm as a personal affront on the part of the Almighty to himself.

No business of any substance was discussed. The two men, British prime minister and Supreme Commander, were there primarily as friends, taking comfort in sharing their common frustration and to draw strength from each other. What I remember most about the incident is the ease with

1

which they communicated. The personal bond between them would never falter, even though the differences in their official positions and conflict between national interests would sometimes cause them to be rivals for power.

The incident I have described above occurred toward the end of their close association. Eleven months later Hitler committed suicide, and Germany surrendered. It had taken a long time to reach this level of intimacy. Churchill's ties with the Americans, however, especially with President Franklin Roosevelt, had begun well before that.

The Anglo-American alliance of the Second World War did not occur by chance; it was to a large extent the product of Churchill's will and determination. Americans in general were opposed to entering the war. So it was up to Britain to woo them. The courting began formally in April 1940, when Churchill was called from the political wilderness to be first lord of the admiralty. He took the initiative when he wrote Roosevelt a letter in which he proposed a private correspondence on "naval matters." Somewhat disingenuously, he hinted that, as first lord in the First World War, he recalled meeting Roosevelt, who had been assistant secretary of the Navy in the United States. Roosevelt had welcomed the idea of a correspondence, and encouraged it even more when Churchill was elevated to the position of prime minister in May 1940.

By coincidence Churchill came to power on the very day that the panzers of Adolf Hitler launched the blitzkrieg on the western front that resulted in the French surrender and the evacuation of the British Expeditionary Force from Dunkirk across the channel back to Britain. Britain itself was left alone, largely disarmed and protected only by the Royal Navy and the Royal Air Force. If Churchill had ever harbored any doubts of Britain's dependence on the United States, he lost them at that time.

Roosevelt proved to be an easy mark for Churchill's flattery and blandishments. He and his wife, Eleanor, were Anglophiles, having hosted the British king and queen at the White House in 1939. Convinced that Britain must survive the war, he did everything politically possible to aid Britain within the limitations imposed by a reluctant American public. In September 1940 Roosevelt signed an executive order transferring fifty "obsolete" American destroyers to Britain in exchange for the use of some naval bases in the Caribbean. In early 1941 he pushed through Congress the Lend-Lease Act, which essentially absolved Britain from paying for the growing supply of armaments the United States was providing them. In August 1941 the two national leaders met at Argentia, Newfoundland, flashing a message to the world that the United States, though neutral in the European conflict, was "neutral on Britain's side." American and British military staffs began joint planning for the day when the United States would enter the war. By later that year, American warships were exchanging fire with German submarines in the North Atlantic. In effect, the Japanese attack on Pearl Harbor on December 7, 1941, and Hitler's declaration of war three days later were merely confirming a situation that already existed. America was already in the war.

Churchill had long been anticipating the day, and he had already laid his plans for an early conference with Roosevelt. He now had a reason for extra urgency: the Americans might change plans and put their strength against Japan, not Nazi Germany. He wheedled a reluctant invitation from Roosevelt, and on December 12, 1941, he and a large staff left Scotland destined for the United States. While at sea he sent a single message to Roosevelt asking him to reaffirm the previously agreed-on principle of "Europe First." On receiving a quick affirmative reply, he knew that he had already accomplished his most urgent aim.

Churchill's party arrived at Hampton Roads on the evening of December 22, and a plane was waiting to fly him to Washington, where Roosevelt and his right-hand man, Harry Hopkins, were out at the airport. Roosevelt invited Churchill to stay as a personal guest in the White House.

Churchill's main aim now was to make friends with Roosevelt, and the president reciprocated, going all out to accommodate his guest. The two quickly became personal friends. Too much so, it was reported, for the taste of Eleanor Roosevelt, who was uncomfortable over the late hours her husband was keeping in playing the genial host. Another unhappy person was General George Marshall, the American Army Chief of Staff, who feared that the persuasive Churchill might lure Roosevelt into participating in ventures of solely British interest, not desirable to the Americans.[1]

Churchill himself was also under great strain. He was forced to tolerate the large Roosevelt family, bent on celebrating a large, happy Christmas despite the war. He was also called on to speak at the traditional lighting of the national Christmas tree on the Ellipse. But he drew the line at the Christmas dinner. He left early to prepare a speech to the joint session of Congress.

The next day Churchill and his physician were driven to the Capitol to address Congress. He went with trepidation, worried about the reception

---

1. Marshall's discomfiture was heightened by the arrival of Churchill's portable war room, which to Roosevelt's delight was set up in the bedroom right across from Churchill. British officers, carrying impressive red briefcases, had free access to the second floor of the White House, while the American staff was disbarred. Roosevelt subsequently set up a war room of his own.

he would receive. Unlike many of his countrymen, who still thought of the Americans as merely "transplanted Englishmen," he knew better. Further, he was still haunted by the fear that the members individually represented constituents whose thirst for revenge on Japan might tempt them to ignore the European Theater. Churchill's worries turned out to be unfounded, however. The American senators and congressmen vied with each other to laud him.

He was at his most eloquent. In one paragraph he summarized what Americans had been thinking but could not, without his oratorical ability, so eloquently verbalize:

> What sort of people do they [the Axis powers] think we are? Is it possible they do not realize that we shall never cease to persevere against them until they have been taught a lesson which they and the world will never forget? He must indeed have a blind soul who cannot see that some great purpose and design is being worked out here below, of which we have the honor to be the faithful servants. . . . The best tidings of all is that the United States, united as never before, have drawn the sword of freedom and cast away the scabbard.

That concise summary of Allied war aims, though inspirational, was overshadowed by some words spoken at the beginning. Referring to his American-born mother, he remarked, "I cannot help reflecting that if my father had been American and my mother British, instead of the other way around, I might have got here [into the American Congress] on my own." Such flattery struck a responsive chord. From that time forward, not only the Congress but Americans in general looked on the British prime minister as one of their own.

Following the Christmas celebrations and Churchill's address to Congress, the code-named ARCADIA conference settled down in earnest. They were breaking new ground in history. Two strong, proud nations, sharing resources though lacking any formal treaty between them, were now planning ways to employ those resources. Most of the issues fell into the sphere of the military organization, in which the Army Chief of Staff, George C. Marshall, dominated.[2] His greatest accomplishment was to establish a system of theater commands around the world, each consisting of troops from all the services of the Allied nations involved. Some British officers resisted the idea, but Marshall, as an enticement, proposed that the

---

2. Marshall accorded General H. H. Arnold, commander of the U.S. Army Air Forces, equal status on the Joint Chiefs.

first theater commander should be British general Sir Archibald Wavell, who would command all the American, British, and Dutch forces fighting Japan in the Far East. Possibly aided by that carrot, Marshall finally won his point.

The ARCADIA Conference had set up procedures and, more important, had affirmed the Anglo-American plan to concentrate the bulk of their forces on what they considered their main enemy, Nazi Germany, and only when Hitler was destroyed turn their combined might on Japan. Churchill and Roosevelt had not seriously discussed how the war in Europe would be fought. Would the Allies invade France, and if so, when? It was here that Churchill, armed with a vital geographical position—Britain—and experienced staffs, virtually dictated the way the European war would be fought. This he managed so deftly that the people of both Britain and the United States had the impression that everything had always gone smoothly, according to a previously agreed-upon plan. Such was far from the case.

In his dealings with the Americans, Churchill always downplayed the fact that British and American war aims were far from identical, emphasizing their partnership as allies against Hitler, Mussolini, and Japan. And so they were. What he seldom emphasized was his determination to preserve the already shaky British Empire, which spread from England, and included Gibraltar, India, Malaysia, and Hong Kong. Americans had no interest in Britain's empire; in fact, our anticolonial tradition gave Churchill little or no sympathy in his effort to preserve it. But they, like the British, tried to brush that issue under the rug unless, as Marshall in particular feared, American troops would be employed to that end. The result was a dichotomy of concepts. Churchill conceived defeating Hitler by first securing the Mediterranean and then squeezing Hitler's Western Europe in a gigantic ring;[3] the American Joint Chiefs of Staff (JCS), to whom Roosevelt delegated all but the momentous decisions, wanted to cross the English Channel from Britain at the first possible moment.

The issue was not immediately addressed on Churchill's return to London because the planners had other things on their minds, trying to send troops and supplies to their meager forces in the Pacific that were falling one by one to Japanese power. One by one, Singapore (which fell while Churchill was in the United States), Hong Kong, Malaysia, and the Dutch East Indies eventually fell to the Imperial Japanese Army and Navy. But the Americans, especially Marshall, wanted action, and Marshall initiated it as early as April, even before the fall of Corregidor.

3. One of the six volumes of Churchill's memoirs was named *Closing the Ring.*

Marshall's staff worked almost around the clock, fighting the war with Japan and at the same time planning for extensive operations in Europe. The overall plan broke down into three phases—or two and a half. The first was a buildup of United States forces in Britain (BOLERO). The second was to launch an invasion of France from Britain in 1943 (ROUNDUP). The third was a long shot, a high-risk attack across the Channel that very same year, 1942 (SLEDGEHAMMER). The last of these was the issue at stake. BOLERO was a basic requisite, and ROUNDUP, Marshall's "Holy Grail," was a year off. SLEDGEHAMMER, if it could be sold, was designed to take the heat off the beleaguered Russians, who were reeling under vicious German attacks in the Caucasus. Russia must not be allowed to fall.

Roosevelt was not immediately convinced. But his respect for Marshall was so great that he was reluctant to turn down the chief of staff's plans arbitrarily. He therefore took the easy way out: he ordered Marshall and his staff to sell the program to Churchill. Roosevelt himself would stay in the background, playing the role of arbitrator.

On April 4, 1942, Marshall and Harry Hopkins, Roosevelt's unofficial right-hand man, flew from Washington to London to meet with Churchill and the British military. When they landed in London on April 8, they were surprised to find Churchill himself at the airport to meet them. They were about to begin their education in how Churchill got his own way.

It seems inconceivable that Churchill would ever give SLEDGEHAM-MER serious consideration. But he did not say no. He invited Hopkins to stay with him, and during the next few days Hopkins conferred with Churchill. Marshall, on the other hand, concentrated on the British Chiefs of Staff (BCOS). This arrangement gave Marshall one great advantage: he was spared the ordeal of conforming to Churchill's late nights. Hopkins, though also a night person, was outclassed.

There was only one bad moment, and it had nothing to do with war planning. On Saturday night—or three o'clock Sunday morning, April 12—the conviviality was interrupted by a message from Roosevelt in which the president offered no sympathy for the failure of the so-called Cripps Mission to India. Churchill had sent Sir Stafford Cripps to visit Indian leader Mahatma Gandhi and persuade him to cease agitating against British rule, at least for the duration of the war. Gandhi had refused. So upset was the prime minister that he berated Hopkins for some time. Yet even that episode did not mar the generally cordial nature of the few days of talks.

Churchill had charmed his guests. Not only Marshall but also the more cynical Hopkins left London on April 18 believing that Churchill had agreed to executing SLEDGEHAMMER in 1942. They were especially inspired by Churchill's rhetoric regarding the "two nations marching shoulder to shoulder in a great brotherhood of arms." They so reported to Roosevelt, who was pleased but remained noncommittal. He was more aware of Churchill's indirect tactics than were his emissaries.

Following that meeting, an amazing four months then passed without direct discussions between the Americans and the British. Nevertheless, the problem would not go away. A series of visitors came to Washington, the most important of whom was Russian foreign minister Vyacheslav Molotov, who pleaded for SLEDGEHAMMER. Possibly to offset Molotov, Churchill sent Admiral Lord Louis Mountbatten, who threw cold water on it.

Churchill came to Washington again in June, but no conclusions were reached. At that time, however, Roosevelt informed Churchill of the establishment of the MANHATTAN PROJECT, a set of scientists and engineers meeting at Oak Ridge, Tennessee. Its purpose was to develop a new super-bomb, based on the energy released from splitting the atom. Churchill offered to contribute what scientific brains Britain had to offer, under the overall direction of the Americans.

Finally, Roosevelt decided to bring the question of SLEDGEHAMMER to a head and again sent Marshall and Hopkins to London, with Admiral Ernest King. Churchill did not mince words. Citing the "War Cabinet," which was really an extension of Churchill's views, he declared that SLEDGEHAMMER in 1942 was out. On notification, Roosevelt was apparently pleased, and he readily agreed that instead of crossing the English Channel in 1942, the Allies would "occupy" French North Africa before the end of the year.

Why these discussions had been so stretched out remains difficult to understand. One possibility, a strong one, is that such an invasion in 1942 was never really in the cards, because the Americans were not yet prepared to participate. Perhaps at the first Hopkins-Marshall visit Churchill was carried away with the thought. As John Keegan has written of the First World War, Churchill was "undiscriminating if a project were grand enough."[4]

Whatever Churchill's thought processes, he had carried the day in what was perhaps the single most important Anglo-American strategic decision of the war: the Mediterranean would be the arena of Allied action for the rest of 1942 and probably into 1943.

---

4. The entire quotation is as follows: "The British Sea Lord, Admiral Sir John Fisher, [was] as ready with bad as well as good ideas. His superior, First Lord of the Admiralty Winston Churchill, was equally undiscriminating if a strategic project were grand enough." John Keegan, *The First World War,* 214.

Once the invasion of North Africa in the fall of 1942 was agreed upon, a commander had to be selected. But who? Oddly, Roosevelt and Churchill quickly decided that he would have to be an American, because the Vichy French occupying Morocco and Algeria had not forgotten Churchill's sending the Royal Navy into Oran Harbor and destroying the French fleet to prevent its falling into German hands after the French defeat in 1940. Many American generals were possibilities for the post, but Lieutenant General Dwight D. Eisenhower was already on the spot as commanding general of U.S. Forces in Europe. Eisenhower was young—not yet fifty-two years of age—and he lacked experience in high command, but Marshall placed a great amount of trust in him and he quickly convinced Roosevelt and Churchill that Eisenhower was the best choice. So Lieutenant General Dwight D. Eisenhower was appointed as Allied Force commander for Operation TORCH.

Churchill, in his memoirs, called the summer and early fall of 1942 "the most anxious months." The two allies were preparing for a high-risk invasion, the largest in history up to that time. Secret messages as to the locations of the landing areas flew back and forth across the Atlantic. Eisenhower, though carrying the title of Allied Commander, was not himself authorized to choose the landing sites. Yet as Churchill discussed his differences with the Americans in Washington, he sensed a partner in this man from Kansas, who saw the problems very much as he did. At one point Churchill recommended coming to Washington and bringing Eisenhower with him. Their personal relationship became close, and strict protocol did not always govern, as when General Mark Clark was planning his clandestine submarine trip to Algeria.[5]

Eventually, plans fell into place, and on the morning of November 8, 1942, five landings were made in North Africa, three in Morocco (Safi, Casablanca, and Port Lyautey) and two in Algeria (Oran and Algiers). The landings were made safely, but many things went wrong from the start. The Vichy French officers felt that their honor as soldiers compelled them to resist. Fortunately, however, the Vichy French defense minister, Admiral Jean-François Darlan, visiting Algiers, fell into Allied hands. Eisenhower made a controversial arrangement with him, whereby the French, under him as governor, would stop fighting the Americans and British and join them against their real enemy, the Germans.

TORCH had assumed a quick seizure of Tunisia, but that expectation soon faded. The Allies had expected Hitler to withdraw from North Africa;

---

5. See chapter 4, "Mark Wayne Clark, the American Eagle."

instead, he decided to stay and defend. The foul weather contributed, and the supply lines were long and rickety. With the hope for a quick, peaceful occupation of Tunisia gone, any chance for the attack on Northwest Europe (ROUNDUP) in 1943 was for all intents and purposes dead. Churchill's "ring" was essentially established.

With the Allies in control of Morocco and Algeria, Roosevelt and Churchill now decided to hold another conference, this time someplace other than Washington. They also hoped that Russian premier Joseph Stalin might join them, but on his refusal the two Western leaders determined to meet at Casablanca in January 1943. Their joint effort began a new phase in Allied planning.

The Allied meeting at Anfa, near Casablanca, French Morocco, was fraught with drama. Although it was kept secret at the time, it caught the public imagination later. Amid the freezing winter at home, two immensely popular leaders were meeting to make great war plans in the warm, luxuriant atmosphere of Morocco. In making the trip, Roosevelt was breaking new ground: no American president had ever flown in a plane while in office, nor had any left the United States during wartime. And by coincidence the block-busting motion picture *Casablanca* was released at that time.

Churchill and the BCOS were the first party to arrive at Casablanca after a dangerous, uncomfortable flight. The American Joint Chiefs arrived soon after. While the military men conferred, Churchill relaxed and swam in the surf. When the president's party arrived on the evening of January 14, Roosevelt invited everyone, political and military, to dinner at his villa. It was an auspicious beginning. For the two political leaders, the few days spent at Casablanca provided a welcome rest, their leisure enhanced by the determination of the military to work their problems out by themselves.

The issues at stake generally centered around troop levels, or, more specifically, the allocation of American forces between Europe and the Pacific. The two main antagonists in the ensuing hassle were General Sir Alan Brooke and Admiral King.[6]

But the main conclusion was clear. It was now impossible to invade France from the United Kingdom in 1943. The recommendations of the Combined Chiefs of Staff (CCS), therefore, were (1) to maintain the war against the German U-boats in the Atlantic, (2) to continue the aerial bombardment of Germany, and (3) to continue to supply the Russians as well

---

6. At one point, an angry Alan Brooke threatened to break off negotiations. Sir John Dill came to the rescue when he warned Brooke that the matter would have to be submitted to Roosevelt and Churchill. "You know," Dill warned, "what a mess they would make of it." Forrest C. Pogue, *George C. Marshall*, 27–30; Arthur Bryant, *The Turn of the Tide*, 449–50.

as possible—no problem there. The main issue, the one that Churchill cared most about, however, was the agreement to "occupy" Sicily after the fall of Tunisia. As a hollow concession to Marshall, the Allies agreed "to assemble strongest possible force in constant readiness to re-enter the continent as soon as Germany is weakened to the required extent."[7] Churchill had once more carried the day.

Important as were the decisions made at Casablanca, the event is remembered chiefly for the cosmetic show of unity between the two French generals, Charles de Gaulle and Henri Giraud, each of whom aspired to be the head of the provisional French Republic for the duration of the war. By force of circumstance, the Americans supported Giraud and the British supported de Gaulle, who was a particular anathema to Roosevelt. But the two Frenchmen respected each other, despite their rivalry, and at the end of the meeting they consented to be photographed together in the garden of Roosevelt's villa. With their respective sponsors beaming, the two Frenchmen stood up from their chairs and, on cue, shook hands. Wags in the press called the stiff but cordial handshake "the shotgun marriage." The episode came to nothing.

It was that same press meeting, however, that showed Churchill's willingness to accord Roosevelt the center stage in public. On an impulse Roosevelt declared to the press that the Allies would accept no terms for an end to the war except "unconditional surrender" on the part of the Axis powers. Churchill later claimed that he had not been consulted in the declaration, but he nodded his approval. The rhetoric meant little to him. He had achieved agreement to go into Sicily after Tunisia. Beyond Sicily, only a few miles away, lay Italy. The British lifeline to India through Suez was now virtually ensured.

The Casablanca Conference over, Roosevelt and Churchill decided to relax just a little longer, and they drove down the heavily guarded two-lane highway to Churchill's favorite vacation spot at Marrakech. There they stayed in the home of an American, Mrs. Moses Taylor, a rabid Republican who for patriotic reasons allowed the leaders to use it. The next morning Churchill impulsively jumped out of bed to accompany Roosevelt to the airstrip for his takeoff home. As the plane left, an aide heard Churchill murmur, "If anything happened to that great man I couldn't bear it. He is the greatest man in the world today. Come, Pendar, let's go home. I don't like to see them take off."[8] That moment represented the high point of the Anglo-American alliance of the Second World War.

· · ·

7. John S. D. Eisenhower, *Allies*, 235.
8. Kenneth Pendar, *Adventure in Diplomacy: Our French Dilemma*, 154.

In one more arrangement, Churchill stuck to his policy of giving the Americans the titles while keeping power in British hands. Two weeks before the Northwest Africa bombings, General Bernard L. Montgomery's Eighth British Army, under the overall command of Sir Harold Alexander, had sent Rommel reeling at El Alamein and would soon arrive in southern Tunisia after pursuing Rommel across the Libyan Desert. When that happened, Alexander would be crossing from what had been designated as the "Eastern Mediterranean" into Eisenhower's "Western." Alexander outranked Eisenhower by a full grade and was far more experienced. When they met, who should command?

Once again, Churchill came up with a scheme by which he could publicly defer to the Americans while keeping real control in his own hands. Since the combined forces would now be operating in Eisenhower's territory, Ike should stay on as overall commander of the theater. But Churchill insisted that Eisenhower's three top subordinate commanders would be British: Alexander for land forces, Sir Arthur Tedder for air forces, and Andrew Cunningham for naval forces. At Casablanca Roosevelt accepted the arrangement, apparently without undue comment.

Eisenhower was understandably pleased to be retained in his position in view of Alexander's qualifications, but he resented the designation of his principal subordinates and also the press announcement of it. American practice has always given the commander the right to choose his subordinates, not to have them dictated to him.[9] Churchill had originally promised to keep the arrangement out of the public eye, but of course it leaked. Eisenhower recognized Churchill's scheming, and he did not forget it. Fortunately, his relations with all three British officers so designated were friendly, even warm. Tedder in particular became his chief advocate, and Cunningham was right behind him.[10]

On May 13, 1943, nearly three months to the day from the last day of the Casablanca Conference, 350,000 Germans and Italians surrendered to the British and Americans in the northern tip of Tunisia. It was a great haul, more men than had surrendered to the Russians at Stalingrad. The prisoners were tough soldiers, and though there were more Italians than

---

9. Churchill once showed Ike a message he was sending to his commanders in the field. Ike said, "If you sent me an order like that, I'd resign."

10. When Churchill became prime minister on May 10, 1940, he wrote a very revealing entry in his diary: "In my long political experience I had held most of the great offices of State but . . . the post which had now fallen to me was the one I liked the best. Power, for the sake of lording it over fellow-creatures or adding to personal pomp, is rightly judged base. But power in a national crisis, when a man believes he knows what orders should be given, is a blessing." Winston S. Churchill, *The Second World War*, 15.

Germans, the loss was a blow to Hitler's Wehrmacht. For the Allies it was already decided that the next Allied objective should be the occupation of Sicily, and the question again arose—what next?

The answer was a foregone conclusion. Italy lay next door, just across the Strait of Messina from Sicily. Despite Marshall's aversion to operations in the Mediterranean, it was practically inevitable that the lateness of the year precluded any action in northern Europe. Failure to pursue the war in the Mediterranean would leave many Allied divisions idle for months, a nearly intolerable situation for the troops. After another meeting in Washington to discuss the issue, Churchill then secured Roosevelt's permission to take Marshall to visit Eisenhower in Algiers, and the invasion of Italy was settled.

In August 1943, Roosevelt and Churchill met with their military staffs at Quebec. The significance of the QUADRANT meeting was far-reaching in that it began serious, concrete planning for the invasion of Northwest Europe in May 1944. A special group was organized under a British officer, Lieutenant General Sir Frederick Morgan, to begin drafting the detailed plans, subject to agreed-upon parameters as to resources. Morgan was given the exotic title COSSAC (Chief of Staff to the Supreme Allied Commander). The Supreme Commander to whom General Morgan was to be "chief of staff" was not named.

On the first evening of the Quebec Conference, Churchill received an unwelcome, though perhaps inevitable, ultimatum from Roosevelt: the commander of the forthcoming Allied invasion (OVERLORD), Roosevelt insisted, would be an American, not a British, officer.[11] The development came as something of a shock to the egocentric Sir Alan Brooke. By reason of their long opposition to Hitler, the British had considered themselves as the senior partners of the alliance. North Africa they had considered a necessary sideshow. There was no doubt at this point that they had been replaced.[12]

The military operations of the summer of 1943 went satisfactorily, though not without troubles. National attitudes did not change. Churchill contin-

---

11. Secretary of War Henry Stimson had apparently put the president's feet to the fire on this matter. A longtime public servant—onetime secretary of state and also previously a secretary of war—Stimson was an avid admirer of George Marshall, whom he obviously expected to be appointed to the position.

12. Chief of the Imperial General Staff Sir Alan Brooke had always presumed that he would command the future Allied Expeditionary Force. His personal disappointment was keen, and he resented Churchill's apparently cheerful acceptance of the inevitable.

ued to take increased interest in the Mediterranean command, while Marshall resisted sending another man, another tank, or yet another bullet to the region. But for Churchill, a source of dismay was in the offing: Roosevelt's obvious decision to begin courting the friendship of Soviet Russia, especially Joseph Stalin, at Churchill's expense.

Roosevelt's decision to court Stalin represented at least the beginning of the end for the close Roosevelt-Churchill relationship. Despite the grief of sentimentalists, however, Roosevelt was only being realistic. The industrial and military power of the United States had grown to the point that this country and the Soviet Union were both overshadowing Britain in importance. Britain was falling into the background. Roosevelt, a cold man behind his disarming smile, was also growing weary of Churchill's doggedness on all issues.

The distancing between Roosevelt and Churchill first manifested itself at Cairo in the fall of 1943, where the British and Americans met, supposedly to prepare themselves for their forthcoming meeting with Stalin at Tehran in late November. To Churchill's disappointment, Roosevelt managed to avoid any significant meetings throughout the entire time, using the excuse that he did not want to appear to be "ganging up on Stalin." The president even went so far as to occupy long periods with Chinese president Chiang Kai-shek discussing Far Eastern matters.

The rift between the Western Allies became more apparent when the American and British delegations finally reached Tehran. On arrival Roosevelt accepted an invitation from Stalin to move the American delegation into the confines of the highly protected Soviet embassy. Roosevelt also lunched with Stalin but avoided any such one-on-one contacts with Churchill.

Such snubs were painful enough for Churchill, but his distress grew even worse when the official meetings began. From the start, he found himself seen by Roosevelt and Stalin as dragging his feet rather than cooperating. Stalin and Roosevelt were intent on launching an Allied crossing into Northwest Europe as soon as possible, and they regarded Churchill as lukewarm, even obstructionist. At the end of the meeting, however, the three powers confirmed that the Allies would invade northern France the following spring, with a fixed date of May 1, 1944.[13] Furthermore, that landing would be accompanied by another assault at Marseilles, with seven divisions to be drawn from Churchill's area of hegemony, the Mediterranean.

13. The date was later put off to early June.

Although Churchill was unhappy about the agreement, he did not consider himself quite powerless. No agreement, to him, was beyond further discussion; no decision, until executed, was absolutely final. Roosevelt saw it otherwise.

On leaving Tehran in early December, Roosevelt and Churchill, with their staffs, returned to Cairo for a short time. There, on December 7, 1943, Roosevelt decided to appoint Eisenhower rather than Marshall as commander of OVERLORD the coming spring. The choice made little difference to Churchill, for it had already been established that the Supreme Commander would be American. Far more important to him was Roosevelt's agreement for the commander in the Mediterranean to be a British officer. Roosevelt had attempted to convince Churchill that the Mediterranean and the European theaters should be combined under General George Marshall, but Churchill had rebuffed the notion in no uncertain terms. He considered the two theaters almost coequal.

Churchill was now the undisputed generalissimo in the Mediterranean. The Allied Commander, General Sir Henry Maitland (Jumbo) Wilson, was his man. Any resemblance to an orderly command chain in the Mediterranean now went out the window. Orders for operations in that region, at least de facto, went from Churchill to his favorite general, Alexander, in Italy, bypassing even Wilson. Never mind the Combined Chiefs of Staff.

The prime minister exercised his new power soon after the Allied leaders left Cairo and stopped off at Carthage. Confined to his bed to fight what the doctors now diagnosed as pneumonia, he fretted and schemed. After a few days, as soon as he began to recover, he summoned Brooke to come to Eisenhower's villa to consult with him on a new operation in Italy. Impatient with Allied progress toward Rome, he revived discussion of a previously rejected plan for an amphibious two-division assault (SHINGLE) at Anzio, near Rome, hoping to force the Germans to abandon their formidable line at Cassino, on the Rapido River.

In drawing up his plans, Churchill felt it necessary to deal with only two people. First, he needed to convince General Eisenhower, departing for London, that he could afford the transfer of some landing craft (LSTs) scheduled for OVERLORD. Then, having secured Eisenhower's reluctant blessing, he proceeded to confirm the agreement with Roosevelt. Wilson, the Allied Commander in the Mediterranean, seemed to play no role, nor did the Combined Chiefs of Staff. SHINGLE, Churchill's project, was executed on January 22, 1944.

Unfortunately, Anzio failed in its intended mission. The German commander, Field Marshal Albert Kesselring, did not abandon the line of the Rapido, and the Anglo-American troops under U.S. VI Corps were unable to break out until the following May, 1944, just before D-day in Normandy. British generals prudently have called the operation a success, since it was Churchill's idea. Its main success, however, was reduced to avoiding destruction of the beachhead.

By the turn of the year, Churchill was well enough to be moved from Carthage to Marrakech. He then returned to London to take his part in preparations for OVERLORD.

During the final stages of planning for OVERLORD, Churchill and Eisenhower, both in London, cooperated much as they had two years earlier. But Eisenhower was now in full charge of OVERLORD, while Churchill still tried to keep as much control as possible in his own hands. Oddly, therefore, his main adversary in the competition for control was his friend Eisenhower.

Eisenhower, while flexible in most matters, was determined that he must be given control of the strategic bombers during the first few months before and after D-day for OVERLORD. His resolve grew out of his frightening experience at the Salerno (Italy) landings the previous September, when he had been denied the amount of airpower he deemed necessary. As the result of that close encounter with disaster, Ike had vowed then that he would never again make another amphibious landing without absolute control of the heavy bomber support he demanded. There was nothing casual about that resolve.

When they had visited at Marrakech, Churchill had seemed to be willing to grant Eisenhower's requirement. Churchill did, indeed, promise to support him—or at least Ike gained the impression that he did. Given Churchill's ability to reverse his opinions whenever he needed to, Eisenhower's impression was probably correct—for the moment.

Eisenhower sensed otherwise when he arrived in London on January 12, 1944. A coolness in some quarters, he discovered, had developed against granting him control of the heavy bombers. To his astonishment, he learned that Churchill himself had developed a case of amnesia regarding his earlier promises. The resistance did not come solely from Churchill, however. The Combined Chiefs were reluctant to relinquish their usual control of the Strategic Bomber Force. And there were conceptual arguments. The strategic airmen believed that Germany could be bombed into submission without the need for executing OVERLORD at all. The tactical Air Force men, who believed that OVERLORD was necessary, were in the minority.

The matter was finally resolved, but only when Eisenhower hinted strongly that he would resign his position as Supreme Commander unless his views prevailed. The Combined Chiefs granted him control of the heavy bombers from April until September, by which time it was presumed that OVERLORD would be secure.[14] Churchill was not a major player in this controversy, but he doubtless would have preferred the CCS position, where he would retain some influence.

Another important controversy grew out of the agreement, made at Tehran, that a landing should be made in southern France simultaneously with OVERLORD. The seven divisions would later come under Eisenhower's command when they linked up with OVERLORD near Dijon, France. Churchill had never reconciled himself to losing seven top-notch divisions that would come from the Mediterranean. Such a loss, he argued, would cripple Alexander's Italian campaign—a buildup of "American" OVERLORD at the expense of Churchill's lake.

Churchill attempted to reopen the issue with Roosevelt, but much to his chagrin Roosevelt considered DRAGOON to be a firm commitment made by him personally to Stalin. Further, Churchill's persistence was wearing thin. The president, therefore, with the concurrence of the American Joint Chiefs, delegated to Eisenhower the chore of representing them in the matter. Unconventional as that action might seem, the prime minister was now forced to present his case to an American general.

Churchill argued against the DRAGOON-ANVIL plan without results, continuing all the way to the first week in August 1944, only eight days before the actual landing was eventually made. His position in talking with Eisenhower was weakened by refusal to admit his real reasons for resisting the proposed venture. Instead he resorted to military hyperbole, painting gory pictures of the beaches of Marseilles running red with the blood of Allied soldiers. Eisenhower knew better; his intelligence had confirmed that southern France was nearly denuded of German troops, and moreover the blood to be shed would be American, not British.

The landing was made, with Churchill personally witnessing it from a British vessel. The results were far-reaching. Many follow-up American divisions were later landed at Marseilles as the European campaign wore on, as well as enormous quantities of the necessary supplies. And from an Anglo-American alliance viewpoint, it signified that Roosevelt was no longer heeding his onetime close ally.

· · ·

14. The matter was greatly eased by the fact that Sir Arthur Tedder, Eisenhower's deputy, was a highly respected airman, and he had great influence with Sir Charles Portal, chief of the Royal Air Force. Informally, Lieutenant General Carl Spaatz, chief of the U.S. Strategic Air Forces in Europe, informed his friend Ike that he would perform any mission Eisenhower wanted, aside from formalities, even after September.

In the spring of 1945 a final issue appeared. After the Americans and British had crossed the Rhine River in late March 1945, Churchill urged Roosevelt to scrap the previous agreements made with the Soviets at Yalta regarding the occupation zones of Germany after the war. To that end he urged that Roosevelt direct Eisenhower to drive straight for Berlin in an effort to take the city ahead of their Russian allies. This was contrary to Eisenhower's plan, however, because he had decided to stop his armies at the line of the Elbe and Mulde rivers. On April 12, aware of Churchill's protests, Eisenhower sent a message to Washington saying that he would, if instructed, "cheerfully" do what he considered unwise from a military viewpoint. But Roosevelt could not take any such action. He died at about the time Eisenhower's message arrived in Washington. The Western Allies stopped at the Elbe.

Wartime operations over, Churchill lost no time insisting that the annoying Supreme Headquarters, Allied Expeditionary Forces, be deactivated. The Anglo-American alliance in Europe was at an end.

Those, in a nutshell, were the differences between Churchill and the Americans in the Second World War, differences that have often been argued back and forth. It must be realized, however, that they were minor compared with the basic friendship and cooperation that bound two allies. Nor did they dampen the friendship between Churchill and Eisenhower, difficult as Churchill may have found his friend to be at times.

They were together shortly before the Potsdam Conference in July 1945, when Churchill was up for reelection as prime minister.[15] Churchill, as the dominant hero in Britain, was confident. He mused to Ike that in some ways it might be well were the Labourites, under Clement Attlee, to win, because individually they were not nearly so well fixed financially as was he. But when the election results reached Churchill at Potsdam, he was shocked to learn that he had been turned out of office. Attlee replaced him while the talks were going on, together with Stalin and the new U.S. president, Harry S. Truman. The British had had enough sacrifice, enough "blood, sweat, and tears."[16] They had stuck by their old warhorse during the war, but now they longed for relief from their sacrifices and more domestic programs from the British government—and that meant the Labour Party.

As for Churchill, though nearing his seventy-first birthday, he did not leave public life. He remained in the political arena for another decade.

15. A conference with Stalin, Churchill, and Truman at Potsdam, Germany.
16. The actual wording had been "blood and sweat, tears and toil."

He reassumed his position as the leader of the Conservative Party and re-sumed the rough-and-tumble of the floor of the House of Commons.

I saw Churchill several times after the war. In October 1946 I was includ-ed on the guest list of a dinner given in my parents' honor at Number 10 Downing Street in London. There Churchill and Prime Minister Clement Attlee seemed to be on cordial terms; after all, Attlee had been Churchill's deputy in the coalition cabinet that ran the war. But I was amused by the fact that the radio that very afternoon had reported one of the two refer-ring to the other as "that wicked man."[17] British politics seemed to be a bit more of a game than American.

As time went by, the world watched Churchill age, though he stayed amazingly active. At an English-Speaking Union dinner in London in July 1951, he appeared to have slowed down dramatically. He was practically deaf—perhaps he was bored. But later in the same year his Conservative Party regained control of the House of Commons, and Churchill became prime minister once again, serving nearly as long a term as he had during the Second World War. His time in office overlapped my father's presi-dency for about two years. He finally retired in 1955, age eighty-one, just before the four-power conference at Geneva.

The most vivid recollection I have of the aging Churchill centers around his visit to the White House in 1959, some eighteen years since he was President Roosevelt's guest in 1941. Several strokes, which he had suffered throughout his life, had crippled him. Hardly able to walk, he could un-derstand almost nothing that was said at the dinner table. When he left the White House after the visit, the entire presidential staff poured out to the northwest gate to send him off in his limousine, the members viewing him half in affection and half in awe.

Yet my father and I had the feeling that Churchill had more book proj-ects in mind. After we moved to Gettysburg, I assisted Dad in writing his two-volume White House memoir. At one point, we decided to repro-duce certain exchanges pertaining to Indochina in 1954 that would require Churchill's authorization. The old man declined, using as his excuse that "these matters should remain secret for a while." Our uncharitable con-clusion was that "for a while" meant "until my own book comes out." A couple of years later, Sir Winston Spencer Churchill, finally knighted, died in London on January 24, 1965. My father flew to London as the guest of the British Royal Family and made the television eulogy at his funeral.

· · ·

17. I do not recall which man had so referred to which.

"Half-American and all British," Winston Churchill was perhaps the strongest advocate of Anglo-American unity of anyone in public life. Probably he would have liked to maintain the close ties that had existed between Britain and America for most of the Second World War. In his endeavors to further that cause, he was not completely successful. A continuation of that relationship, the Americans realized, would have served the interests of Britain but not necessarily those of the United States.

To adapt his own words, Churchill could be a difficult ally. But it would have been far worse to fight Hitler without him.

Secretary of State John Foster Dulles (Library of Congress)

# 2

## John Foster Dulles

### The Presbyterian

*Date and time: Mid-July, 1955, late afternoon.*

*Place: An anteroom of the Council Hall of the Palace of Nations, Geneva, Switzerland.*

*Circumstances: The members of the delegations of the great four-power summit meeting of the United States, France, Britain, and the Soviets—the "Open-Skies" meeting[1]—are having a cer-emonial cocktail, predictably more business than social, after the end of that day's meeting.*

*Cast of characters: British prime minister Sir Anthony Eden, American secretary of state John Foster Dulles, and Major John Eisenhower, who is between military assignments and acting temporarily as his father's aide.*

*The two statesmen, each holding an empty glass, are confer-ring seriously. Major Eisenhower, demonstrating more zeal than wisdom, approaches them with a cheery, "May I refresh your drinks?"*

*Eden springs up as if called from a trance, smiles brightly, and says, "Oh, no, thanks."*

*Dulles does not bother looking up. He glowers into his empty glass and growls, "Had one."*

I smiled to myself. This was just Dulles being Dulles. I would have been astonished had he reacted differently. The small vignette illustrates the way President Eisenhower himself, in later years, described him: "Foster

---

1. The Soviets were represented by four men who declared themselves to be on coequal status: Nikita Khrushchev, Nikolai Bulganin, V. M. Molotov, and Georgi K. Zhukov.

[Dulles] was all business when there was business to be discussed. For this reason he was sometimes considered by strangers as abrupt, even brusque. This often made him a target for the venom of smaller men, especially anyone who felt slighted by his serious, almost sharp form of address. This circumstance partially distorted the average man's picture of Foster who, in truth, was filled with human kindness and understanding."[2]

This characteristic explains to a large extent why Secretary of State John Foster Dulles, an able and dedicated man, was never a popular figure. His dour manner, abruptness, and occasional self-righteousness—the popular caricature of the Presbyterian minister his father had been—caused him to be criticized, sometimes vilified, and at other times a subject for humor. He was, however, admired and appreciated by the man who counted most to him: President Dwight Eisenhower.

Actually, Dulles was a man of extraordinary abilities. He was arguably the most experienced diplomat that America could boast at the time, and Eisenhower would have extended that assertion to encompass the entire history of the nation. His background in foreign affairs ran back to the days when he was a student at Princeton University at age nineteen. The year was 1907, and he secured some time off from his studies to accompany his grandfather former secretary of state John W. Foster to the Second Peace Conference at The Hague.[3] From that time on, Foster Dulles's activities never wandered far from the field of foreign affairs.

Deciding to make international law his profession, Dulles attended George Washington University Law School, and by 1919, at the age of thirty-one, he was a member of President Wilson's delegation at the Versailles Peace Talks. Going into law practice in New York, he specialized in cases involving international negotiations. From time to time he served in government, exercising his expertise under presidents of both political parties. Though he was a Republican, his crowning achievement before being appointed secretary of state had been reached under President Harry S. Truman. In 1951 he had conducted the difficult negotiations that led to the treaty officially ending the Second World War with Japan. In Republican circles Dulles was Mr. Foreign Policy itself, so when Eisenhower was elected president, Foster Dulles was almost automatically selected to be secretary of state. In that position, Dulles had reached his apotheosis. Secretary of state was his lifelong ambition. He had no desire to be president.

Dulles took up his new duties with a bang. Within a week after taking office in January 1953, he embarked on a mission to several European capitals, the first of many trips that he would make in his six years as

2. Dwight D. Eisenhower, *Waging Peace*, 365.
3. He served under President Benjamin Harrison.

secretary.[4] He was well prepared to do so. During the month before the Eisenhower inauguration, he and Dulles had consulted frequently. By the time inauguration day arrived, they knew at least the first things they wanted to accomplish.

Eisenhower had two reasons for urgency. First of all, he was concerned that the Western European nations might need assurances of his own continuing support. He had left his post as Supreme Commander of the NATO military forces less than nine months before, but the main issue of the ensuing political campaign had been the war in Korea. Now Ike needed to reassure the NATO nations that he had not forgotten the primacy of Western Europe.

But Eisenhower was concerned about another matter. Unconfirmed reports had reached him that the Europeans were showing signs of dragging their feet in ratifying the European Defense Community, central to the success of NATO. The EDC, as it was called, was the device that would make it possible to amalgamate the land forces of the various nations into a unified military unit, including forces from West Germany. Certain European leaders had denied any such apathy, but Eisenhower wanted a firsthand report.

Dulles's trip took him to Rome, Paris, London, Bonn, the Hague, Brussels, and Luxembourg—all the nations on the western front. At every capital he sent back a message describing his activities. On February 3, 1953, for example, he reported: "Had a useful visit at Paris. Yesterday devoted to talks with French officials largely in relation to EDC. While political difficulties are great, Stassen and I feel that there is a real determination on the part of the present government, particularly [French president] Mayer and [defense minister] Pleven, to push this to a successful conclusion. There is still a hard road ahead, but we feel that ultimate success is possible and even probable."[5]

The trip was an unqualified diplomatic success, but the aspect most noted by the public was an unfortunate remark Dulles had made just before his departure. After pointing out that the United States had invested forty billion dollars in Europe since the end of World War II, he had added, "If, however, there were no chance . . . of getting effective unity, and if in particular France, Germany, and England should go their separate ways, then certainly it would be necessary to give a little rethinking to America's own foreign policy in relation to Western Europe."[6] The result was a serious

---

4. Dwight D. Eisenhower, *Mandate for Change*, 141, estimates that Dulles's total mileage would come to a half-million miles.
5. Ibid. Harold Stassen, director of the Mutual Aid Agency, accompanied Dulles.
6. Ibid.

misunderstanding. Though Dulles had prefaced his remarks by saying that he believed unity was going to be achieved, the word *rethinking* came to be associated with the term *agonizing reappraisal.* Never mind that the secretary was representing the views of his boss, President Eisenhower. The Europeans were less upset with the substance of Dulles's remark than with the way he expressed it.

At the same time that Dulles was causing uneasiness in Western Europe, he was unfortunately doing just the opposite to the Eastern Europeans behind the Iron Curtain. Unwittingly, he was giving an unrealistic glimmer of hope for release from the bondage under which they were held by the Soviet Union. Though generally an advocate of the policy of "containment" promulgated by diplomat George Kennan in 1949, Dulles, as an international lawyer, refused to admit the justice of Soviet occupation of the captive nations. In various remarks, therefore, he unwittingly gave the false impression that the United States might take some direct measures to begin freeing Poland, Czechoslovakia, Hungary, and even the Baltic countries. Apparently, he failed to follow Ike's repeated warning always to use the words *by all peaceful means.*

The subject peoples heard only what they wanted to hear. The cold facts were, as most people realized, that pushing back the boundaries of the Soviet Empire could be accomplished only by military force, not diplomacy —and military force was out of the question. In the Hungarian uprising of 1956, the results would be tragic.

Though Dulles warned of the possibility of "massive retaliation" against any Soviet military aggression toward the West, he and Eisenhower were fully aware that an exchange of nuclear stockpiles between the two superpowers would mean the end of civilization. The Americans had no real fear of such an eventuality, however, because the Central Intelligence Agency's reconnaissance flights (U-2) had produced solid evidence that the Soviets, despite their bluster, were really weak from a military standpoint. Inevitably, Eisenhower and Dulles believed, the Russians would back down in any confrontation.

Nevertheless, Dulles seemed to enjoy bluffing, and that foible led him to make the unfortunate statement that has become almost synonymous with his name. It had to do with the Far East, the Formosa Strait, between Taiwan and Communist China. There, two small islands named Quemoy and Matsu, located within range of Chinese Communist artillery from the mainland, attained great significance because they still flew the flag of Generalissimo Chiang Kai-shek's Republic of China.

When Chiang's Nationalist regime had escaped to Taiwan in 1949, it still claimed that it, not Mao's government, was the legitimate government of the entire country. Though the Nationalist regime was utterly dependent on American military and economic support for its survival, Chiang had always turned a deaf ear when urged to vacate those two worthless little pieces of land. Quemoy and Matsu were, he insisted, symbols of the ambitions of his followers to return someday to the mainland.

The impasse between the United States and Chiang was still unresolved when Eisenhower took office. The United States, though it had committed itself to defend Taiwan, had never extended that commitment to defending Quemoy and Matsu. President Eisenhower, as a poker player, never made a public comment on what he would do if the Chinese Communists attempted to take the little islands.

In late 1955 the Chinese Communists decided to do some bluffing on their own. Peking began making a series of threats against Quemoy and Matsu but took no overt action. Faced with the prospect of possible destruction by the American Strategic Air Command, they held off doing anything more dire than threaten. Eventually, they tired of the whole exercise and quieted down.

Dulles apparently took this Communist back-down as a personal triumph, and he made no secret of his elation. In the January 1956 issue of *Life* he crowed, "The ability to get to the verge without getting into war is the necessary art. If you are scared to get to the brink, you are lost. We walked to the brink, and we looked it in the face."

The effect on a nervous American public was electrifying. Governor Adlai Stevenson, preparing for a second run at the presidency later that year, made the most of it. He coined the term *brinkmanship,* a term that has become part of our language. Even I, as a young infantry officer at nearby Fort Belvoir, felt the impact. "If the secretary hadn't been so damn quotable by using the word *art*," I remember thinking, "he could have said the same thing, and it would not have been noticed." But then again, that was just Dulles being Dulles.

Dulles's public image was a joy to the newspaper cartoonists. His dour expression, wire-rimmed glasses, and invariably dark suit and black hat made him easy to caricature. I still chuckle over one cartoon by Herbert Block (Herblock), the cartoonist of the *Washington Post.* Dulles was known to detest meetings between heads of government, and as one of them approached, Herblock showed him looking especially sour, taking out flight insurance at the door of an elevator before a sign with an upward arrow that read *SUMMIT.*

On one occasion the president himself participated in a scene that brought on a widespread chuckle. It occurred following a NATO summit meeting in December 1957. The conference, held in Paris, had been important. Among other things it had secured the agreement by the NATO nations to allow the deployment of American intermediate-range atomic missiles on their soil. This was a vital step, in the light of growing Soviet intercontinental missile capabilities, so vital that Ike, on his return, decided to make a personal report to the nation. However, doing so would be difficult, because in late November, he had suffered a small stroke,[7] and he had not recovered sufficiently to feel comfortable in rendering a complete, thorough report on television.

Eisenhower and Dulles came up with a scheme. The president and secretary would appear together in the Oval Office of the White House. The president would open the program by giving a short summary of the meeting and would then introduce the secretary to provide the more detailed report.

Unfortunately, they made one serious mistake. Instead of Ike's leaving the screen after making the introduction, he stayed in the picture. While Dulles droned on in his pontifical way, Eisenhower found it impossible to sit stone-faced and attentive. He chewed on the end of a yellow pencil, examined every detail of the ceiling of the Oval Office, and appeared to be doing everything except listen. Among the amused viewers was former president Harry Truman, who happily remarked to the press, "I think I was as bored as the president was." At least the episode produced one time during Eisenhower's presidency that Truman referred to him by his proper title.

By no means do I intend, in a short essay, to give a full description of the six years during which John Foster Dulles was the secretary of state. Such an account would be lengthy, and my knowledge insufficient. Nevertheless, it might be well here to share some impressions I received of Dulles over years of observation.

Primarily, I have been struck by the misconceptions under which the public has labored regarding the respective roles played by president and secretary in the conduct of foreign affairs. The most important fallacy was the idea that Dulles's policies, especially the unpopular ones, were all his own. Many, perhaps most, initiatives may have been originated by Dulles, but the secretary assiduously avoided acting on any major matter without

---

7. There were no appreciable lasting effects from the stroke. Though laid up for a few days, he was able to attend service for Thanksgiving and then leave for Paris on Friday, December 13, much to the dismay of my superstitious mother.

first attaining Eisenhower's approval. Only on one occasion, which I will describe later, did Dulles take an important step without prior consultation. At all other times, to the best of my knowledge, he checked in detail first.

Dulles was sensitive on this point, even more so than was Eisenhower, because the experience of his uncle Secretary of State Robert Lansing had made him aware of the danger of exceeding his authority. Lansing had been secretary under President Woodrow Wilson between 1915 and 1920. When Wilson became incapacitated by a stroke in 1919, Lansing, as the ranking member of the Wilson administration,[8] held several meetings of the cabinet while Wilson was confined to the second floor of the White House. Lansing went even further when he suggested calling on Vice President Thomas Marshall to take over Wilson's duties temporarily. As a result, Lansing received word from the president's sickbed that his resignation as secretary was desired. Eisenhower was not so touchy as Wilson, of course, but Dulles could not be sure. Even so, in spite of that caution, it was noticeable that Dulles did not overemphasize Ike's primacy in foreign affairs when being questioned by the public.

The impression I had was that Dulles regarded himself as the president's lawyer in foreign matters. As such, it was up to him to give his client honest advice and then, once the client had made his decision, to act aggressively on his behalf. It was not important to either man whether the lawyer possessed more expertise in the technicalities of his field than the man he represented. Eisenhower was not concerned about such things. He expected his experts to be just that—experts.

The one instance in which Dulles acted without Eisenhower's concurrence occurred in June 1956. Negotiations had been going on between the American government and Colonel Gamal Nasser, president of Egypt, for the United States to provide a substantial loan to construct a huge dam at Aswan, on the Nile River. Nasser, playing the West off against the Soviets, became so difficult that Dulles, unable to contact Ike, terminated negotiations for the contract. He acted on his own because the circumstances were extreme: the president was undergoing a life-and-death intestinal operation at Walter Reed Army Hospital.

Nasser, infuriated by Dulles's action, responded by nationalizing the Suez Canal, which had hitherto been regarded as international property, despite its location in Egyptian territory. A series of complicated but futile negotiations followed. Eventually, later in the year, the world-shaking

8. In 1920 the vice president was not considered to be a working member of the presidential administration. He had no office in the White House or the Executive Office Building across the street. His sole duties had to do with presiding over the Senate.

"Suez Crisis" erupted. Britain, France, and Israel attacked Egypt to seize the canal. To their surprise, Eisenhower, recovered from his illness, halted them by submitting a resolution in the United Nations, forcing their withdrawal.[9]

I was not assigned to the White House at the time, but I later studied the communications on the subject while assisting my father in writing his memoirs of the White House years. In the files I found at least two memoranda that Ike later wrote to Dulles, asking if perhaps we had made an error in canceling the Aswan loan in the first place. The answers to both notes vehemently denied any error. The entire affair, as far as Dulles was concerned, had been conducted in a most brilliant manner. I have never run across an issue in which John Foster Dulles admitted a mistake.

The Suez Crisis cast new light on a major principle that Dulles and Eisenhower would follow in the conduct of foreign policy. In a nutshell, no nation should gain anything by force, allies or not. When Britain and France and Israel invaded the Sinai Peninsula and Port Said on the Suez Canal, Dulles had Eisenhower's complete backing in submitting a resolution in the United Nations condemning the action but not the nations themselves. Following the withdrawal of the three nations, the United States went all out to help supply oil for Western Europe for the winter ahead. (Nasser had closed the Suez waterway by sinking ships in critical places.) In short, the three offending nations were in violation of that principle. Those who expected the United States to ignore the rule of international law out of friendship for selected nations were put on notice.

Thus far I have dealt with Dulles and his dealing with the public. In my opinion, however, his greatest contribution to the conduct of the Eisenhower administration was the moral support he gave his boss in dealing with difficult issues. His ability to do so was enhanced by the fact that Eisenhower accorded him a great deal of respect.

Contrary to the general impression, the two actually spent a considerable amount of time alone together, with no third party allowed. They met every evening that both happened to be in Washington, conversing informally in the Oval Office for about an hour.

These meetings came to follow a certain routine. In decent weather—or even halfway-decent weather—Ike would lean back in his swivel chair at

---

9. The "good cop-bad cop" routine worked to my advantage some years later when, in 1972, I visited Israel. Granted an audience with former prime minister Ben-Gurion, I was warned that he might take me to task for the actions of my father's administration. By contrast, Ben-Gurion was the soul of cordiality. I was advised that the Israelis blamed Dulles, not Eisenhower, for American actions fifteen years before.

about five o'clock, pull on his golf shoes, and walk the few feet between his desk and the glass door leading out onto the portico.[10] Then, on the practice green that some friends had built for him, he putted, chipped, and hit sand trap shots for an hour or so. At about six he returned to his desk, where Dulles would be waiting. They would then discuss the day's business in detail, undisturbed by staff officers or record takers.

Besides the concrete decisions they would reach, they often would exchange broad ideas. Usually, after an hour, Dulles would leave, and Ike would head back to the White House mansion for the evening cocktail and visits with personal friends. Dulles was never present at these social gatherings. Ike kept his business and his pleasure distinctly separate.

Those intimate conferences were highly important to both men, because along with specific decisions to make, they fostered mutual support. They were ideal for Dulles, who by nature was a vest-pocket operator who resented allowing any underlings to get between them. Up until his death in 1959, Dulles was the only man, to the best of my knowledge, who ever saw the president alone. All others were accompanied by a staff officer taking notes.[11] The position of national security adviser had not yet been established.[12]

For a man as self-assured as my father, the need for such support may seem strange. Dulles was also self-assured. But people in power are human, and most all can use occasional reassurances. Dulles in particular needed to know he was pleasing his boss. One late afternoon—I do not recall exactly when—my father made a casual statement to me as we were walking down the portico between the White House and the West Wing. "Well," he said, "I've got to go give Foster some encouragement. He doesn't look it, but he takes the public criticisms hurled at him much to heart. I've got to reassure him."

---

10. In those days the floor of the Oval Office was soft tile. Ike was unconcerned with the fact that those tiles became heavily pockmarked from the spikes on his shoes. Perhaps he regarded inflicting such indignities on the hallowed office as a kind of subconscious revenge for being consigned to the Oval Office at all. In any event, Ike's spike holes were, I understand, great novelties for subsequent presidents to show visitors.

11. General Andrew Goodpaster generally took the bulk of Ike's meetings. After my arrival at the White House in 1958, I relieved him of many of them, especially those that were more routine. But routine in the White House has its own meaning. It included such guests as King Hussein of Jordan.

12. Up to the Kennedy administration, there was no national security adviser, a position about which I still harbor doubts. During the Eisenhower administration, matters of long-term planning were handled by Gordon Gray, the director of the National Security Council staff. Immediate national security matters were handled by General Goodpaster. Their areas of interest often overlapped. It worked only because both of them were gentlemen, who lunched together frequently and bent over backward to inform each other.

It was, however, a two-way street. Ike held Foster's views in such high regard that he had no difficulty listening while Dulles mused aloud over matters more wide-ranging than merely foreign relations. Ike had a nearly uncanny ability to learn through his ears and a similar ability to change his mind when new, convincing arguments presented themselves. So important were these philosophical give-and-take sessions that Ike, in publishing the second volume of his memoirs, devoted seven pages to them out of a thirteen-page chapter devoted solely to Dulles.

Not surprisingly, given the times, their most immediate concern was the Soviet Union. They were both baffled, according to Ike's description, as to why the Soviets had turned down a series of proposals for the control of nuclear arms and other measures to avoid a nuclear holocaust. These proposals, in the Americans' view, were self-enforcing and much to the advantage of both nations. Dulles also reviewed the past history of relations between East and West, and even took into consideration what they called the "Slavic temperament," about which I doubt that either man was a consummate expert. They never came up with an answer. They were certain, however, that the leaders in the Kremlin, being human, were as interested in continuing to live as were they. Therefore, they concluded that nuclear war was well-nigh impossible.

Both men were basically idealists who had devoted their lives to their country. Dulles expressed himself as baffled that such a thing as corruption could exist. Why, he wondered, would anyone risk his reputation for mere money? This question is totally valid, though Dulles, with all his service, had never been in want; his life had been privileged.

But of all the remarks that my father quoted in his description of these late-afternoon musings, one sticks out in my mind most: "Representative government is still on trial."[13]

The Fates were not kind to Foster Dulles, and death from cancer cut short his tenure in the office of secretary of state. The period of his sickness was less than a year, however, and he was mercifully allowed to stay active to the very end, making contributions up to within days of his ultimate passing. Exactly when the seriousness of the cancer condition became known is not clear. Eisenhower, in *Waging Peace*, gives the impression that he was unaware of it until February 1959, after the secretary had returned from an extensive trip to the Western capitals of Europe.[14]

---

13. D. Eisenhower, *Waging Peace*, 371.
14. "When the secretary arrived home and after we had met for extended consultations, he sent me a note that held disturbing implications. It requested permission to turn over temporarily his duties as Secretary of State to Under Secretary Herter because of the need for an operation for a recently developed hernia. He had also, he indicated, not wholly

Ike's recollection, though written only a few years after the fact, may have been faulty. Or possibly the stoic Dulles, anxious to avoid worrying his boss, had previously withheld the news. Vice President Richard Nixon, in his book *Six Crises*, describes what Dulles went through. He had been well aware from the outset that his condition was terminal, during the European trip he had been unable to sleep at night without heavy sedation, and he had been unable to keep food down during the daytime. Yet Ike recalled that Dulles had not mentioned his physical condition in their extensive visits after Dulles's return. Perhaps a description of his condition did not meet the secretary's definition of what belonged in a business meeting. In any case, Dulles's request to turn over his duties "temporarily" was accepted in early February 1959, and he never returned to the State Department.

After a temporary release from Walter Reed Army Hospital, Dulles went to stay at the Florida home of Douglas Dillon, a wealthy businessman who was then serving as an assistant secretary of state. Perhaps the pain was too severe for him to remain out of the hospital, however, for he soon returned to spend his last days in the Presidential Suite at Walter Reed.

At Walter Reed, Dulles nominally resumed his duties as secretary of state. When British prime minister Harold Macmillan came to Washington, Eisenhower immediately took him out to visit the secretary. The Berlin crisis was at its height, and Dulles was aware of Macmillan's proclivity to be conciliatory to the Soviets. Eisenhower described the scene aptly:

> Foster made a forceful plea that we avoid giving the people of the world the impression that we were frightened of the Soviets or that the Soviets were in the "driver's seat." Foster asked wryly why we spent $40 billion a year or more to create a deterrent and defensive power if, whenever the Soviets threatened us, our only answer would be to buy peace by compromise. "If appeasement and partial surrender are to be our attitude," Foster said, "we had better save our money." He admitted that we could not prevent Khrushchev from strutting across the stage and making grandiloquent speeches, but we could avoid the impression that whenever he sounded conciliatory we should rejoice, and whenever he sounded threatening, we would become "fearful as though he were the Lord of Creation."

Eisenhower added admiringly, "Whatever treatment he had been given in the hospital had done nothing to dull his mind."[15]

· · ·

---

thrown off the effects of an abdominal inflammation which had appeared the previous December. I could not but feel apprehensive." Ibid., 343.
  15. Ibid., 353.

On April 15, 1959, Secretary of State Dulles submitted his final resignation to an aggrieved Eisenhower, who appointed Governor Christian
Herter in his place. At the same time he swore Dulles in as a "consultant."[16]
Dulles did not consider his position as a consultant an empty title. Though
he admonished Herter against allowing any "interlopers" to come between
himself and the president, he offered free and frank advice.

He continued to offer advice right up to the end. Perhaps the man who
benefited most was Vice President Richard M. Nixon, who was preparing
to leave on a mission of personal diplomacy to Moscow. The trip to Russia
was not supposed to entail any business, but Nixon knew that it would
be impossible to be in the presence of Premier Nikita Khrushchev and get
away with small talk. Nor did he want to.

Nixon went to others for background on the Russians and their attitudes,
but he found his conferences with Dulles to be especially rewarding. Their
last meeting was just four days before Dulles died.

Nixon, fortunately, made detailed notes of the meeting. He later described Dulles as he sat propped up in the drawing room of the Presidential Suite sucking constantly on ice cubes to dull the burning in his throat.
The specific advice that Nixon was seeking was simple: "What above all
else should I try to get across to Khrushchev?" Dulles gave the matter
long consideration, longer even than usual. Finally he replied, as Nixon
recollected:

> Khrushchev does not need to be convinced of our good intentions. . . . He
> understands us. But what he needs to know is that we also understand
> him. . . . He says he is for peaceful co-existence. What he means, as he has
> shown in Hungary, is that while a revolution against a non-Communist
> government is proper and should be supported, a revolution against a
> Communist government is wrong and must be suppressed. Thus the peace-
> ful co-existence which he advocates represents peace for the Communist
> world and constant strife and conflict for the non-Communist world.

"[Khrushchev] must be made to understand that he cannot have it both
ways," Dulles went on. "If we are to have peaceful competition of economic systems and political ideas, it must take place in the Communist
world as well as ours." He predicted that Khrushchev would deny that
the Soviets were connected with Communist activities in other countries,
which were simply spontaneous acts of people's resentment against capi-
talistic regimes. In response, Dulles advised that Nixon should point the
record out to him, chapter and verse, to show him that we were not taken

16. Ibid., 357.

in at all by the "mock innocence of Soviet leaders." "[Khrushchev] should be told," Dulles concluded, "that until he puts a stop to those activities, his call for the reduction of tensions and for peaceful co-existence will have a completely false and hollow ring."[17]

Nixon never saw Dulles again. But the "consultant" had provided him material for the world-famous "Kitchen Debate" that followed later that summer.

On Tuesday, May 22, 1959, the president sent for me. As I entered the Oval Office, I could see that he was unusually somber. He explained to me what was on his mind.

Foster Dulles was about to die, the boss said, and he wished dearly that there were some unique way that he could express his appreciation for his services, but such was impossible. He should have had a special medal struck for Dulles months ago, he said, but when such a project should have been started, he and Dulles were presuming that the secretary would recover from his illnesses.

That left only the option of presenting the Medal of Freedom. Though that was the highest decoration available for presentation to civilians, it was inadequate, in Ike's mind, because it had been presented to others before him. The only way to make an award unique, he concluded, was to personalize it with a note from himself, which I, as his son, would deliver to Walter Reed. "Present it to the secretary in person, if you can," he said. I hastened to draft a short note, and since I was now expert at imitating Dad's writing style, he signed it immediately and sent me on my way.

As I went up the elevator to the all-too-familiar Ward 8, I felt uneasy, unsure of what I was going to say. But there was no time to plan. When I reached the drawing room of the ward, I met three women: Dulles's wife, Janet; his sister Eleanor Dulles; and his secretary Phyllis Bernau, who was practically part of the family. They greeted me cheerfully, even brightly. They seemed delighted with the medal.

Mrs. Dulles then tiptoed into the bedroom where Dulles was lying in the dark. "The secretary is sleeping," she reported. "But I will give him this medal when he wakes up. You don't need to stay around."

I was struck by the bravery of these women. And as I rode back to the White House I had the distinct feeling that, with all Mr. Dulles's foibles, and as many times as I had chuckled about him, I had been in the presence of greatness.

17. Richard M. Nixon, *Six Crises*, 241–42.

**President Harry S. Truman (Library of Congress)**

# 3

# Harry S. Truman as Commander in Chief

**I don't know if any of you have had a bale of hay fall on you. Well, I feel like the sun, the stars and all the planets just fell on me. Don't expect too much of me.**

**—Harry S. Truman**

President Franklin Roosevelt died on the afternoon of April 12, 1945, at Warm Springs, Georgia. (To us in Europe it was Friday the thirteenth, local time.) Vice President Truman was at the Capitol in the office of House Speaker Sam Rayburn when he was summoned to the White House. On the way, thinking of the condition of the president's health, he feared the worst.

His worst fears were realized. Ushered immediately to Mrs. Roosevelt's office on the second floor, he was met with startling news. "Harry," the first lady said, "the president is dead."

"Is there anything we can do for you?" Truman asked.

"Is there anything we can do for you?" she replied. "You're the one in trouble now."

That evening at seven o'clock, Harry Truman was sworn in as thirty-third president of the United States. As quoted above, he felt a crushing burden as he spoke to the assembled reporters right afterward. Having accepted the vice presidency under a man obviously as sick as Roosevelt was, Truman had to have known that this moment would come. But when it did, it was still a fearsome shock.

The American public was no less dismayed. Most people, I conjecture, reacted first with sympathy for Roosevelt himself. It seemed a shame that the president, with the war so obviously coming to victory, had not lived to savor the results of the goal he had been striving for. Though many of us had never been particularly fond of Roosevelt personally, he was at least a known quantity. His successor, Harry Truman, was not. I got the sinking feeling that he would never be able to replace FDR.

Though he had been vice president for nearly three months, Truman was a virtual unknown. Unlike FDR, he lacked what might be called "presence." True, he was known to be capable. As a senator from Missouri, he had held a responsible position as a sort of watchdog over the money being spent on the war effort, and he was known to have performed his duties well. But as a vice president he had been serving under a president who shared the limelight with nobody. His image in the papers had been dominated by one photo, playing an upright piano with the actress Lauren Bacall sprawling on top of the instrument, showing a good bit of leg.

After the first reaction, however, all of us in the European Theater went on about our duties. I myself could not imagine that within a little over a couple of months, I would meet the new president in person.

The end of the European war found me in Cheb, Czechoslovakia, and about a month later, in early June, I received orders to report to Supreme Headquarters, now moved to Frankfurt, Germany. I was to act as my father's personal aide on a Roman triumph he was making to the United States. His party consisted of about fifty "typical" soldiers and airmen, chosen as representatives of America's armed services in Europe.

One of the events on the itinerary was a dinner in the East Room of the White House, with President Truman as host. It was not a high-pressure affair; the president shook hands with his guests, but if there were speeches, I do not recollect them. After the evening was over, my father, who had stood by the president in the receiving line, described what Mr. Truman had been forced to put up with. Each young guest, experiencing his big moment, seemed to have some word of wisdom to share with his C in C. As an old politician, Truman seemed to enjoy it.

After our return to Europe, something of the same nature took place about a month later. My father briefly attended the Potsdam Conference on July 18, 1945. Present were the Big Three, Truman, Churchill, and Stalin. Their purpose was to discuss the joint strategy for the war against Japan and to confirm arrangements for the future of Germany. Dad, whose part of the war was finished, played only a minor role. We were there only one morning. At breakfast Dad introduced me again to the president, making some faint apology. Mr. Truman responded with some folksy assurance like "He's always welcome here," or something like that. When he was among people he liked, Harry Truman could be the soul of congeniality.

· · ·

Potsdam was the last meeting of the Big Three before Japan's surrender.[1] During the meeting, word came that the Americans at Alamogordo had made a successful test of the atomic bomb. An elated Truman broke the news to a seemingly unimpressed Stalin, who undoubtedly had been watching our progress through spies.

Back in the United States, Truman's principal task was to assure the public that American policy had not changed with Roosevelt's death. Immediately on taking office he announced that the San Francisco Conference, at which the new United Nations organization was to be inaugurated, would go on. But within days after returning from Potsdam, he was faced with the difficult question of how to employ the new superweapon. Should it be used against the Japanese population, and if so when and where? Truman decided quickly, and on August 6, 1945, the first atomic bomb was dropped on Hiroshima. Nagasaki met the same fate two days later.

The results were decisive. This new weapon gave the Japanese government the justification, without losing undue face, to surrender in what was increasingly a hopeless war. I never questioned the rightness of the decision, and I never heard anybody else in uniform protest Mr. Truman's decision at the time. Truman himself never gave the slightest inkling of regret, at least in public.

Once the Japanese surrender was signed aboard the battleship *Missouri* in early September 1945, the American public began to act much as it had at the end of every war in their history. A near panic erupted to demobilize and bring the troops home. In previous wars the nation could afford such a luxury, but in 1945 we faced a powerful Soviet Union, enigmatic and progressively more hostile. Despite that potential threat, President Truman fell short, in my opinion, by failing to resist the public's outcry. In Europe, by the end of 1946, American land forces in the U.S. zones of Germany and Austria had been reduced to a single infantry division and a constabulary of perhaps the size of a mechanized cavalry regiment.[2] The rationale for this precipitate redeployment lay in our recent alliance with the Russians against Hitler. In addition, we were at that time the sole possessors of the atomic bomb and harbored the unrealistic hope to remain so. But I cannot escape the feeling that Truman took the easy route and

1. In the middle of the conference, the reader may recall, the British electorate turned Mr. Churchill out of the office of prime minister. His defeat was totally unexpected. Clement Attlee, the new prime minister, represented Britain for the concluding portion of the conference.

2. One infantry regiment, the 26th, was assigned to guard the Nuremberg trials, where top-ranking ex-Nazis answered for their war crimes and some paid with their lives. Another regiment, the 18th, occupied all of Germany, including the American Zone of Berlin, way behind the Soviet lines. The third regiment, the 16th, occupied all of Austria.

succumbed to political pressure. We were fortunate that we did not pay dearly for so denuding our forces in Europe.

When the brief "honeymoon" between the West and the Soviet Union came to an end, the so-called cold war set in. Historians differ as to when it began, but the Soviet threat was recognized by early March 1947. On the twelfth, President Truman announced a policy commonly called the "Truman Doctrine." The United States, it declared, would resist encroachment against freedom anywhere in the free world. The action was no mere rhetoric; words were accompanied by the unprecedented step of granting military aid to Turkey and Greece, both of which felt threatened by internal rebellions obviously supported by the Soviet Union. The results were salutary, and the rebellions were eventually put down. To us today the amount of aid allocated sounds small—some four hundred million dollars split up between the two countries.[3] But its success represented the first stemming of the expanding Soviet tide.

On January 1, 1947, General of the Army George C. Marshall assumed the post of secretary of state. Though Marshall held that office for only two years, retiring on January 1, 1949, it was during his tenure that many of the most noteworthy actions of the Truman administration were taken.

Here I digress for a moment to mention Truman's warm relationships with Marshall and Eisenhower at that time. Though Truman could never attain Roosevelt's stature with the public, he came into the presidency better equipped for the position than he or the public realized. He had spent valuable years in the United States Senate, and his knowledge of the ropes of politics was invaluable. Nevertheless, the burden of the responsibilities that had fallen on his shoulders was crushing. In need of loyal and capable assistants, he looked to these two Army officers for unstinting support. He once said to my father, "If you and General Marshall both recommend that I do something, I'll do it." Eisenhower protested: "In General Marshall and me you have two men with the same background, the military. You need another viewpoint." The president remained unmoved.[4] It was also about this time, in front of witnesses, that Truman made a strange offer

---

3. It is difficult to translate 1947 dollars to those of today. If we presume that today's dollar is worth about a dime in 1947 currency, the figure would come to about four billion dollars.

4. This situation has always puzzled me. For one thing, if Harry Truman was so daunted by the presidency, why did he accept nomination as vice president under Roosevelt, who quite obviously was not fit to survive his term? Also, if Truman was so dependent on Marshall, why did he put his favorite general in exile in China for more than a year?

to Eisenhower that he would do his best to get him any job he wanted, "including this one [the presidency]." Eisenhower, of course, demurred.[5] That cordial relationship lasted for years. With Marshall it never ended.

It was during the next year, 1948, that General Marshall, with Truman's backing, conceived a plan officially designated the European Recovery Plan, but popularly known as the Marshall Plan. In essence it was a more ambitious version of the Truman Doctrine of a year before. It provided seed money for the reconstruction of Europe. It was a huge success, and Marshall was awarded the Nobel Peace Prize five years later for his role in conceiving and implementing it.

With the passage of time it is easy to forget the difficulties the executive branch had to cope with in selling the plan to Congress. In that year the Republicans held a majority of more than two-thirds of the seats in both houses of Congress. Isolationism was strong. For that reason, the presence of Marshall, whose prestige at the moment greatly exceeded that of Truman, was critical. Fortunately, he was aided by Senator Arthur Vandenberg, a former isolationist. I have always thought that President Truman was generous in insisting that the European Recovery Plan be named after Marshall, not himself.

If the name Truman and the year 1948 are mentioned in the same sentence, the memory will probably jump to his reelection over Republican Thomas E. Dewey in the presidential election that year. It was perhaps the most surprising upset in American political history, and it took years for the Republicans to recover from it.

Truman's victory was all the more remarkable because he was unpopular with the public, and less so among the pundits. Circumstances were stacked against him. The inevitable letdown after the end of the recent war contributed. Moreover, victory had failed to bring about a secure peace.

5. "At 3:30 today had a very interesting conversation with General Eisenhower. Sent for him to discuss the new Secretary of National Defense. Asked him if he could work with Forrestal. He said he could. . . . After the discussion on Forrestal was over Ike and I talked politics. He is going to Columbia University in New York as President. What a job he can do there. . . . Ike and I think MacArthur expects to make a Roman Triumphal return to the U.S. a short time before the Republican Convention meets in Philadelphia. I told Ike that if he did that he (Ike) should announce for the nomination for President on the Democratic ticket and that I'd be glad to be in second place, or Vice President. I like the Senate anyway. Ike & I could be elected and my family and myself would be happy outside this great white jail known as the White House." Harry S. Truman Diary, July 25, 1947. Prepared by the staff of the Harry S. Truman Library.

The public therefore tended to associate Roosevelt with victory and Truman with the gloomy current situation. Personality also entered the equation. It has been remarked that "the American people never forgave Harry Truman for not being Franklin Roosevelt." Roosevelt had been a father figure of dignity and reassuring confidence. Realists may have scoffed at his cheery statement that he could "take care of Uncle Joe [Stalin]," but the public believed in Roosevelt—and wanted to believe the claim. In Truman the public saw none of that aura.

To top matters off, the public seemed ready for a change in the party occupying the White House. The overwhelming Republican control of both houses of Congress served as an omen in that direction. The Republican ability to pass the Twenty-second Amendment to the Constitution, which limited a president to two terms, was obviously directed toward preventing another Roosevelt, who had been elected four times.

All this added up to what seemed a hopeless prospect for Truman's reelection in 1948. Desperate Democrats even approached my father, asking his permission to be proposed to replace Truman on the Democratic presidential ticket. I was present one evening when one of the Roosevelt sons, probably James, telephoned my father at Columbia University, urging him to run as a Democrat.[6]

But the pundits and the Republicans underestimated the "Man from Missouri." Overconfident, the Republicans selected a colorless team that pleased their leaders rather than the citizens in the street. For president they nominated Thomas E. Dewey, governor of New York, a onetime crime buster who had run unsuccessfully against Roosevelt in 1944. For vice president they named Earl Warren, governor of California. Sure of success, Dewey and Warren adopted a campaign strategy of saying as little as possible. Nobody held Dewey's defeat of 1944 against him; he had been running against the unbeatable Roosevelt.

In contrast, Truman conducted a vigorous if lonely campaign, shrewdly attacking those issues where the "do nothing" Congress had taken measures unpopular with the general populace. The press, however, did not seem to notice and remained as confident of a Republican victory as were the Republicans themselves. I can recall an article in *Life*, the headline of which read, "The Truman Train Stumbles West," referring to the medio-

---

6. Truman reportedly learned of this movement and took James Roosevelt to task: "Your father asked me to take this job. I didn't want it. I was happy in the Senate. But your father asked me to take it and I took it. And if your father knew what you are doing to me he would turn over in his grave. But get this straight: I am going to be the next President of the United States." Steve Neal, *Harry and Ike: The Partnership That Remade the Postwar World*, 128–29.

cre crowds that greeted the president's whistle-stop campaign across the country. Truman himself seemed to remain confident, but few took his optimism seriously.

On election night we of the American public settled down by our radios expected to hear news of a coronation, not a contest. We discounted the first returns, which indicated that Truman was leading; after all, they were voters from the cities, Democratic territory. I cannot recall at what point in the evening we realized that the trend to Truman was real.

The Democratic victory was no landslide, but it was definite. Truman and vice presidential nominee Alben Barkley won a popular vote of a little more than 24 million, attaining 303 electoral votes. Dewey and Warren garnered a little more than 22 million, for a total of 189 electoral votes. Two third parties, one led by Strom Thurmond and one led by Henry Wallace, drew about 2.5 million, with Thurmond's Dixiecrats garnering 39 votes in the Electoral College. The support for Thurmond and Wallace came from the extreme wings of the Democratic Party, at Truman's expense. Without those two drains, Truman's majority would have been greater.

The trend toward these results came too late for Colonel Robert R. (Bertie) McCormick's conservative *Chicago Tribune,* the morning headlines of which read "Dewey Defeats Truman." The photograph of a widely grinning Truman holding up a copy of that paper for the cameramen has become one of our most famous political photos. It remains a source of grief to Republicans, especially to those of us who did not vote. The freshman English faculty at West Point consisted of eleven young officers, ten of whom were Republicans. Only one of those eleven had voted: the lone Democrat.

To the outside observer, the upset victory appeared to exert a profound effect on Harry Truman. Having now been elected president in his own right, he lost a great deal of his previous humility. The cry, "Give 'em hell, Harry" now dominated his demeanor, producing a defiance and cockiness that never left him, despite the trials ahead.

Truman was allowed little or no time to savor his political victory, for in early 1949 he developed difficulties with the Department of Defense that reached the point of confrontation.

Two years earlier, in 1947, the experience of the Second World War had helped him to reorganize the military services. The old War Department and the Navy Department were combined, and the U.S. Army Air Force, previously part of the Army, was established as a separate service. All three—Army, Navy, and Air Force—were subordinated to a single executive department. The reorganization had not been easy. The Army and the new Air Force favored it, each for its own reasons, but the Navy had strongly resisted being forced to report to the president through a secretary of defense. As a sop to induce the admirals to sign on, Truman agreed to appoint as the first secretary of defense James Forrestal, the former secretary of the Navy. On July 16, 1947, President Truman signed the National Security Act of 1947, establishing the National Military Establishment (later the Department of Defense).[7]

The organization of the Department of Defense, however, represented only the beginning of the president's troubles with defense matters. A competition for resources soon began among the three services. The budget for the total defense establishment was first set at fifteen billion dollars, but each service demanded a larger portion of the total than the others were willing to concede. The most difficult point of contention arose between the Air Force and the Navy over the best means to deal with the impending Soviet threat. The Air Force contended that the answer lay in the heavy bomber, the B-36, whereas the Navy contended that the counter to Soviet airpower lay in its own huge aircraft carriers. Defense Secretary Forrestal, who had switched his viewpoint from his days as secretary of the Navy, called on General Dwight Eisenhower, now retired and president of Columbia University, for assistance.[8] President Truman agreed, so Eisenhower made the trip from New York to Washington periodically, averaging a couple of days a week. At that time, Ike could see firsthand the wear and tear on Forrestal's personality under the strain.

In the meantime, the Truman administration continually lowered the defense budget, with Forrestal fighting him every inch of the way. Finally in March 1949, the president sided with the Air Force and asked for Forrestal's resignation, replacing him with Louis Johnson, a man more compatible with his own views.[9] Forrestal broke down with overwork and frustration. He was hospitalized at the Bethesda Naval Hospital, and after a few weeks of ineffectual treatment, he died by a plunge from a window in a presumed suicide.

Eisenhower stayed on as unofficial Chairman of the Joint Chiefs of Staff, but finally, when Truman reduced the defense budget to a total of eleven billion dollars, he declared himself no longer able to be a part of the ex-

7. The act did more than establish the National Military Establishment. It also established the National Security Council and the Central Intelligence Agency.

8. In May 1948 my father had been able to persuade the president to allow him to leave his post as chief of staff of the Army about a year and a half before his regular stint of four years was up. He then accepted the post of president of Columbia University.

9. By and large the Air Force position versus that of the Navy prevailed, although the Navy did thwart the rather extreme Air Force ambition to control naval aviation.

ercise. Truman seems to have accepted Ike's departure cheerfully. I have often wondered how we develop fixed ideas that Republicans are always promoters of economy and Democrats are always big spenders.[10]

It did not take long before Truman's parsimonious defense budget brought about near disaster. On June 25, 1950, the Communist army of North Korea crossed the artificial border of the thirty-eighth parallel of latitude and drove southward into South Korea, quickly taking Seoul and threatening to overrun the entire peninsula. Truman decided that the United States must aid South Korea.

The ensuing days were tense and dramatic. On his own authority Truman ordered the Air Force to support the hopelessly outnumbered and outclassed Republic of Korea (ROK) Army. A couple of days later he called on the Security Council of the United Nations for authority to go into Korea with ground forces and to name General Douglas MacArthur to command.[11] So the 24th U.S. Infantry Division, currently stationed on occupation duty in Japan, landed at Pusan and raced up toward Seoul to intercept the North Koreans. The two sides made contact at a point just south of Seoul on July 5, where the Americans were cut to pieces, as were several following divisions.[12] Truman has been justly praised for this bold action, but he should never be forgiven for allowing the American armed forces to sink to such a sorry state of readiness.

The next two months of the summer of 1950 were brutal for the American and Allied troops in Korea. The U.S. Eighth Army, in overall command, fought a delaying action back to a tight little defensive line around the southeastern port of Pusan, protected on the west by the Naktong River. The beachhead was eventually manned by a total of eight American divisions. By early September 1950, however, the situation swung in favor of MacArthur's UN Force. The North Korean supply lines were overstretched and subject to American airpower. The UN Force was now strong. General MacArthur decided to attack. He combined a two-division amphibious landing at Inchon, near Seoul, with a simultaneous breakout

10. In 1963, when I was assisting my father in writing his presidential memoirs, I consulted with Dr. Gabriel Hauge, his brilliant chairman of the Council of Economic Advisers. In the course of a discussion of fiscal policy, Hauge said casually, "It all depends on the preoccupation of a given party at a given time." That I considered heresy. I have since realized, along with other Americans, how right Gabe Hauge was.

11. He secured approval by an incredible set of circumstances. The Soviet representative, home in Moscow in protest over some dispute, was not there to cast a fatal veto.

12. The confusion was great. A friend of mine, heading for duty in Japan, found his ship diverted to Korea. He descended the gangplank at Pusan carrying his golf clubs.

from the Pusan perimeter. The North Koreans collapsed, and MacArthur's forces drove triumphantly across the thirty-eighth parallel and into North Korea,[13] not stopping until his forces on the east reached the Yalu River, the boundary between Korea and Manchuria.

At that point, however, MacArthur made a fateful error: he ignored reports that Communist Chinese troops had crossed the Yalu River from Manchuria and were hiding in the mountains of North Korea. Shortly after Thanksgiving, 1950, the Chinese attacked, driving the American X Corps back into the sea. Fortunately, naval superiority made it possible for the corps to be evacuated and brought around to Pusan to start all over again. The United Nations forces resumed the attack northward and once more had the communists on the run.[14] In late 1951 the Communists proposed peace talks, and Truman halted the drive north. The two sides then settled down on a line close to the original, roughly following the thirty-eighth parallel of latitude. There, along the present-day Demilitarized Zone, the United Nations and the Communists fought a low-level war of attrition until a truce was signed in late July 1953.

Despite the heavy losses of that brutal war—33,000 Americans killed and 103,000 wounded over the course of three years—the most remembered episode of the war occurred not on the battlefield but in Washington and Tokyo: President Truman's relief of General MacArthur.

The story of the "MacArthur firing" was a complicated affair, described in my chapter on MacArthur. In my personal view, MacArthur's brilliant mind was hobbled by his egotism; insubordination permeated his soul.[15] Since Truman often gave the impression of deference to his subordinates, MacArthur apparently grew to consider himself invulnerable to the president's wrath. He protested Truman's policy of limiting the Korean War by prohibiting any firing by UN Forces across the Yalu into China. That restriction obviously precluded any hope of driving back to the line of the Yalu a second time.

13. MacArthur's decision to go beyond the original goal, of expelling the North Koreans from the south, has been a controversial one, and the American Joint Chiefs of Staff were very much involved. That his move was not overridden can be attributed to a divided committee trying to control a subordinate on the spot who knew what he wanted.

14. The Eighth U.S. Army, although consisting principally of American and South Korean units, had representatives from many nations. The British Commonwealth provided an entire division. The Turks provided a brigade. The French and Belgians sent a battalion each, as did the Greeks. The United Nations force was truly that: a UN formation.

15. Ambassador Averell Harriman, in 1975, told me, to my mild surprise, "Even Roosevelt handled MacArthur with kid gloves."

MacArthur had a right to complain in private, but his mistake lay in taking his case to the public. When faced with such public defiance, Truman recalled him from command. The means employed by the president may have been ham-handed, but the action, painful as it was, had to be taken.[16]

The public reaction to the firing of an icon, a hero of our greatest war, was explosive. MacArthur returned to Washington and accepted an invitation to address a joint session of Congress, in which he pulled out all the stops, exercising to the fullest his talent for self-dramatization. It was said, and I think with reason, that the president could not go safely in the streets of Washington that day for fear of being attacked. Even Truman biographers admit that by the act of firing MacArthur, Truman irreparably damaged the remainder of his presidency.

The Communist aggression in Korea carried consequences far beyond Korea itself; it sent shock waves all across Europe and the United States, spreading fear that the Korean War could spread to Europe. Faced with that possibility, real or imagined, representatives of a dozen Western nations —Europe, plus the United States and Canada—met to devise an alliance whereby they could defend themselves. Fortunately, the North Atlantic Treaty Alliance had been signed the previous year (1949) in response to the Communist takeover of Czechoslovakia. Though the text of the NATO Treaty had contained strong wording—"an attack on one is to be considered as an attack on all"—it had thus far resulted in no concrete actions. The United States, for example, still deployed the single infantry division and large cavalry regiment to occupy all of Germany and Austria.

The NATO Treaty provided the framework for action. Accordingly, all countries involved pledged to raise their defense budgets dramatically and deploy substantial forces along the line of contact between the communist and western countries.[17] They agreed to place those newly organized forces under the command of a single military officer, and it was agreed that the commander had to be American, specifically General of the Army Dwight D. Eisenhower.

That demand from the Europeans presented an awkward situation, both for Truman and for Eisenhower. Eisenhower had now been out of uniform since 1948 and expected to spend the rest of his active days as president of

---

16. See chapter 7 on MacArthur.

17. The countries involved were the United States, Canada, Britain, France, Italy, Belgium, Netherlands, Luxembourg, Norway, Denmark, and Iceland. Germany did not gain admission until 1954, and Spain much later.

Columbia University. On the other hand, he realized that this was a true national emergency, and, though unhappy with the prospect, he fully realized that his status as a five-star general on active duty for life made him available for recall at any time. The trustees of Columbia University supported Ike's request for leave and promised to keep his position open for him. In a year or two, they were assured, he could hand the NATO command over to some younger general who could serve a full tour.

Truman was also in an awkward position. In recalling Eisenhower from retirement, he laid himself open to critics who could accuse him of conveniently removing a political competitor. Although Eisenhower had taken himself out of the 1948 presidential race, he had now been a civilian for nearly three years and might have changed his mind. Sending Eisenhower to Europe to command NATO could be seen as a political ploy.

But both Truman and Eisenhower quickly agreed that the crisis in Europe was dire, so Eisenhower was appointed. After a quick trip to survey the situation, he arrived in Paris to assume full command in early 1951.

It was at this time that Truman and Eisenhower worked together at their best. Their most serious hurdle was to convince the Republicans in Congress, many of whom were reluctant to finance the force levels the United States needed. The NATO defenses would depend on the United States, as the country already under partial mobilization. Truman and his advisers decided that the proper American contribution should be six "equivalent" divisions (one being the constabulary).

Congress, however, saw a military buildup as a threat to its constitutional power to "raise and support" armies. Some members also questioned why this country, already providing the vast bulk of the forces fighting in Korea, should be asked to assume such a heavy burden. The leader of this group was Robert A. Taft of Ohio, currently the foremost contender for the Republican presidential nomination in 1952. Taft, though lacking enough Republican votes to deny the president's desires in a vote along party lines, could probably marshal enough Democratic votes. As a last resort Taft could even use a filibuster. Truman and Eisenhower saw, therefore, that they must convince Taft of the need for reinforcing Europe—or at least refrain from resisting it.

Eisenhower, who had set aside any vague political ideas that he might have had, assumed the chore of persuading Taft to support the NATO concept. Aware that Taft feared him politically, he set up an appointment with the senator. At Taft's request, they met in an obscure office in the Pentagon. There Ike outlined the situation and asked for cooperation. To his disappointment, he received no satisfaction. Taft later relented, however, possibly because Ike withheld his original intention of taking himself out of politics by a Shermanesque note he had in his pocket. The force level of six equivalent divisions eventually passed Congress.[18]

Ike's wholehearted support may have been misleading. Truman could well have assumed that Ike was with him on other matters, even that Ike was underneath it all a Democrat.[19]

Possibly due to President Truman's prudent policy in Korea, the war in Korea remained localized. In the meantime, throughout the year of 1951, however, General Eisenhower in Paris found himself invaded by a host of visitors, nearly all of them political and most of them Republican, urging him to come home to run for president.[20] At first Ike stoutly refused those blandishments, but as time wore on, his resistance began to weaken. By the turn of the year 1952, however, he was still very much wavering.

On December 18, 1951, Truman sent Eisenhower a handwritten letter couched in terms far from the peppery style he is popularly known for. Its subtleties, however, are rife:

Dear Ike:

The columnists, the slick magazines, and all the political people who like to speculate, are saying many things about what is to happen in 1952.
As I told you in 1948 and at our luncheon in 1951, do what you think best for the country. My own position is in the balance. If I do what I want to do, I'll go back to Missouri and maybe run for the Senate. If you decide to finish the European job (and I don't know who else can), I must keep the isolationists out of the White House. I wish you would let me know what you intend to do. It will be between us and no one else.
I have the utmost confidence in your judgment and your patriotism. My best to you and Mrs. Ike for a happy holiday season.

Most sincerely,
Harry Truman

It was a remarkable letter, if only for the optimism the president seemed to feel for his own political prospects. And despite Truman's alleged preference to leave the presidency, his hint about Ike's "finishing the European

18. See Dwight D. Eisenhower, *At Ease: Stories I Tell to Friends*, 370–72.
19. In April 1951, while observing a tactical maneuver, Ike heard of Truman's firing of MacArthur. Notably, Eisenhower supported Democrat Truman's action wholeheartedly.
20. Many of the visitors were friends from his days in New York. Some among them were Democrats, including Senator Lloyd Bentsen, later secretary of the Treasury and Democratic nominee for the vice presidency. One nonpolitical visitor was the popular radio host Arthur Godfrey, who came to ask if he could make use of his wide audience to further understanding of NATO.

job" implies that Truman may have felt that he could defeat any other rival in a presidential election.

Eisenhower replied on January 1, 1952, in cordial terms. He was "deeply touched," he wrote, by Truman's confidence in him. "It breathes," he went on, "your anxious concern for our country's future." He, like Truman, would desire a return to private life. And finally, "I do not feel that I have any duty to seek a presidential nomination, in spite of the fact that many have urged to the contrary. Because of this belief, and because particularly of my determination to remain silent, you know, far better than I, that the possibility that I will ever be drawn into political activity is so remote as to be negligible." That exchange marked the culmination of the warm relationship between Truman and Eisenhower, and practically its end.

In the next few weeks, however, the situation changed. In early February, members of the burgeoning Citizens for Eisenhower movement demanded that he declare himself a Republican. They needed that simple statement so that they could enter his name in the upcoming New Hampshire presidential primary. When Ike did that, he had practically crossed the Rubicon.[21] Then followed Republican primaries in Wisconsin and Nebraska, in which his showings were spectacular. Finally, Ike gave in, returned home in mid-1952, and after a hard and dirty nomination battle with Senator Robert Taft was nominated at the Republican Convention at Chicago in July.

The Democratic primaries, for their part, demonstrated once and for all that Truman's status with the party was low. The American electorate by early 1952 was heartily sick of the Korean War, with the casualties it exacted every day. Further, the public had not forgotten Truman's relief of MacArthur. And finally, Truman's image suffered from the buffoonery of an old crony, Major General Harry Vaughan, who was accused of petty corruption. Such things, trivial as they sound today, gave the impression of a sleazy White House.

Truman was understandably disappointed over Eisenhower's Republican affiliation, and as time went on, he began to develop a severe animosity toward his former friend. The rift was inevitable. The Democratic candidate, Governor Adlai E. Stevenson, had no record to run against, so the Republicans were forced to attack the "mess in Washington." Any president is touchy about criticism of his performance as his office nears

---

21. In New Hampshire Eisenhower won over Senator Robert A. Taft by forty-seven thousand votes to Taft's thirty-six thousand. Democratic senator Estes Kefauver, of Tennessee, garnered 55 percent of the Democratic votes. Truman brushed the results aside by saying that New Hampshire was, after all, a Republican, not a Democratic, state.

the end, and Truman was infuriated. The lavish admiration he had once showered on Eisenhower was now completely reversed.

The president did not suffer in silence; he launched attacks against Republicans in general and Eisenhower in particular. One incident was particularly hurtful. Truman took advantage of a serious blunder that Eisenhower and his staff committed with regard to Senator Joseph McCarthy, who had just been renominated for senator by Wisconsin Republicans. McCarthy had attacked General George Marshall for his performance as Truman's secretary of state, and Eisenhower had planned to include a gratuitous paragraph in a speech. He deleted the paragraph at the request of the Wisconsin governor, and word got out.[22] The mistake was real, and Eisenhower always regretted it, but Truman twisted the knife with such venom that any possibility of a resumption of friendship between the two men disappeared. The animosity was heightened just after Eisenhower's election in November, when Truman offered the president-elect the use of his presidential airplane to make Ike's promised trip to Korea, "if you still want to go." Whether Truman intended the subtle dig or not, Eisenhower took the offer as an insult to his own integrity. He used another Air Force plane.

In early January 1953, I had the dubious distinction of coming briefly to Mr. Truman's attention—unfortunately, in an unfavorable light. It resulted from a misunderstanding.

On January 8, 1953, I received orders in Korea to proceed to Kimpo Airport and thence to the United States.[23] Though no purpose was given, it was obviously to attend my father's inauguration as president. I was alarmed; I feared that my absence from the 3rd Division would cost me the very desirable position I held on the division staff. I sent a message to my father, pleading for him to get the orders canceled. He never answered.

The situation was soon resolved, however. The division chief of staff informed me that, given the circumstances, General George Smythe would hold my position open. I lost no time in commandeering a small plane, making my way to Kimpo, and heading home.

On the morning of January 20, 1953, as my father rode with Truman down Pennsylvania Avenue, Dad asked a question that had been puzzling

22. The incident has been written up countless times. Suffice it to say that Eisenhower, having praised Marshall lavishly a few days earlier, did not believe that the deletion of a paragraph from a speech was an act of disloyalty. He had misjudged appearances when the alteration of the speech became public knowledge.

23. I had spent the entire autumn (and therefore the election) in Korea, where the war was still in progress.

all of us: where did my orders to return home come from? General J. Lawton Collins, chief of staff of the Army, had no idea. Truman answered brusquely, "Tell him that crotchety old man in the White House did it." That explained nothing, but we surmised that Truman had instructed his military aide General Vaughan to make the arrangements. Vaughan had gone directly to the Adjutant General, bypassing conventional channels.[24] I was reported as being angry at Mr. Truman for ordering me home, whereas I was far from it. He had risen above his feud with my father and decided that I ought to be there. I have always been grateful for his kind gesture.

The exchange between presidents had done nothing to melt the iciness between them. As I wrote of the occasion some years ago, "The atmosphere, while correct, was hardly warm. Though I stood almost next to Mr. Truman, he never spoke. Nor did I, out of respect for his desires. The atmosphere was a bit chilly, in fact, with little of the handshaking among guests that have seemed to characterize other such ceremonies, even the Kennedy inauguration of 1961."

On January 20, 1953, immediately after the Eisenhower inauguration ceremony, former president Harry Truman left Washington by train with his family, bound for Independence, Missouri. In those days, without Secret Service protection for former presidents, he seemed a slightly pathetic figure. He did not, however, intend to drop out of politics. He had opposed the nomination of Adlai Stevenson by the Democrats in 1952, and in 1956 he attempted to secure that nomination for Governor W. Averell Harriman of New York. But even his own party paid little attention to his efforts.

Harry Truman lived nearly twenty years after leaving the White House. After his early attempts to influence politics, he was not very visible. Much was made of a short visit between my parents, Mr. Truman, and his daughter, Margaret, at the funeral of John F. Kennedy in late 1963, but nothing came of it—nor did anyone intend that it should. He wrote his memoirs and supervised the building of his presidential library, which was located only a couple of blocks from his house in Independence, Missouri.

In March 1972, only a few months before Mr. Truman's death, I was a member of a group from the National Archives that paid a call on him and Mrs. Truman in conjunction with a visit to the Truman Library. At that point the old gentleman was completely deaf, and he sat reading books in their modest living room while his charming wife, Bess, entertained us

---

24. It took me nineteen years, on a visit to Independence, Missouri, for me to confirm my theory, which turned out to be correct. Mr. Truman, incidentally, had a completely different version of the conversation down Pennsylvania Avenue. This version comes from my father.

with a few minutes of pleasantries. He died later that year after witnessing the landslide reelection victory of his archnemesis, Richard Nixon.

For those of us who remember the dark cloud under which Truman left the presidency, it is sometimes difficult to understand the exaggerated praise, bordering on idolatry, that many have since heaped on his presidency. Part of the answer, I think, can be attributed to a change in what we expect in a president. In 1953 the public expected a higher level of dignity than is now the case, and in that regard Truman fell far short of his predecessor, Roosevelt, and his successor, Eisenhower. What people saw was a very ordinary-looking man, who made no bones about his fondness for bourbon whiskey and poker games with cronies, who often acted impulsively, and who sometimes employed what was then considered gutter language in public.

Neither the unpopularity then nor the glorification later is valid. In my opinion, Truman's administration should be regarded as simply a moderate, if cautious, handling of the nation's interests through extremely dangerous years. That is how we ought to remember him for today, with thanks.

General Mark Wayne Clark (Library of Congress)

# 4

# Mark Wayne Clark, the American Eagle

## A Very Personal View

General Mark Wayne Clark, known to the Army as "Wayne," was a true enigma. In terms of accomplishments, he was one of the giants of the Second World War. Such notables as George C. Marshall, Dwight D. Eisenhower, and even Winston S. Churchill swore by him for his drive, his bravery, and his imagination. Yet his fatal flaws of vanity and ruthlessness have caused him to be highly underrated. Some critics almost hold him in contempt.

Though I came to know General Clark fairly well, and even considered him a friend, I could never understand the contrast between his capabilities, on the one hand, and his insane lust for publicity, on the other. Why a man of such shrewdness could be so tone-deaf to his image among the people he was trying to impress defeats me.

In that respect, the officer to whom Clark bore the greatest resemblance was Douglas MacArthur. MacArthur's use of the vertical pronoun—"I shall return"—and Clark's ostensibly "giving his wife the city of Naples for her birthday" are infuriating to the soldier dying in the trenches. But both Clark and MacArthur appeared to be unaware of what their egos were doing to their lasting reputations.

Unlike many other officers who became generals in the Second World War, Clark was not part of my early years in Washington. He was not a West Point classmate of Dad's, and he had not served in the 19th Infantry, where so many of the family friends met.[1] But they had been in the famed Roughneck "F Company," and doubtless had known each other there. I recall hearing his name fleetingly in the Philippines. Apparently, Clark, already known as a "comer," was pulling strings to get Ike back to Fort Lewis, where Clark was in the 3d Infantry Division. He also was of help in mundane matters of the move home. I believe that Clark had left Fort Lewis for duty with the Army General Staff in Washington before our family arrived, but from then on Ike and Wayne were something of a team.

I first met the future general Clark during the early fall of 1940, when, following graduation from high school, I attended a West Point preparatory school in Washington. The Clarks invited me to dinner at their quarters at the Army War College, now Fort Leslie J. McNair. It was a pleasant evening with the Clark family, which included his wife, Maurine (Renie); his son, Bill; and his daughter, Ann. The atmosphere was warm. Clark was a tough man on duty, but he was an affectionate family man at home.

My most vivid memory of the evening came when Colonel Clark and I climbed into his car for the twenty-minute ride back to my school. Side by side in the front seat, I observed my host closely, aware of my father's prediction that he would undoubtedly become one of the prominent generals of the coming war. The figure behind the wheel, however, bore no resemblance to my mental picture of a general. What I saw was a gaunt, eagle-beaked man in a crumpled fedora, hunched over a steering wheel. His annoyance at having to drive me back to school was obvious. He brightened up when I volunteered to take the Mount Pleasant streetcar back to school. That trivial incident, however, left an image in my mind.

A little over a year later, on December 7, 1941, the Japanese attacked the U.S. battle fleet at Pearl Harbor, and America entered the war on the side of the British. By that time Clark, who had received his brigadier generalcy before Eisenhower, was chief of staff of the Army Ground Forces, and Eisenhower, a week after the attack, found himself on the Army General Staff, War Plans Division. Though Army Ground Forces was not technically part of the War Department staff, the two men worked closely together under the careful tutelage of General George C. Marshall. During the spring of 1942 he sent the two together to inspect the condition of the U.S. forces that were in the United Kingdom. When they submitted a critical report, Marshall asked for their recommendations as to who should head up the fledgling European theater of operations. Eisenhower recommended Clark; Clark recommended Eisenhower. Marshall sent them both, with Eisenhow-

1. Walton Walker, Wade Haislip, and Leonard T. Gerow were among them.

er to command the theater and Clark to command II Corps, expecting to invade Europe that year.

Marshall could have a sense of humor. "It appears," he said, "that you boys got together."

Though the Anglo-American Allies suffered one defeat after another throughout the first half of 1942, the tide began to turn after the American naval victory at Midway in the Pacific during June. Soon thereafter the Allies began planning for TORCH, an "occupation" of French North Africa. It was to be commanded by my father, Lieutenant General Dwight D. Eisenhower, with Major General Mark Clark as his deputy. Ike's prediction that Clark would be an important figure in the coming war had already been borne out.[2]

Churchill has called the period between July and November 1942 "the most anxious months." And so they were. Finally, however, after much backing and filling, a date for TORCH, the North African landing, was set in early November. In the last tense days of October, as TORCH was drawing near, Eisenhower received a message from Washington directing him to send a prominent American officer to meet some French officers at an isolated spot on the Mediterranean coast some miles west of Algiers. Such a contact was a godsend, because the bulk of the French army occupying Algeria and Morocco had sworn allegiance to the German puppet at Vichy, Marshal Henri Pétain. The Vichy government was supposedly "neutral," but it was at Hitler's mercy. The Allied invasion, therefore, needed all the help it could get from any officers willing to help in eliminating French resistance to the landings. General Marie Émile Antoine Béthouart was one known to be in sympathy with the Anglo-Americans, and someone needed to exchange information with him and his followers.

The mission would be highly risky. If the conspirators were to be caught, all of them, American and French, would be imprisoned at best and quite possibly shot as spies. Nevertheless, despite that risk, Clark let it be known that he expected to head the small delegation.

It may have been here that the Churchill-Clark relationship was born. Since this was an all-important meeting for both Britain and America, Eisenhower called Churchill at his weekend retreat, Chequers, and practically demanded that the somewhat incensed prime minister join them

2. As a matter of trivia, I have often wondered why Clark had elected to be known as "Mark" rather than "Wayne." My guess is that the name "Wayne" sounds too friendly and informal. "Mark" has a stronger impact on the listener. In any case, I feel sure that the change was calculated.

in London. Once Churchill recognized the drama and significance of the operation, he threw himself into the planning with zest, giving Clark his personal assurances that the whole resources of the British Empire were behind him. Clark had already come to the attention of Churchill, who saw in the American's large nose and gaunt face and neck the "American Eagle." Churchill's friendship would mean a great deal to Clark in the coming years and months.

The result was a true adventure tale. Clark's party of five[3] was delivered by a British submarine, the *Seraph,* at the appointed location off the Algerian coast but had to wait a day submerged before they could go ashore, with oxygen so thin that a match would go out for lack of it. They used canvas kayaks to carry them through the surf and up the cliffs. On hand were Béthouart and American consul general Robert B. Murphy, the sponsor of the meeting. Though Clark was unable to disclose the planned date of the invasion—Béthouart's main interest—he was able to secure extremely important information regarding the conditions in North Africa.

The conspirators were in peril all the time. The French police came to the door. Fortunately, they were suspecting only smugglers. While Clark's party hid in an abandoned wine cellar, Murphy, pretending to be drunk, dissuaded the police from entering. Clark and his party soon made their way back to the *Seraph* and were delivered back to London. Churchill and Eisenhower were delighted to see them.

Word of the meeting had to be kept secret until the success of the Allied landings on November 7. For a short time the episode caught the public imagination, during which Clark was in his element; he recounted every detail to the astonished reporters, and even his wife at home held a press conference on the subject. The story soon soured somewhat, however, because Clark, carried away by the presence of reporters, overplayed it using self-deprecating humor that was not so self-deprecating.

Eventually, the episode—or rather Clark's recounting of it—hurt his reputation. In the desperate early days of the North African fighting, levity was not popular. Clark's bravery and accomplishment were tarnished by his thirst for personal publicity. It was the story of Mark Clark's career in the Second World War.

Unfortunately for the Anglo-Americans, the mind-set of the Vichy French officers turned out to be even more hostile than they had expected. When the Americans landed on the night of November 7, 1942, they met with determined French resistance. Although all the landings were successful

---

3. The other four were Colonel Lyman L. Lemnitzer; Captain Jerauld Wright, USN; Colonel Archibald Hamblen; and Julius Holmes, State Department.

in securing bridgeheads, it appeared possible that the Anglo-Americans would be lucky to subdue men they thought should be their allies, not their real common enemy, the Germans. Ensconced in their forward headquarters in the British bastion of Gibraltar, Eisenhower and Clark were concerned as to what to do next.

At this juncture a rare stroke of good luck eased the issue: the Americans in Algiers unexpectedly captured Admiral Jean-François Darlan, the defense minister of the Vichy French government, who had come over to visit his sick son. With Darlan in American hands, the hope arose that he, as their military superior, might carry the authority to order the French in North Africa to cease resistance. With that in mind, Clark left Gibraltar on November 9, headed for Algiers to negotiate with Darlan.

Darlan, though a helpless prisoner, had his price. In exchange for his ordering the French commanders to cease resistance, the Allies would have to recognize him as the governor of French forces in North Africa. Clark tentatively agreed, and Eisenhower quickly approved. Darlan issued the order, and the French troops ceased resistance.

Eisenhower, and to a lesser degree Clark, was taking a great personal risk in making this agreement. Darlan had earned an unsavory reputation in both America and Britain as a Hitler collaborator, a man universally despised. No sooner was the agreement announced, therefore, than protests arose in both Allied capitals. The reaction reached such a crescendo that for a time it appeared as if Eisenhower's position as Allied Commander was in jeopardy. Eisenhower had anticipated the reaction but had decided that the safety of his command required him to take the risk. The action was later accepted, if not applauded, by both Roosevelt and Churchill. In one of the important decisions of the war, Clark had been a major player.

December 1943 was an eventful month, with the fighting raging in Tunisia in the face of miserable weather, a long and rickety supply line from Algiers to the front, and unexpectedly fierce German resistance. Finally, during a trip to visit General Sir Kenneth Anderson, commanding the British First Army, Eisenhower sadly suspended offensive operations against Tunisia for the rest of the winter. That same night, in Algiers, Admiral Darlan was assassinated. Eisenhower quickly replaced him with the American-supported General Henri Giraud.

In all this Mark Clark had almost no role to play. Harboring an overweening obsession to command a field army, he convinced Eisenhower that he should leave Allied Force Headquarters and take command of the U.S. Fifth Army, which was being organized in Morocco with the mission of defending the American rear and training for future operations. The official date of the organization, January 4, 1943, made the Fifth the first

American Army organized overseas in the Second World War. On the evening of January 5, Eisenhower hosted a farewell dinner for Clark, and the next day the ambitious lieutenant general left for Oran, where he took a plane for the thousand-mile flight back to Morocco. It was a good arrangement; Clark was one of the best organizers in the U.S. Army, and his mission with Eisenhower was completed.

Then, in February 1943, the Tunisian front blew up. Field Marshal Erwin Rommel, retreating from El Alamein with Montgomery's Eighth British Army in cautious pursuit, hit the American II Corps, on Anderson's right flank, and inflicted a humiliating defeat on the Americans at Kasserine. Eisenhower decided to replace Major General Lloyd Fredendall, who had proved himself incompetent. He offered the command of II Corps to Clark, but Clark was unwilling to step down a notch from command of an army to that of a corps, at lesser rank. Ike turned to Major General George S. Patton, commanding I Armored Corps, also in Morocco. Patton, as Eisenhower had expected, seized the opportunity to fight, even though his command would soon be elevated to the status of the Seventh Army.

Clark's refusal made an impression on Eisenhower, who placed a great premium on a general's selflessness and zeal to fight. The incident passed over, and outwardly Ike was unaffected. But from that time on, he viewed his friend with just a touch of reservation.

Clark and his Fifth Army not only missed the Tunisian campaign but missed the Sicilian campaign as well, which was conducted during the months of July and early August 1943. When Churchill was finally able to secure American agreement to invade Italy after the fall of Sicily, Clark finally had his mission: the Fifth Army would go into battle at Salerno, near Naples, on the Italian peninsula. With that decision began the period in Clark's service for which he is best remembered, from the landing at Salerno on September 9, 1943, to the fall of Rome on June 5, 1944.

Unfortunately for Clark's reputation, the entire Italian campaign was a thankless, costly operation, for which he has borne too much of the blame. It began with a near disaster at the Salerno landing on September 1943 and went on through the cold and rainy winter campaign of 1943–1944, including the disaster at the Rapido, and even Anzio. Though the bulk of the blame for these nightmares belongs to others, Clark's need for public acclaim, already mentioned, soured the troops under his command. But he also had another serious fault, his apparent distrust of his top subordinates. Having been sky-rocketed into high command so suddenly, he found that his top subordinates—Ernest Dawley, Fred Walker, and Troy Middleton, for example—were all senior to him on the regular promotion list.[4] Walker and Middleton, for example, had even been his instructors at the Army service schools. He therefore resorted to finding ways to re-move these very capable men, one by one. The result was that he lost their services but also incurred the wrath of other capable officers who were loyal to them. When it came to dishing out blame, then, Clark received no loyalty or even charity.

The first near disaster, AVALANCHE, should probably never have been attempted. It was undertaken as a compromise that should not have been made between Churchill and General George C. Marshall, who was resolved that no more forces should be sent to the Mediterranean. As a result, the operation was made on a shoestring, limited by lack of shipping to about four divisions, in the face of sixteen German divisions in Italy. Even Eisen-hower's main reliance, overwhelming airpower, was drastically limited. He went only on orders.

Here was Clark at his best. Despite the high risks of the operation, he showed no undue apprehension, at least to the correspondents. On the voyage between Bizerte and Salerno, he met with the newsmen to give them a briefing on the plans. One, the popular Quentin Reynolds, was par-ticularly taken by him, describing him as "lanky and likeable." According to Reynolds, Clark grinned as he asked the correspondents to sit down. When he called for opinions of the plan, Reynolds blurted out, "My God, it's daring."

"Sure," Clark agreed. "We're spitting in the lion's mouth. We know it." He then went on to explain the several alternate plans and why the Allies had chosen this one. "We may get hurt," he concluded, "but you can't play with fire without the risk of burning your fingers."

As Reynolds concluded, "When we left General Clark we felt a little better because of his quiet air of confidence. Clark at forty-six looks thirty-six—if that. He had never commanded large units in combat, but Eisen-hower had picked him. General Eisenhower didn't make mistakes—and he was sold on Clark."[5]

The Fifth Army was only half-American. It consisted of the British 10 Corps on the left and the American VI Corps on the right. It landed at Salerno the night of September 9, 1943, resisted only by the German *16th*

---

4. Major Generals Troy Middleton, commander of the 45th Infantry Division; Ernest Dawley of the VI Corps; and Major General Fred Walker of the 36th Infantry Division. Just after the disaster at the Rapido on January 20, 1944, Clark relieved all the key officers of Walker's 36th Division without consulting Walker himself. He did not dare remove Walker until the fall of Rome on June 5, 1944.

5. Quentin Reynolds, *The Curtain Rises*, 281–83.

*Panzer Division.*[6] On the second day German Field Marshal Albert Kesselring moved the bulk of the *16th Panzer* to the front of the British 10 Corps, allowing the Americans to push forward and take some critical high ground. In the meantime, however, the Germans began moving six divisions or parts thereof toward the beachhead.

On the night of September 10, Clark made an error he would never forget. Underestimating the German forces facing VI Corps, he sent two infantry regiments of the 45th Division forward up the Sele River valley, where the next day they were hit by the Germans on all sides. For a while the newly arrived *29th Panzer* threatened to break through the Allied position to the sea. The crisis came on Monday, September 13, 1943, when only two American field artillery battalions from the 45th Division stood between the German spearheads and the sea. By the end of the fourteenth, however, the crisis had eased; additional Allied divisions were arriving, and General Eisenhower had been able to convince the Combined Chiefs of Staff that he needed more by way of heavy bomber support.

Clark's first experience in high command exerted a profound effect on him. For one thing, it made him cautious. Perhaps more important, it confirmed his natural distaste for his British associates. Montgomery, the commander of the Eighth Army, Clark thought, had been inexcusably slow in driving up from the toe of the Italian boot to join the battle. Most infuriating was a memo from Alexander's headquarters in Sicily. In press releases, the memo said, Montgomery's operations should be "played up," but the Americans "may be mentioned."[7]

The Fifth Army reached the Rapido River in the last months of 1943. Even before reaching that obstacle, the high command, goaded by Churchill, conceived Operation SHINGLE, an amphibious seventy-mile end run to a beach near the resort town of Anzio, thirty miles from Rome. It was one part of a giant one-two attack, the other component being an all-out assault by the II American Corps and 10 British Corps upon the German Gustav line along the Rapido and Garigliano rivers. The Rapido crossing was planned for January 20, 1944, and the Anzio landing was to take place two days later. The two attacks, the Allies hoped, would induce German Field Marshal Kesselring to withdraw to a line north of Rome. Unfortunately, that hope was based on a false premise, and two regiments of the 36th Infantry Division were temporarily destroyed as fighting units.[8]

---

6. Field Marshal Albert Kesselring had anticipated Allied plans.
7. Mark W. Clark, *Calculated Risk*, 209–10.
8. The attack of the British 46th Division on its left was to be deferred for a couple of days

The failure had been anticipated by the troops. The crossing was to be made at a point where the Rapido was unfordable, its current swift, its banks steep, its crossing sites dominated by German strongpoints. The approaches on the near side of the river led across wide, flat, open, soggy ground. Major General Fred Walker, the 36th Division commander, protested. But Clark had no authority to cancel or delay it. In the eyes of his superiors, its importance to the success of SHINGLE overrode all other considerations.

Despite the sacrifice of Walker's men, SHINGLE was also, on the whole, a failure, even though it began with great promise. The British 1st Infantry Division and the U.S. 3d Infantry Division encountered very little resistance on the beaches, but Kesselring refused to abandon his nearly impregnable line of the Rapido. Instead, he secured additional German divisions from northern Italy, the Balkans, and even France, and soon had the Anzio beachhead hemmed in with superior numbers. As with Salerno, the bridgehead was at times in danger of being overrun. It would be four months, early May 1944, before the Allies would be able to build up the power to break those positions, at great cost.[9]

By early May 1944, both the American Fifth Army and the British Eighth Army were ready to launch their final attack to take Rome. Simultaneous attacks would be launched from the Cassino line and from Anzio. Clark's Fifth Army, now consisting of the French Expeditionary Corps on the right and the American II Corps on the left, was faced with crossing the Garigliano River on the Allied left flank.

On the night of May 11, the Rapido front erupted with artillery and air attack. The French crossed the Garigliano into the Liri Valley, and the American II Corps, with less spectacular but still substantial results, also crossed and began its way up the coast road known as the Appian Way. The Fifth Army advanced about twenty-five miles in eleven days, well over half the distance to the Anzio Beachhead.

Here was where Clark made his most controversial decision. In planning for the breakout from Anzio, Alexander, as commander in Italy, was presented with two options. Truscott's VI Corps at Anzio could drive northeast to cut Route 6, the German main line of retreat, or it could turn to the left and drive northwestward straight into Rome. From a military

---

in order that the 36th might take high ground that dominated the British crossing sites. The American 34th Division was on the right of the 36th.

9. Both Eisenhower and Montgomery had departed the Mediterranean theater for London in December 1943 for top command positions in OVERLORD, the invasion of Northwest Europe.

viewpoint, the first of these two alternatives, to cut Route 6, held the best promise of destroying the German army on the Rapido. Once that was accomplished, the city of Rome could be expected to fall of its own weight. Alexander selected that option and issued explicit orders for Clark to execute it.

Clark, however, had other ideas. Though he never openly contested Alexander's order, he executed the other alternative without informing Alexander. He turned his main effort to the left, thus ensuring that his beloved Fifth Army took Rome, all important to Clark.

His insubordination was obvious to those who knew the facts. Clark's blunt and no-nonsense subordinate Lucian Truscott, commander of VI Corps, had this to say:

> I was dumbfounded. I protested that conditions were not right. . . . This was no time to drive to the northwest where there was no evidence of any [enemy] withdrawal. . . . [We] should put our maximum power into the Valmontone Gap to ensure the destruction of the retreating German army. I would not comply with the order without first talking to General Clark in person. He was not in the beachhead and could not be reached even by radio. There was nothing to do except to begin preparations. Such was the order that turned the main effort of the beachhead from the Valmontone Gap and prevented the destruction of the German X Army.[10]

In December 1944, the death of Field Marshal Sir John Dill, the British representative on the Combined Chiefs in Washington, brought about a drastic change in the Allied command structure. General Sir Henry M. Wilson, the theater commander in the Mediterranean, was transferred to Washington to replace Dill. Alexander was sent from the Italian battle to Algiers in place of Wilson. On Churchill's recommendation, Clark was elevated to the post of commander, Fifteenth Army Group. It was a monument to the prime minister's devotion to the Allied cause that he supported an American, not a British, officer, for that important position. Churchill had never lost his admiration for the man he called the "American Eagle."

The Italian campaign may have become a "secondary" theater once OVERLORD was launched in northwestern France, but any campaign commanded by Clark would inevitably remain much in the news. Clark would see to that. And with the addition of such highly publicized divisions as the 10th Mountain, the Fifteenth Army Group broke into the Po

---

10. Lucian K. Truscott Jr., *Command Missions,* 275.

Valley in the spring of 1945. On April 29, 1945, Heinrich von Vietinghoff, who had replaced Kesselring as German commander in chief, surrendered all German forces in Italy, effective May 4.

With the end of hostilities, Clark's divisions were soon sent back to the United States. Italy, as an Allied "cobelligerent," was not subject to occupation. The American portion of Clark's Fifteenth Army Group crossed the Alps and became the U.S. component of the Allied occupation of Austria, a command separate from that of Allied forces in Germany.

My account now becomes personal, for I came to know General Clark fairly well during the Vienna occupation.[11] I reported to his headquarters in January 1946, about eight months after the end of the war. Thereafter, he played the role of proconsul, in which role he cut a remarkable figure.

The Allied forces in Austria were set up much along the lines of those in Berlin. As in Germany, Austria was divided into four national occupation zones, one for the Russians,[12] one for the Americans, one for the British, and one for the French. Also as in Germany, the Russians had overrun and occupied the nation's capital, with the result that the country was being administered from a city located well behind the Russian lines. Vienna, like the country, was also divided among the four powers.[13]

When I reported to General Clark in January 1946, his headquarters was located in an elaborate office called the "Bank Building." In contrast to the rather rustic Fifth Army command post he occupied in Italy, U.S. Forces, Austria was truly a higher headquarters. Everyone wore formal duty uniform (blouses and neckties) and kept regular office hours.[14] I do not recall much about my interview with Clark, but the general had already selected a job for me. I was to join the Allied Secretariat, a group that, in cooperation with its counterparts, prepared agendas for four-power meetings, wrote up the minutes for those meetings, and kept journals. The officers were intelligent, sophisticated people.

11. The tour of Italy in which I accompanied my father and Clark the previous September was a pleasant but not a significant event.

12. Technically, the correct designation is *Soviet*. However, we used the term *Russian* in our daily business (except with them, of course). It is also handier.

13. In this instance, however, there was a fifth zone, the center of the city. One borough, the First, inside the "Ring," was considered international. In that area, each power took responsibility for guarding the treasures inside the "Ring," rotating every month. The Americans were fortunate, at least for pleasant living, in that they occupied the western area of the city, which included both the Vienna Woods and the wine community of Grinzing, made famous by the onetime residence of Ludwig van Beethoven.

14. One of Clark's aides was Bernard Rogers, a future Army Chief of Staff and later Supreme Allied Commander of Europe (SACEUR).

The most memorable duty in the Allied Secretariat entailed keeping minutes of the four-power meetings. Admittedly, very little of a concrete nature could be accomplished in these rituals, because the Russians controlled all the important infrastructure of the country.[15] Feeding the Austrian population was a real problem. International agreements had set a level of 1,550 calories per individual a day, which in itself was low.[16] But the daily ration fell short of that. The trouble was largely due to the failure of the Russians to meet their share of even that modest quota, thus adding to the suffering of the populace.

Nevertheless, though Clark had few cards to play in the meetings of the Control Council, he dominated the four-power meetings of the Allied Control Council by sheer force of personality. He made a regular habit of arriving just a little bit late. Then, rather than hurrying apologetically to his place at the table, he would saunter around the table to have a word with each of his three counterparts. Towering over the addressee, he would laboriously question each about the health of his family and indulge in other pleasantries. He would then move slowly on to the next.

That bit of showmanship seemed to impress the Russian, Marshal Ivan S. Konev, who with his shaved head, flat face, and light-blue eyes resembled the conventional idea of a Russian peasant rather than a commander of vast armies. Clark spent less time patronizing the Frenchman, Marie Émile Antoine Béthouart,[17] and even less with Sir Richard McCreery, his onetime subordinate for whom he bore little love. I was astonished at Clark's performance. If there was any officer in the American Army who could play the role of emperor of Japan half as well as Douglas MacArthur, I conjectured, it would be Wayne Clark, now a far different figure from the disconsolate man in a crumpled hat behind the wheel of a car in Washington six years earlier.

In May 1946 General Clark apparently decided that it was time for me to take command of an infantry company occupying Vienna. He promoted me from my rank of first lieutenant to that of captain and arranged for me to be assigned to the 1st Battalion, 5th Infantry, which was just then arriving from the "Zone" of Austria. On receiving my orders promoting me to captain, I was instructed to report to Clark's office in the Bank Building for a procedure whereby the honor might be duly solemnized. I was a

---

15. One important matter was that of Danube River shipping, which the Russians kept well tied up, whether on purpose or from incompetence, I do not know.

16. At first we Americans were puzzled by the listlessness of the people on the streets, but we soon realized that they were simply tired, underfed.

17. It was Béthouart, it will be recalled, who had met with Clark on the Algerian coast in October 1942.

little bit baffled—promotion to captain was not a momentous event in the Army—but I was in no position to question the order.

When I arrived as directed, I was ushered past the tall, immaculate MP guards and instructed to join a group of perhaps twenty other young officers and men. Soon the general appeared, and the procedure began. Each of us in turn was photographed while being congratulated for some accomplishment or other. It was a well-oiled machine: each honoree stepped up, saluted, shook hands with a beneficent-looking general, and then left, to be followed by the next. A few months later, when my company had achieved a touch of success, I was decorated with a minor medal and reported to the Bank Building for a repetition of the ceremony.

Rumor had it that General Clark experienced a small altercation with one of his honorees, the lady who headed the local chapter of the American Red Cross. It seems that the Red Cross bakery had just produced the two millionth doughnut since its arrival in the city, and that landmark event deserved to be observed. The young woman had a request: she asked that the photo be taken from her left in order that the Red Cross patch on her shoulder would show. Her request was denied, however. General Clark was well aware that the left side of his face photographed to his best advantage, and that consideration took precedence over the lady's shoulder patch. I understand, if the story is true, that some words were exchanged before the outgunned Red Cross official gave up.

Chance had it that I saw General Clark occasionally on a social basis during this time. Clark's entourage included a group of young officers, some of them his aides. I usually managed to avoid that set, preferring to socialize with the members of my own unit, the 5th and later the 16th infantries. Occasionally, however, the Clarks held social gatherings that were command performances. There, on the tennis court of Clark's sumptuous residence, I was impressed with the general's agility, assuming, as does any young man, that an oldster who had turned fifty was ready for the wheelchair. At all such functions Clark and his wife, Renie, were great hosts, pleasant and unpretending. Clark was always dignified, but he was no stuffed shirt.

In 1947 Clark returned to the United States to assume a series of relatively routine assignments—commanding general of the Sixth Army at the Presidio of San Francisco and later chief of Army Field Forces at Fort Monroe, Virginia. I saw him occasionally then, but the meetings were not memorable. In 1952 he assumed command of the Far East Command, which had been set up originally by General Douglas MacArthur. The Korean War against the Red Chinese and the North Koreans was now well into its third year.

In December 1952 my father, as president-elect, made the visit to Korea that he had promised during the recent election campaign. Clark, as Far East commander, joined him. For three days I was detailed from my regular assignment with the 3d Division to accompany my father during his visit. Of the many conferences that ensued between them, one I remember with particular amusement. Clark reported one evening on a conference he had recently held with Syngman Rhee, president of South Korea. Rhee, a nearly indispensable asset to the cause of the United Nations, suffered from one serious obsession, his intense animosity toward Japan. The Japanese had occupied Korea from the early twentieth century until the end of the Second World War, and as an activist against them, Rhee had often been imprisoned and tortured. If Rhee hated the Chinese and North Korean invaders of his homeland, he hated the Japanese more.

By the time of the visit, the Americans, under UN authority, had built up a sizable South Korean army, consisting of some ten divisions. Japan, still disarmed after the Second World War, had none. Rhee, according to Clark, sought his advice on a scheme he was considering: to invade Japan with the army now at his disposal. But he had his doubts. "I don't really think that this is the time to invade Japan," Rhee said.

"No," said Clark with his customary suavity. "It would really be most inappropriate."

I next saw General Clark in his headquarters in Tokyo, about six weeks after the Korea visit. I had been called to the United States to attend my father's inauguration as president in January 1953, and I was on my way back to rejoin my division in Korea. My presence in a combat unit was viewed with much discomfort by many generals, but I had pleaded with my father to let me return to my old division. Dad had delegated the decision to Clark.

I can still remember Clark's face, as he sat slouched behind his desk, a bit annoyed by being put on the spot. My usual rejoinder, that I "played it cool," did not satisfy him. His brow darkened. Then, with very measured words, he said, "Well, I think I had better put some teeth into that." He then proceeded to outline what the limits of my travel in Korea would be, limits that made it just barely possible for me to do my job. But I accepted them and then headed quickly back to the 3d Division.

Clark retired from the Army the next year, at age fifty-seven. He had not attained the traditional pinnacle of an Army career, that of chief of staff, but he had commanded multinational forces in two wars, earning him a significant place in history. On his retirement he assumed the position as superintendent of the Citadel, the Military College of South Carolina. I have no idea of how successful he was as a college president, but he remained a celebrated figure.

As to his relations with the Citadel itself, my guess is that Clark remained relatively aloof from the day-by-day operation of the school, as he seemed to be aloof from his troops in Italy. He was, however, popular in the community. The bypass around Charleston, a major artery, is named "Mark Clark Highway."

Politics brings about strange situations. At one time in 1970, when I was American ambassador to Belgium, General Clark visited Brussels as president of the American Battle Monuments Commission. By protocol the ambassador is always considered the highest-ranking American within the country, so for the time of his short stay, I was officially—and only temporarily—his senior. When we climbed into my car, therefore, Clark insisted on sitting on my left, despite my pleas that he occupy the right, the seat of honor. As I looked at the still-slender figure in a now loose-fitting uniform, I was all too conscious that I had been a cadet at West Point while this distinguished officer had commanded the Fifth Army on the beaches of Salerno. But despite my protests, Clark would have it no other way. Things were always correct with Mark W. Clark.

In October 1982, while I was writing a book about the command structure in the Second World War, I felt an impulse to write to General Clark to observe the fortieth anniversary of his daring submarine visit to Algiers.[18] The eighty-six-year-old retired general answered cordially, offering to show me around Charleston. I was never able to take advantage of that kindness, because the general died a couple of years later.

In the 1990s my wife, Joanne, and I visited the Citadel in Charleston. It is an impressive, comfortable campus, and we enjoyed the Sunday-afternoon drive. At a prominent place is a memorial consisting of the periscope of the *Seraph*, the British submarine aboard which Clark made his clandestine trip to the Algerian coast in 1942. At one spot we spied a lone grave a short distance from the road. It had to be that of Mark Wayne Clark. An impulse grabbed me.

I jumped out of the car, walked up to the grave, paused in silence for a few moments, and saluted.

18. J. Eisenhower, *Allies*.

General George S. Patton Jr. (Library of Congress)

# 5

## George S. Patton Jr.

### A Zest for War

On the morning of December 19, 1944, General Dwight D. Eisenhower strode into the gloomy school building in Verdun that housed the main headquarters of General Omar Bradley's Twelfth Army Group. He had called a meeting of all the senior commanders of Bradley's command. More than just the building was gloomy; the weather outside was a dark gray, and the tactical situation facing the American Army in Europe was also dark. Adolf Hitler's gigantic Ardennes counteroffensive had been launched three days before, and German General Hasso von Manteuffels's *Fifth Panzer Army* was about to surround the all-important road junction at Bastogne. The news had reached the United States, and near panic reigned from across the ocean.

This was the first commanders' conference since the so-called Rundstedt Offensive had been launched,[1] and the various commanders had received no news to be optimistic. Perhaps to their surprise, they found the Supreme Commander in an upbeat mood. "The present situation is to be regarded as one of opportunity for us and not disaster," he admonished. "There will be only cheerful faces at this conference table."

Ike's optimism, which had been based on the latest intelligence estimates, gave everyone a lift. His remark was overshadowed, however, by the falsetto voice of an ebullient George S. Patton, commander of Third Army, then threatening the Saar. "This bastard," he shouted, "has put his cock in a meat grinder and I've got ahold of the handle." Everyone chuckled. George fought wars with professional competence but with zest. Immediately, Eisenhower and Patton, as the two men who controlled

---

1. It was actually Hitler's plan. Runstedt disapproved.

the means to fight, began planning to launch a counterattack northward toward Bastogne. Eisenhower asked how soon Patton could launch an attack. "Three divisions in two days."

Eisenhower was doubtful of Patton's ability to move so quickly but did not press the point. He would settle, he declared, for an attack of three divisions to jump off in three days. Patton excused himself and went to the telephone. Reaching his Third Army headquarters, he gave a simple code word, representing one of the three anticipated options he had left with his staff that morning. Thus was launched Third Army's attack to relieve Bastogne, a feat that was completed exactly a week from the meeting at Verdun. This was Patton the tactical genius at his best.

Unfortunately, the average soldier—the GI in the foxhole—did not share Patton's zest for battle or for military discipline. For the most part, the men saw Patton as more of an oppressor. Cartoonist Bill Mauldin, the most noted spokesman for the American infantryman, once depicted Willie and Joe, his two rough-hewn heroes, sitting in a jeep reading an impressive road sign. The sign was ominous: "You are now entering Third Army." It went on to present a list of fines to be exacted upon offenders of regulations: No helmet—$25. No shave—$10. No tie—$25. Windshields up—$25. The sign concluded, "Enforced! Ol' Blood and Guts." Willie thereupon says to Joe, "Radio the ol' man we'll be late on account of a thousand-mile detour."

I can well appreciate the attitude behind Mauldin's cartoon because I shared a similar reaction. Just after the war in Europe ended, the bulletin board at 1st Infantry Division headquarters displayed an order: "Beginning immediately, all personnel will wear a necktie as part of the regular uniform." We all groaned, hating to add a necktie to our already uncomfortable woolen shirts, and we feared more of the same. We now knew that the division had come under the authority of Third Army, commanded by Patton, the strictest martinet in the European Theater.

Both pictures of Patton—professional and eccentric—are valid, because Patton was a man of multiple personalities. On one side was the craftsman of battle, a man who could keep the location of every unit and every supply dump of the Third Army in his mind at the same time. And then there was the fanatic for military punctilio. But behind them was also George Patton himself, the man respected by his peers, but also chuckled at. It is that side of the man that I would like to throw some light on.

Patton's otherwise multiple personality is best understood by realizing that all his facets were governed by his total devotion to the military, the bad aspects as well as the good. To Patton, an all-out attack on an enemy position, a hot-blooded pursuit of a defeated foe, and the wearing of the proper uniform were all part of a single package: the military way. He was determined to follow the military way under all circumstances.

Hand in hand with his devotion to the military, however, Patton also harbored a burning ambition for personal recognition. Sometimes the obsession carried a humorous aspect. His son, George, my friend and contemporary, once told of an incident that occurred during the mid-1930s, when his father was commanding the 3d Cavalry Regiment at Fort Myer, Virginia.[2] One day, according to young George, he heard the sounds of sobs emanating from his father's upstairs study. George climbed the steps, knocked on the door, and asked what was the matter.

Colonel Patton turned and pointed to a book sitting open on his desk. "I see here," he moaned, "that Napoleon was a general at the age of twenty-six, and here I am, at the age of fifty, only a lieutenant colonel." The son left, knowing that the period of anguish would soon pass.

There were rumors that Patton actually dreamed that he was the reincarnation of various great commanders in history, especially of the Roman Scipio Africanus, who demolished the Carthaginian Hannibal at the Battle of Zama in 202 BC.[3] I did not know the general well enough to offer an opinion on the matter, but frankly I doubt it. We were all aware, however, that Patton studied such battles thoroughly. Perhaps his imagination allowed him to relive the experiences of the men of ancient conflicts.

Patton's adherence to the rigid code of military propriety evidenced itself from his earliest days as a cadet at West Point. He was comfortable with his own code with little regard for the opinions of others. This he demonstrated during his first class (senior) year, at which time he was the battalion adjutant, the second-highest-ranking cadet in the corps. One day, in the absence of the battalion commander, Patton was charged with marching the cadets to the Cadet Mess for the noon meal. After all were in their assigned seats, the officer in charge came through the door. Instantly, all the cadets stopped eating and sat stiffly at attention, faces straight forward. The young officer had apparently committed some act the cadets thought merited a gesture called "silencing."[4]

2. Fort Myer, Virginia, is situated next to Arlington Cemetery, across from Washington. Whatever regiment is located there is considered elite, especially for ceremonial duties.

3. The Battle of Zama (202 BC) was the final battle of the Second Punic War between Rome and Carthage, in which Scipio defeated Hannibal.

4. In my experience, such occasions were rare. One example, however, sticks in my mind. A certain young officer was in the habit of late-dating the cadets, who by regulation were required to drop off their ladies at the Thayer Hotel at midnight. Word got around, and the cadets not only silenced him but also gave him the sobriquet of El Lobo. The officer mended his ways and eventually lived down his disgrace, but it was a painful experience.

Patton would have none of it. In his own words, "I felt that the Cadets were misinformed upon this officer, and in any case, I was against 'Silence.' I therefore called the Corps of Cadets to attention and marched them home without lunch. The officer, who was somewhat young and inexperienced, criticized me for my action until I explained why I did it."[5] As with nearly all such actions in his career, Patton's superiors took no action against him, even though he often stretched the bounds of his authority.

There was nothing self-effacing or stoic about Patton's view of his own importance as an individual. He scorned the concept of the officer as a mere instrument of some invisible and faceless higher authority. Rather than waiting for others to decide his fate, he made use of every friend who had reached a position to advance his interests. In 1942, the first year of American involvement in the Second World War, my father, Patton's onetime junior partner, happened to be assigned to a position in the War Department where he could recommend officers for various important commands. Patton's letters at that time could be termed obsequious. To his credit, he always asked only for the chance to fight. That was in contrast to many other ambitious but less pugnacious officers. He would gladly step down to a lesser position if the demotion brought with it a chance for battle. Ike, who knew him well, was pleased but not surprised.

Patton's career was launched largely by his use of a personal relationship with Brigadier General John J. Pershing, future commander of the American Expeditionary Force (AEF), when they were both stationed on the Mexican border in 1915.

Pershing, commanding the Eighth Cavalry Brigade at Fort Bliss, Texas, was in a vulnerable emotional condition. He had recently lost his wife and three of his four children in a tragic fire and as a grieving widower was keeping proper company with Patton's older sister, Ann (Nita) Patton.[6] The thirty-year-old Lieutenant Patton, Nita's kid brother, managed to build up at least an acquaintance with the general.

That acquaintance might have amounted to nothing were it not for a twist of fate. On March 9, 1916, the bandit Pancho Villa crossed the border from Mexico and raided Columbus, New Mexico, killing seventeen Americans. An enraged public demanded that Villa be punished. President

5. George S. Patton Jr., *War as I Knew It*, 368.
6. Pershing had undergone a devastating bereavement the previous year when his wife and three daughters had perished in a fire in the Presidio of California, where he had left them, supposedly to keep them safe. Only Warren Pershing, age six, survived. He was away at the time.

Woodrow Wilson reluctantly ordered Pershing to track Villa down and bring him back, dead or alive.

Pershing made up a troop list, but it did not include Patton's unit, the 8th Cavalry Regiment. Patton, however, was undaunted. Determined not to miss the action, he presumed upon his tenuous social acquaintance to secure an audience with Pershing. When they met in Pershing's tent, Patton asked the general to take him along. Pershing apparently felt no pressing personal obligation, and he put the case bluntly: "Everyone wants to go. Why should I favor you?"

Patton's answer was quick: "Because I want to go more than anyone else."

The next morning Patton's telephone rang early. Pershing was on the line. "Lieutenant Patton, how long will it take you to get ready?"

"Right now."

"Well, I'll be goddamned," Pershing muttered. "You are appointed aide."

Thus began a friendship that lasted for the rest of both of their lives.

Once on Pershing's staff, Patton set out to ensure that his new boss would have no cause to regret his action. He performed various missions, some of them hazardous, with such temerity and good judgment that Pershing once told a protesting major that whatever Patton ordered were his orders.[7] On another occasion Patton took five men to ambush Villista General Cardenas, a man he knew Pershing wanted. Having successfully ambushed Cardenas and two others Villistas, Patton strapped the bodies across the front of his automobile and drove them through Villista territory straight to the general's tent. Pershing was both surprised and pleased. From then on he referred to Patton as his "bandit." The episode reached the newspapers, and Patton now, for the moment at least, basked in the public notice he craved.[8]

The Punitive Expedition lasted a little less than a year, only about three months of that time in active pursuit of Villa. The rest of the time was spent training in a fixed camp. In early February 1917, President Wilson recalled the Punitive Expedition from Mexico in anticipation of America's entry into the war on Germany. Within a few months Pershing was headed for France as the commander of the American Expeditionary Force. Captain Patton was still at his side as an aide. Once in France, however, Patton did not stay long. There were no hard feelings in his departure, far from

7. Ibid., 370.
8. John S. D. Eisenhower, *Intervention*, 288–89.

it. From the beginning the two men had agreed that his position as aide was only a device to get Patton overseas. Patton joined the fledgling Tank Corps, which was just in the process of being formed.

Patton was in his element with the tanks. Promoted to major, he was soon given the command of the 1st Tank Brigade, part of the AEF Tank Corps under Brigadier General Samuel Rockenbach. In late September 1918, Patton's brigade was given the most important tank mission in the Meuse-Argonne, that of supporting General Hunter Liggett's I Corps for the main effort up the Aire River toward Varennes. Liggett, in turn, attached the brigade to the 35th Division.

Patton's service in the Meuse-Argonne campaign was short but dramatic. His style of command did not conform to Rockenbach's conception of a brigade commander's proper role. Two weeks earlier, in the two-day battle of Saint-Mihiel, Rockenbach had reprimanded Patton for taking too many chances. Now he exacted a promise that Patton would stay close to brigade headquarters. Patton did not keep his promise long, however, and he was soon up at the front of the column, assisting in removing a tank that was stuck crossing a stream, under enemy machine-gun fire. Patton got his men to working by threats and personal example.

During a brief lull, Patton and his tankers continued, with Patton on foot. They soon met further heavy fire, and Patton experienced what he later termed a vision: "Just before I was wounded I felt a great desire to run. I was trembling with fear when suddenly I thought of my progenitors and seemed to see them on a cloud above the German lines looking at me. I became calm at once and saying aloud, 'It is time for another Patton to die' called for volunteers and went forward to what I believed to be certain death. Six men went with me. Five were killed and I was wounded so I was not much in error." Before allowing himself to be carried to the aid station, Patton demanded to be taken to the 35th Division headquarters to report the situation. He had, he announced, placed the brigade under the command of his trusted subordinate Major Sereno Brett.[9] His diary shows more pride in his assessment of the danger than grief for the men who had entrusted their lives to him.[10] He spent his time in the hospital planning the use of tanks in the next war.

· · ·

9. As an aside, Brett later became the closest companion to Dwight Eisenhower in the noted Army cross-country truck convoy of 1919.

10. There were exceptions, but only among persons to whom he was personally attached. When an aide was killed in North Africa, Patton kneeled by the body, kissed the dead boy on the forehead, and snipped a lock of hair to send to his mother. George S. Patton Jr., *The Patton Papers*, 203.

Patton in person was a human and likable man. He was the only officer in the Army that the austere George Marshall referred to by any other than his last name: "Georgie." He had an impish sense of humor and could laugh at himself—so long as nobody accepted his self-deprecation too readily.[11] He was no stuffed shirt. Except in times of emergency, he personally joined his staff every evening for a cocktail and dinner. As I recall, about thirty persons were present, including a couple of Red Cross girls who billeted at Army headquarters. There he played the genial host, often answering incoming telephone calls himself. One evening, so the story goes, a stranger, who obviously did not know who was on the line, shouted, "Is that you, you old sonofabitch?" Patton, unperturbed, took a gaze around the room and came back, "Which sonofabitch do you want?"

He was fond of his ugly white bull terrier, Willie. One day when I was one of his guests, he boasted that Willie, in a fight, had bitten off his adversary's ear. Patton beamed with pride. "When we got in the car," he crowed, "Willie threw up Jonahs and tossed the bloody ear all over my clean uniform." In almost the same sentence, however, he gloated over having caught a couple of soldiers speeding in a jeep and delighted in recounting the hiding he had given them. Patton had many sides.

In peacetime Patton's personal wealth set him apart from his fellows. He was, for example, allowed to maintain a string of polo ponies wherever he was stationed. When he attended the Command and General Staff School at Fort Leavenworth, an understanding Army excused him from the required equitation course. During those years, after the Army disbanded the Tank Corps, he was back with the horse cavalry.

Patton is noted for his strong language, which among men could be scatological. In mixed company he abandoned vulgarity and confined himself to blasphemy. He would begin a party using swear words until he discovered that nobody was paying any attention. Then he ceased swearing. Still, he had to be the center of attention. My mother, Mamie Eisenhower, once said she could detect "Georgie's" peeking out of the corner of his eye to see how his audience was reacting to his antics.

Ironically, the warrior who risked his life so cheerfully on the battlefield never quite overcame a haunting fear of some hidden cowardice. His recklessness on the back of a horse was a manifestation. And he went so far as to buy a sailboat that he sailed, with a crew, from California to Hawaii.

---

11. Eisenhower liked to tell of a meeting between King George VI of Britain, Patton, and himself. The king asked Patton how many men he had killed with his ivory-handled revolvers. Patton pulled some number out of the air—twenty or so. Ike looked at him sternly and exclaimed, "George!" Patton came back, "Oh, about six." The revolvers had probably never been fired.

As he explained to my father in the early 1930s, "I'm the world's biggest coward, and I have to prove myself from time to time."[12]

Patton's service in the First World War had not been forgotten. When the Second World War approached, he was recalled to the tanks and assigned to the newly formed Armored Service—and on to greater things.

When one thinks of Patton, the image comes to mind of the flamboyant uniform he wore in the Second World War. His getup, however, comprised only regular-issue equipment. With the exception of the ivory-handled revolvers he substituted for the regulation Colt .45 automatic, he wore only items the government issued. His helmet liner, though highly polished, was regular issue. His brass-buttoned jacket and riding breeches were standard cavalry uniform. His large belt was the regular "general officer's belt."

What made Patton's uniform seem spectacular was his ostentatious display of the four stars of a general. He managed to pin twenty stars on his uniform—four on each of his two shoulder straps, four each on the two tabs on his shirt collar, and four on the helmet liner. He always wore the ribbons for all his many decorations. To top it all, he developed what he termed his "war face," a rather peevish look that seems to the observer to be a bit juvenile, though the beholder tends to laugh with him rather than at him.

Patton always considered proper attire part of being a soldier. He referred to Generals Terry Allen and Teddy Roosevelt Jr. as "no soldiers." Never mind that the two had exhausted themselves (and the 1st Infantry Division) fighting grueling, successful battles in Tunisia and Sicily. They may have won battles, but in uniform and attitude they made no effort to conform to his strict disciplinary standards.[13]

Patton's mercurial nature contributed to both his success and nearly to his downfall. Just how emotional he could be was driven home to me one evening when I was his houseguest at Bad Tolz just after the fighting in Europe. During dinner the general broke into tears twice over things he himself had just said. When it was time for me to take my leave, he courteously accompanied me to the door. There, with moist eyes, he expressed

---

12. The above anecdotes are drawn from memory of conversation with my mother and father in the 1930s.

13. To be fair, both Omar Bradley and Dwight Eisenhower disapproved of Allen's and Roosevelt's informal ways, but they never went so far as to consider the two "no soldiers." One is reminded of a remark a sergeant allegedly made to a colonel, "Sir let's get this war over and go back to Fort Riley and do some real soldiering."

gratitude to my father for making the fulfillment of his military dreams possible. "I owe these four stars to Ike," he said.

I knew, of course, that in the heat of battle, Georgie Patton was often highly critical of General Eisenhower, usually for being overly influenced by the British. Eisenhower accepted Patton's moods as simply part of his nature.[14]

When the European campaign of the Second World War ended in May 1945, many of Patton's friends were concerned about how he would fare in the humdrum of a peacetime army. He was not slated to be shipped to MacArthur's command in the Pacific, so he settled in with his Third Army for occupation duty in Bavaria. Predictably, within weeks he had managed to shock newspaper reporters by offhandedly alleging that the Americans and British should have continued the European war—joining the Germans against the Russians.

Finally, in October 1945 Patton made a statement that hit a raw nerve at home and abroad. Frustrated by the difficulties of administering Bavaria without the skills of those men who had been Nazis as a condition of employment, he compared Nazis and non-Nazis to Republicans and Democrats.

That was too much. With great regret, General Eisenhower found it necessary to remove him from the command of his beloved Third Army. As my father told me the evening of the action, he did not do so "for what George has done so much as what he will do next." As it was, a gentle way was found to ease the blow. The Fifteenth Army, at Bad Nauheim, had recently been converted into a study group officially called the Theater General Board, the mission of which was to evaluate the performance of the Army during the European campaign. Its director was leaving, and Patton was eminently qualified for that type of work, and it involved no demotion.

14. In *Crusade in Europe,* Dwight Eisenhower wrote, "During my investigation [of one of Patton's indiscretions to the press] George came to see me and in his typical generous and emotional way offered to resign his commission to relieve me of any embarrassment. When I finally announced to him my determination to drop the whole matter and to retain him as the prospective commander of the Third Army, he was stirred to the point of tears. At such moments, General Patton revealed a side of his make-up that was difficult for anyone except his intimate friends to understand. His remorse was very great, not only for the trouble he had caused but, he said, for the fact he had vehemently criticized me to his associates when he thought I might relieve him. His emotional range was very great and he lived at either one end or the other of it. I laughingly told him, You owe me some victories. Pay off and the world will deem me a wise man" (225).

The whole matter was of some concern to me personally. I felt sorry both for my father and for Patton, and I was also uncomfortable because I was assigned as a member of the board, under the command of the man my father had just fired. I winced when Patton arrived on the scene and immediately set up a reception to meet all the Fifteenth Army officers.

Patton had been deeply hurt by my father's action in relieving him, but he did a class act in hiding his feelings.[15] With his usual delight in surprising an audience, he got up at the reception and declared, "I have looked at your reports and have been SHOCKED." Then, after a pause, he finished very softly, "by the excellence of your work." When we went through the receiving line, the general pulled me aside for just a few moments of pleasantries.

Patton may have been pleased with the work done so far by the Theater General Board, but if so, his approval did not prevent him from recasting many reports to the distinct advantage of Third Army. He also declared that he wanted to go back to the United States by the turn of the year.

It was not to be. In mid-December 1945, Patton was fatally injured in a car accident near Darmstadt, on the way to a hunting trip. Those who delight in conspiracy theories have had their day with that incident, but there is no question that it was a true accident. Both car drivers—Patton's own and the soldier driving the truck that plowed into him—were unscathed.

For a week the general, paralyzed from a broken neck, held on to life in the Army Hospital at Heidelberg. Even though I was not on his personal staff, I was kept in on the latest news, probably through aides. For a while we were heartened by reports of Patton's impish humor. At one point he refused to do something the doctor directed until he was given a shot of whiskey. Mrs. Patton arrived on the scene, outwardly the picture of confidence. "I've seen Georgie in these scrapes before," she assured us, "and he'll pull out of this one." But it was no use. On December 21, General George S. Patton died. Many of us from Fifteenth Army Headquarters took jeeps down to Heidelberg to attend the funeral.

Then occurred a small incident that to me represented the Army as a family. In her grief Mrs. Patton sent for every army brat she could find so that on her return home, she could report on our well-being to our parents. General Patton was buried in the American cemetery in Luxembourg.

• • •

15. A few days after Patton's relief, he and Ike attended a football game together. I was one of those who, on seeing the photo of them together in the stands, really believed that no hard feelings existed.

Most of the prominent generals of the Second World War have faded from memory, but George S. Patton's reputation has grown. His tragic and untimely death doubtless did much to promote his reputation, because the public was never given the chance to tire of him. As with other prominent public figures who have died at the height of their power—Abraham Lincoln, Franklin Roosevelt, and John Kennedy—his mystique was never dulled by the everyday exposure that eventually relegates most heroes to the commonplace.

Yet there can be no question as to Patton's prowess as a soldier. Military scholars such as Roger Nye and Martin Blumenson tend to see him as something more than merely an outstanding Army commander. Carlo D'Este names his biography *A Genius for War*. Blumenson even goes so far, in his book *The War between the Generals*, to suggest that Patton, not Omar Bradley, should have commanded Twelfth Army Group in Europe. Though I disagree on that point, Blumenson was a capable scholar; his judgment illustrates the degree to which the Patton mystique has grown since his lifetime.

Patton's reputation has also been enhanced by a good amount of orchestration, especially the efforts of his wife and family. In 1947 Houghton Mifflin published a book carrying his byline titled *War as I Knew It*, which obviously carries material from Patton's diaries. Also within a couple of years, a shiny bronze statue of the general appeared one morning across the street from the Cadet Library at West Point, much to the surprise of many members of the post garrison.

While Patton's abilities are unquestioned, it was his flamboyance, once a cause for criticism, that has caused him to be especially remembered. He is good copy, as evidenced by the lavish motion picture of 1970 *Patton*. It did not portray the real Patton, but it was great theater.[16]

Now men who once fumed over the discipline of "Ol' Blood and Guts" take pride in their service with him. They often approach me with a swagger and a look of self-satisfaction. "In World War II," they whisper proudly, "I wuz wid Georgie Patton in Europe."

16. The producer was Frank McCarthy, a graduate of the Virginia Military Institute, who served as unofficial aide to General George C. Marshall throughout the war. After leaving the Army, Frank returned to Hollywood, where he had been previously. He also produced the less successful motion picture *MacArthur*. I once asked Frank why he substituted Scott's booming voice for the little chirp that the real Patton had. I had some historical quarrels. Frank's answer was clear: you give the public what they want.

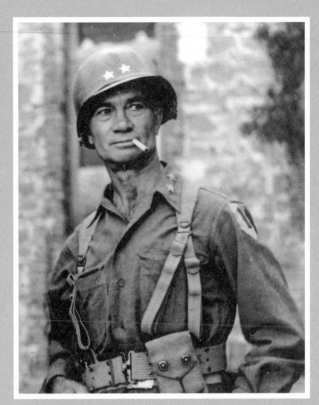

Major General Terry
de la Mesa Allen
(Eisenhower Library)

Brigadier General
Theodore Roosevelt Jr.
(U.S. Army)

# 6

# Terry Allen and
# Theodore Roosevelt Jr.

## The Terrible Two

On May 8, 1945, the day World War II ended in Europe, the atmosphere at the 1st Infantry Division at Cheb, Czechoslovakia, was remarkably subdued. Many of the division staff were veterans of two and a half years of hard combat in the Mediterranean and northern Europe, and I surmised that many were murmuring silent prayers of thanks for having survived. Others were looking skyward, laughing, where some enterprising American pilot in a German M-252 jet was performing wild acrobatics, confirming that the war in Europe was over.

As a newcomer to the Big Red One, I gazed around, taking everything in. My eye fell on an odd sight. In the front yard of the small hotel that housed division headquarters stood a large oak tree on which had been nailed a four-foot sign in the form of the division shoulder patch. A dapper young captain by the name of "Obie" Knight was busily tacking a glossy, eight-by-ten-inch photograph of Brigadier General Theodore (Teddy) Roosevelt Jr. to the upper-left-hand corner of the sign, preparing to photograph the sign and the glossy together. After two and a half years of war, this was the souvenir that Knight wanted to keep.

Roosevelt had been assistant division commander under Major General Terry Allen for only a year, from mid-1942 to July 1943. Together they made perhaps the most colorful pair of characters of the Second World War. They were rivals for the esteem of the men of the division, and they did not particularly like each other. Yet they worked together in harmony and mutual confidence. For some reason Roosevelt seems to have captured the imagination of the division more than the division commander, but Allen was definitely the boss.

Allen and Roosevelt had two attributes in common: they were both great fighters, and they shared a fanatical devotion to the 1st Division. Otherwise, their backgrounds could not have been more different.

Teddy Roosevelt Jr., oldest son of President Theodore Roosevelt, was an ambitious man, and he intended to follow in his distinguished father's footsteps, into national politics. He had the right credentials. Born in 1887 at Sagamore Hill, the family home in Oyster Bay, Long Island, he attended the right schools, including Harvard, and in his early adult years he exhibited a genius for making money in various enterprises on Wall Street and in industry. By 1917, at age thirty, he had amassed a fortune.

At the same time, however, Roosevelt had always taken a keen interest in the military. Even though sickly as a child, he had been strongly encouraged by his father to take military training. According to young Ted's later accounts, the elder Roosevelt recounted tales of heroic battles and imbued in him the conviction that America's elite should be at the forefront in the defense of the country.

It is not surprising, then, that in 1915 Ted Roosevelt entered the officer's training camp recently established by Major General Leonard Wood at Plattsburgh Barracks, New York.[1] Then, in 1916, with the war raging in Europe, Congress formally established the Officers' Reserve Corps. Roosevelt eagerly accepted a commission.

Former president Theodore Roosevelt did all he could to encourage Ted and his brothers to do their parts. When the United States entered the war in early 1917, he wrote to Major General John J. Pershing, who was then organizing the American Expeditionary Force, offering the services of all four of his sons to go overseas as privates in the 1st Division. Pershing accepted the two oldest, Theodore and Archibald, but not as privates. Ted, the elder, went in as a major, Archie as a lieutenant. Both were assigned as combat infantrymen.

The 1st Division, which represented almost the entire Regular Army, was being sent almost untrained to France as a token force. Since it was assumed that the division's first action must be successful, it was given much preparation, after which it was assigned to a period of low-level combat in a "quiet" zone. The Saint-Mihiel sector, devoid of action since 1914, was chosen. By May 1918 the division was ready for full-scale battle, first at Cantigny, north of Paris, then Soissons, and even later in the Meuse-Argonne. Ted Roosevelt grew along with the rest of them. He was wounded in the attack on Soissons in July and was decorated with the Distinguished Service Cross. By the time of the Armistice he was, at age

1. Wood was enthusiastically supported by former president Theodore Roosevelt, Ted's father.

thirty-one, a lieutenant colonel in command of the 26th Infantry, with which he would always be associated. Archie Roosevelt was not so fortunate. In contrast to Ted, who recovered, he incurred a wound in the knee from which he never fully recovered.[2]

When Theodore Roosevelt Jr. returned home to New York at the end of the war, he set out to exploit his laurels as a military hero to promote his political career. He was only moderately successful. In 1919 he was elected to the state assembly, and in 1921 President Warren G. Harding appointed him to be assistant secretary of the Navy, a position his father had held twenty years earlier. There his career nearly came to an end when he was remotely involved in the infamous Teapot Dome scandal. Despite his innocence, Roosevelt's reputation was tainted. Undaunted, he ran for governor of New York against the popular Alfred E. Smith, but was trounced.

In 1929 Roosevelt was called back into government service, this time in the civilian sphere. President Herbert Hoover appointed him to be governor of Puerto Rico and later governor-general of the Philippines. His tenure in Manila was cut short by Hoover's defeat in the presidential election of 1932, and the new president-elect, his alienated cousin Franklin D. Roosevelt, readily accepted his resignation.[3]

Throughout the years between the world wars, Roosevelt had retained his active reserve commission. He attended summer training at Pine Camp, New York, the Officers' Infantry Advance Course at Fort Benning, and the Associate Course of the Army's Command and General Staff School at Fort Leavenworth, Kansas. As a result, as the Second World War approached Ted was well prepared to perform active duty as an Army officer. As a colonel in the reserve, he was called into service on April 21, 1941, nearly eight months before Pearl Harbor. Whether by his own design or by the imagination of some historically minded personnel officer, he was assigned command of his old regiment, the 26th Infantry. Shortly thereafter he received the star of a brigadier general, but contrary to custom was kept with the 1st Infantry Division.[4]

Major General Terry de la Mesa Allen, the commanding general of the 1st Division, had followed a path that bore no resemblance to that of Roosevelt. Allen had spent most of his career as a regular cavalryman on the western frontier. He came from an Army family. His father and grandfather

2. Kermit Roosevelt served with the British, and the youngest brother, Quentin, was killed in the Aviation Corps.

3. Relative or not, Ted Roosevelt was a realist. When asked about his relationship with Franklin Roosevelt, he humorously replied, "Fifth cousin about to be removed." In that he was correct.

4. Because of the new armored divisions, the Big Red One was now officially the 1st Infantry Division. I will often omit the word *Infantry*.

before him had been soldiers, his father a graduate of West Point. Terry was born in 1888 at Fort Douglas, Utah, near Salt Lake City. His mother, Conchita de la Mesa, was the daughter of Colonel Carlos de la Mesa, a Spanish officer who had fought for the Union in the American Civil War.

Young Terry, growing up in the West, has been described as "saddle-hardened before he was ten." Associated with regular troopers, he had all the minor vices—chewing tobacco, smoking, cussing, and fighting. In 1907, in common with most Army sons, he applied for and was accepted as a cadet at West Point in the class of 1911.

The West Point disciplinary system, however, did not agree with Terry Allen. He acquired the nickname "Tear Around the Mess Hall Allen," and often he flagrantly flouted the normal military rules, such as breaking ranks to pet a puppy. His demerits were high. It was academics, however, that spelled his doom; he failed in both Ordnance and Mathematics. After two years as a cadet, he was dismissed.

Once released from the rigidity of West Point, however, Allen pulled himself together. He graduated from Catholic University in Washington in 1912, in the process winning a competitive examination for the Regular Army. On November 12, 1912, he was commissioned a second lieutenant of cavalry. On duty with the cavalry on the Texas border the following year, he captured a group of smugglers, thus experiencing his first taste of action.

Allen served with the infantry in the First World War, not his regular branch of cavalry. In the Saint-Mihiel campaign of September 1918, he was decorated with a Silver Star for "distinguished and exceptional gallantry," and he was wounded in the jaw. He was said to have been disappointed that the war ended in November 1918, because he was just learning his job as battalion commander. After serving in the occupation of Germany, he returned to the United States and the cavalry in 1920.

In his postwar career, Allen continued to follow a pattern of ups and downs. At the Command and Staff School in 1926, he graduated 221st out of a student body of 241. His drinking was often excessive,[5] and he barely finished the course. Once again on active duty, however, his soldierly qualities again became evident. In 1928 he was assigned to the Weapons Department of the Infantry School, Fort Benning, along with such future luminaries as Joseph Stilwell and Omar N. Bradley. There he came under the watchful eye of Colonel George C. Marshall, who noted Allen's prow-

5. On a personal note, my father, Dwight Eisenhower, attended the same class, standing number 1. So noteworthy was Allen's drunkenness that it was a shock to the Army wives that Allen stayed in the Army, let alone was later promoted to command a division. When Allen's photo appeared on the cover of *Time* during the war, I remember my mother remarking, "Well, you don't have to wear socks in Tunisia."

ess with infantry weapons. In 1940 Marshall, as the newly appointed chief of staff, promoted Allen to the rank of brigadier general in the Army of the United States.[6] He assumed command of the 1st Infantry Division in June 1942. There he met Roosevelt, presumably for the first time.

## The Landing at Oran

Under Terry Allen in the Mediterranean, the 1st Division saw combat at Oran, Algeria; Gafsa, El Guettar; Hill 609 in Tunisia; as well as Sicily later on. It would be impossible to describe all the actions. One that illustrates the way that Allen and Roosevelt worked together, however, involved the Oran landing the night of November 7, 1942, in Operation TORCH.

TORCH was the code name for the invasion of French North Africa. But though the Americans and British harbored hopes that the Vichy officers would greet them as liberators, they wisely decided to land as if they expected to be resisted—which turned out to be the case. Rather than landing in the town, Allen decided to split the division and land at points east and west of the city proper. He assigned the western landing to Roosevelt with the 26th Regimental Combat Team.[7] He himself would command the rest of the division.

The conduct of the two task forces, both successful, illustrates the difference in the way that Allen and Roosevelt operated. Roosevelt, the dramatist and romantic, landed in the early morning. Spotting a soldier taking refuge behind a hillock, Roosevelt shouted, "Come on! Follow me." He then drove forward in his jeep, the name "Rough Rider" painted below the dashboard, ignoring the machine-gun bullets that were hitting the sand all around. As he rode out ahead of his troops, he shouted back that he was going forward to find a French commander who might be willing to surrender. "If I'm not back in two hours," he yelled, "give it all you've got!!"[8] He soon returned, however, safely but with no surrender. The French were not in that kind of mood. Not for a while yet.

To the east, Allen landed the rest of the division on a beach near Arzew, about twenty-five miles away from Oran. To give him the punch he needed, General Lloyd Fredendall, the task force commander at Oran, had

---

6. As a matter of casual interest, the United States Army (USA) and the Army of the United States (AUS) are two different animals. USA designates the regular army, the ranks therein being permanent. AUS involves the temporary rank awarded in times of emergency, particularly war. Thus, General Eisenhower, in mid-1943, was a general (four stars) in the Army of the United States but still only a lieutenant colonel in the USA.

7. The regimental combat team was a task force consisting of an infantry regiment (hence its name), with its normally associated artillery battalion, a company of engineers, some tanks, and other necessary units. The task organization was used only when distances made fighting as a unit infeasible.

8. Rick Atkinson, *An Army at Dawn,* 85–87.

given him William O. Darby's 1st Ranger Battalion and a combat command from the 1st Armored Division.[9] Two parallel roads led from Arzew to Oran, so Allen sent the 18th Infantry along the direct road and the 16th on the parallel road farther south. Once the infantry had secured the beaches, the plan called for the armor to sweep southward to cut off the city and prevent any reinforcement by the French.

Allen's approach to his job carried none of the romance of Roosevelt's. He indulged in no histrionics. Instead of appealing to patriotism and the lore of the Rough Riders,[10] Allen varied his appeals for action according to his audience. When he spotted troops he believed were spoiling for a fight, he would shout, "Boys, I've just sent a signal to the French to put in their first team." He tantalized a company lying exhausted in a ditch with a promise: "There are a lot of good-looking girls in that town ready to welcome the liberating Americans." To those he considered laggards, he simply threatened, "Take Oran or you don't eat."[11]

Despite the hopelessness of resistance to the Allied landings, the French troops defending Oran still insisted that their honor as officers required them to put up at least a token resistance. Unaware that peace negotiations were going on between Clark and Darlan in Algiers,[12] they held out fiercely. Thus on the morning of November 9, a day after the landing, the 18th Infantry remained stalled in front of the town of St. Cloud, only a few miles from Arzew. At that point, Allen realized that to reduce St. Cloud would take an all-out effort. Urged on by an exasperated regimental commander, he massed his artillery and tank support, ready to level the town.

Before letting loose with all his power, however, Allen paused. His objective, he reminded himself, was Oran, not St. Cloud. Furthermore, he knew that this small town was full of innocent civilians cowering in the stone buildings. He therefore changed his orders, instructing a disappointed regimental commander to stop and "contain" St. Cloud with a single infantry battalion. The rest of the 18th Infantry was to follow along the parallel road assigned to the 16th. His humanity and good common sense were rewarded. No enemy attack emanated from the bypassed St. Cloud.[13] Terry Allen was admiringly called the "fightingest general in the world," but he was no butcher.

On the morning of November 10, Allen's armor had swept around and entered Oran from the south, with the infantry, on the outskirts, not far be-

9. The 1st Armored Division will henceforth be referred to as the 1st Armored.

10. In the Spanish-American War of 1898, Roosevelt's father had made his name for his heroics at San Juan Hill with the Rough Riders.

11. Ibid., 127.

12. See chapter 4, "Mark Wayne Clark, the American Eagle."

13. Ibid., 127–28.

hind. In the late morning, men of the 16th Infantry spotted a tank up ahead but wisely held their fire. It was one of their own, and it had a message: the French command in Algiers had agreed to an armistice, the cease-fire to take effect at 1215. Taking Oran was the toughest nut of all the five major Allied landings.[14]

For the next few weeks following the landing at Oran, Allen and Roosevelt were doomed to frustration due to lack of action. The supply situation made it impossible for the Allied high command to employ even those meager forces closer to Tunisia. All supplies to the Tunisian front had to be delivered on a rickety single-track railway and a small dirt road, both of which ran from Algiers, five hundred miles away. On December 24, 1942, therefore, General Eisenhower ordered Lieutenant General Sir Kenneth Anderson, the British officer in tactical command of the Tunisian front, to suspend his futile effort to take Tunis and go on an aggressive defensive.

Anderson built up a thin defensive position on a north-south ridge called the Western Dorsal, which joined in the north with another range of hills called the Eastern Dorsal, meeting at a point just south of Tunis. As the dorsals ran south, they separated, with the Eastern running parallel to the Tunisian east coast. In the north, facing Tunis, was Anderson's British First Army, a force that, despite its impressive designation, comprised only a little more than a reinforced armored division. In the center, on Anderson's right, was the French XIX Corps under General Alphonse Pierre Juin. On the south was the U.S. II Corps, which consisted of only the 1st Armored and the 34th Infantry divisions. The two were spread out over a vast area.[15] There things stood until after the second week of February, when Rommel and von Arnim turned their retreating forces on the stretched-out and green American troops at Faid and Kasserine passes.[16] In this action, bits and pieces of the 1st Division played creditable supporting roles, but never as a coordinated force.

On March 6, 1943, after the Kasserine disaster had been brought under control, General Eisenhower relieved General Fredendall as commander

14. The Oran landing carried with it a tragic aspect. An auxiliary landing was made straight into the port area of the town, expecting a quick French surrender. Instead, they were met by rockets, machine-gun fire, and antitank guns. The casualties came to 189 dead and 157 wounded out of an original 393 men. The survivors were all captured.

15. For a while General Eisenhower hoped to launch a limited offensive from Tebessa, Algeria, the American base, toward the sea at Gabes. That operation died, however, because the British managed to get it canceled at the Anglo-American Casablanca Conference in January.

16. The German forces in Tunisia were split between Field Marshal Erwin Rommel and Colonel General Jürgen von Arnim.

of II Corps and replaced him with Major General George S. Patton Jr. With Rommel now preoccupied with defending against the advancing British Eighth Army, and with the Western Dorsal now restored, General Sir Harold Alexander, the newly arrived overall ground commander, began planning for the last phase of the campaign. In general it called for the Americans and the French to confine their action to pushing forward from the Western to the Eastern Dorsal. There they were to stop. Their mission was passive, to confine the retreating Germans to a channel in which Montgomery's Eighth Army, driving northward from the Mareth line, would act as a projectile in the barrel of a gun.[17]

Patton, anxious to attack, considered this plan an implied insult to American arms. A man who at best bore the British little love, Patton decided to modify the orders. He would drive southeastward from the main American base at Tebessa to Gafsa, hoping possibly to continue to the port of Gabes. To lead the attack, he chose the 1st Division, the only unit in his command that did not need rehabilitation. For the first time since the landing at Oran, the 1st Division had been given a chance to operate as a single unit. The members of the division were delighted.

### Gafsa—El Guettar

The 1st Division attack toward Gafsa was launched in mid-March 1943. Code-named Operation WOP, it was officially touted as a move to support Montgomery's triumphant march northward.[18] In reality Patton had no intention to so limit the mission. His fighting blood was hot. "Gentlemen, tomorrow we attack," he told his commanders. "If we are not victorious, let no one come back alive." Patton then retired to his tent to pray.[19]

Terry Allen, the man in charge of the actual fighting, moved his three combat teams from their assembly point near Tebessa early on the morning of March 17. They covered the fifty miles to Gafsa by late morning without meeting resistance.[20] Shortly after noon the town was declared secure. Patton was disappointed. "The dagoes beat it," he complained. It is doubtful that many of the foot-slogging soldiers felt the same disappointment.[21]

Despite the easy start, however, Allen was far from content. Gafsa was not much of a prize; it consisted of only five hundred French settlers and

17. The Mareth line ran along the Tunisian-Libyan border.
18. The term *wop*, probably out of use now, was a derogatory name for Italians in general and recently arrived immigrants from Italy. Many were illegal. Hence, the initials stand for "without papers."
19. Ibid., 434.
20. James Scott Wheeler, *The Big Red One*, 185.
21. Atkinson, *An Army at Dawn*, 434.

some local Arabs. Further, the flat territory was not fitted for a strong defense. So despite Alexander's orders to stop in place, Allen decided to "reconnoiter" El Guettar, some eleven miles down Route 15. Darby's Rangers pushed forward and occupied El Guettar without incident by the late afternoon of March 18.[22] Allen also moved some of his artillery up close in anticipation of further attacks southeastward.

Meanwhile, the situation was changing on the rest of the Tunisian front. Montgomery, who had expected to sail through the German defenders at the Mareth line in the South, discovered that the First Italian Army and the German Afrika Korps were still capable of fighting; he needed help. Alexander therefore ordered Patton to do what he had already done, to push on to El Guettar.

Contact with the fleeing enemy had been lost, however, and intelligence indicated that many Germans and Italians were not far off. "It's all going like maneuvers," Allen mused. "It can't be right." Perhaps unbeknownst to Allen, the II Corps intelligence officer was reporting, "Rommel probably will attack us with whatever he has left after dealing with Eighth Army. Probably not earlier than 24 March."[23] They were right. Von Arnim had decided to attack and destroy the Americans. The unit he selected for this task was the famed *10th Panzer Division.* It would follow Route 15 toward El Guettar on a collision course with the 1st Division.

Early on the morning of March 23, 1943, Ted Roosevelt was awakened by the sound of gunfire. He had slept with his boots on, and in short order he had made his way to the command post of the 18th Infantry, atop Hill 336,[24] which provided a magnificent view. There he learned that a full battle had been in progress since seven o'clock. The Germans, he noted, were employing their best tanks—Mark IVs—and the attack was being supported from the air by German JU-88s, ME-109s, and FW-190s.[25]

Without waiting for instructions, Roosevelt took charge of the immediate battlefield. First he ordered two battalions of the 18th Infantry to move left, where the threat to the division's flank was serious. He then sent for the 601st Tank Destroyer (TD) Battalion. The critical threat would come from the estimated fifty German tanks rumbling up Route 15.

At the division command post, only two miles from the front, Terry Allen had no intention of evacuating his position despite the threat. When someone suggested pulling back, he snapped, "I will like hell pull out."

22. Wheeler, *The Big Red One,* 186.
23. Atkinson, *An Army at Dawn,* 438.
24. The command post was named "Wop Hill," consistent with the name of the operation.
25. Gerald Astor, *Terrible Terry Allen,* 165–66.

Then he added, "And I'll shoot the first bastard who does."[26] He then joined Roosevelt on Hill 336.

The battle raged throughout the morning. American artillery, which he had moved forward from Gafsa, poured rounds into the advancing German tanks. Infantry employed machine guns, grenades, and bazookas. The greatest damage to the Germans was done by the 601st Tank Destroyer Battalion, with its outclassed 75 mm guns, later joined by the 899th TD Battalion with its more substantial 3-inch guns. A report later revealed the extent of the loss: "All the guns of Companies B and C of the 601st Tank Destroyer Battalion and 7 guns of the 899th Tank Destroyer Battalion were lost. 30 and possibly 50 enemy tanks were knocked out."[27] Eventually, the Germans pulled back. Nobody expected them to give up so easily.

At 3:00 p.m. that same day, a British radio intercept team broke the code of the *10th Panzer*. From a message they learned that six battalions of German infantry were prepared to attack in forty-five minutes. A little bit later a second message came through delaying the attack until 4:20 p.m. Patton, at II Corps, despite the need to protect radio security, distributed that critical warning to his commanders. He then hopped in his jeep and drove up to Allen's command post. What happened then was typical Terry Allen. His dander up, he grabbed a microphone and transmitted a radio message to the Germans: "What the hell are you waiting for? We have been ready since 4:00 P.M. Signed 1st Division."

Patton was disgusted. "Terry," he yelled, "when are you going to learn to take this damn war seriously?"[28] Patton was wrong. Terry Allen was taking the war seriously indeed. His taunt was part of his fighting make-up. Besides, Patton himself had first betrayed the breaking of the German code when he sent his earlier warnings. In any event, Allen was unrepentant.

The infantry of the German *10th Panzer Division* came on schedule, but seemed to move forward reluctantly. This time the Americans were ready. Armed with VT fuses, the American artillery wrought tremendous slaughter.[29] The Germans fell back, and the field belonged to the 1st Division and attached elements of the 9th Infantry Division. Elated, Allen gave a press conference, basking in the success. He was proud, he said, that the 1st Division had fought off the enemy without tanks (giving inadequate credit to the decimated tank destroyers) and condescendingly forgave the Allied air forces for their lack of help. The battle had, he pointed out, been fought under the air forces of the Germans.

26. Atkinson, *An Army at Dawn*, 440.
27. Astor, *Terrible Terry Allen*, 166.
28. Atkinson, *An Army at Dawn*, 442.
29. The variable timed (VT) fuse, set to explode before hitting the ground, greatly increased the lethality of an artillery shell.

The casualties had not been light, and it was estimated that American losses had been heavier than those of the Germans. Nevertheless, the Americans had stopped the best the Germans had. Allen's men, however, could go no farther than El Guettar. Attrition was heavy in the vicinity until April 7, two weeks after the beginning of the battle. The most important thing was that American pride, so wounded at Kasserine, had been restored.

Despite the fact that the 1st Division had fought well, an ominous cloud was on the horizon; the division was showing an excessive lack of formal discipline. Neither Allen nor Roosevelt cared for appearances—far from it—and they both seemed to revel in playing the part of fighting roughnecks. Furthermore, apparently vying for the cheers of their men, each of the generals dropped broad hints, if not promises, that the 1st would soon be sent home to the United States or given an extended rest. They also encouraged their men to feel contempt for those "rear echelon bastards" in Oran, the headquarters and service men who had been wearing the comfortable khaki uniforms while they were wearing the itchy wools. The breakdown in discipline was not yet acute, but the seeds had been planted.

Following the action at El Guettar, Montgomery's Eighth Army finally broke the German position at the Mareth line. When that happened, the Americans found themselves with their front devoid of enemy. Alexander's plan for the last drive made military sense: Montgomery was to drive up the Tunisian coast to meet Anderson's British First Army holding Tunis, Bizerte, and Mateur. But the Americans still needed more successes to build national confidence, so Eisenhower gave Alexander a direct order to move the American II Corps northward and give it a place in the line for the final drive.[30] Alexander placed the II Corps, now under Omar Bradley, on the north, to drive from Beja to Mateur, about thirty miles beyond. Final plans for the very last push awaited developments. If II Corps reached Mateur ahead of Anderson, Bradley could then continue on to Bizerte, a little more than twenty miles farther on. Alexander probably did not expect that to come about.

Bradley's front was about sixty miles across, and he had four divisions to work with—the 1st, 9th, and 34th infantry divisions and the 1st Armored. The front afforded only two usable roads to Mateur, both leading through

30. Allen claimed that the original idea had been his; Bradley later did the same; even Eisenhower seemed to believe that the idea had come to him independently. In any event, Eisenhower's headquarters was the only one with the authority to issue an order to Alexander. Eisenhower did that, and Alex took it in good humor.

rough country. On the north (left), Bradley assigned Manton Eddy's 9th Infantry Division, which had attained some experience at El Guettar. On the south road, between Beja and Mateur, he planned to make his main attack with Harmon's 1st Armored and Allen's 1st Infantry Division. But until the high *djebels* (ridges) to the north and south of that road were cleared by the infantry, Harmon's tanks could not proceed. The valley through which these three divisions was to drive was called the Mousetrap, an apt nickname.

The main *djebel* dominating the Mousetrap was Hill 609, on the north, about five miles from the line of departure. Bradley assigned its seizure to Charles W. Ryder's 34th. The 1st was tired and understrength, and the 34th was still smarting from its previous humiliations, needing a success to regain its self-respect.

The attack jumped off on Friday, April 23, 1943. The 34th Division took six days to accomplish the task through difficult terrain. Meanwhile, the 1st Division, in the Mousetrap, achieved a breakthrough for Harmon's tanks, and the Americans were in Mateur by the end of May 2. Since the British to the south had run into unexpected trouble, II Corps pushed on to Bizerte. Tunis fell to the British on the same day, May 7. It took about five additional days to round up all the Axis troops, whose numbers came to an astonishing 250,000 men, 125,000 of them German.[31]

Through it all, the relationships between Allen and his superiors were often strained. Through the years, he and Patton, as fellow cavalrymen, had been friends. Yet Patton could never condone Allen's informal dress and apparent contempt for discipline. As a result, Patton always believed that Allen should be relieved of command, though it is noticeable that, when planning for the invasion of Sicily about two months away, Patton insisted that the 1st Division be included. Bradley was likewise exasperated by Allen's ways but was less harsh in his judgment.

When the Sicilian campaign was completed in August, Bradley decided that the time had come to relieve both Terry Allen and Teddy Roosevelt from their posts with the 1st Division. It was not that either one of them had failed in combat—the 1st Division was considered to be worth several inexperienced divisions—but that its discipline had to be restored. Back in Oran, immediately after the end of the Tunisian campaign, the men of the division had perpetrated riots and disorder that could be neither ignored nor tolerated. Bradley knew that the 1st was slated to lead the assault on Northwest Europe in the coming Normandy invasion, and it had to be whipped into the best shape possible. That meant a new commander.

31. Dwight D. Eisenhower, *Crusade in Europe*, 156.

Bradley's first thought had been to relieve Allen alone, on the theory that the commanding general was responsible for everything pertaining to the division. On second thought, however, Bradley concluded otherwise. He realized that, in his words, "There had developed in the 1st Division an unintentional rivalry between Terry Allen and Ted Roosevelt. . . . Allen would feel deeply hurt if he were to leave the division and Roosevelt were to remain. He might have considered himself a failure instead of the victim of too much success."

Bradley sent for the two generals to report to his command post in Nicosia, Sicily. Bradley described their arrival:

> En route [to the command post] they were ticketed by a corps MP for violation of the uniform regulations. Terry had been sitting in the front seat [of the jeep], holding his helmet between his knees while his unruly black hair blew in the wind. An MP flagged him down. He reddened when he saw Allen's two stars. "I'm sorry, General," the MP said, "but my orders are to ticket anyone riding without a helmet. My captain would give me hell if he saw you going by."
>
> Allen grinned, but Roosevelt objected.
>
> "See here, my boy, don't you know that's General Allen of the 1st Division?"
>
> "Yes, sir," the MP replied. "And you're General Roosevelt, sir. But I'm going to have to give you a ticket too, sir, for wearing that stocking cap." Ted shrugged in despair and peeled off the cap.[32]

When the two reached II Corps headquarters, Roosevelt lost no time in telling Bradley that the men of the 1st Division got along better with the Krauts up front than with Bradley's people in the rear.

The following session was extremely difficult for Bradley, but he reported that the two "rebounded from the blow like good soldiers." Perhaps they would not have been so soldierly had one, but not the other, been relieved. Be all that as it may, their days with the 1st Division—and with each other—were over.[33]

Fortunately for the Allied cause, the high command—Eisenhower, Patton, and Bradley—were well aware of the fighting qualities of both Allen and Roosevelt. Orders therefore portrayed their removals as routine, calculated to provide them a well-earned rest. As a result, the two

32. Omar N. Bradley, *A Soldier's Story*, 155–56.

33. It is difficult to ascertain exactly which officer is responsible for any personnel action, because each views himself as accepting the recommendations from subordinates, taking the action, and securing the approval of his superiors. In this case, for example, General George Patton, Bradley's superior, had been after Allen's scalp for some time. But he left it to Bradley to break the news to the two officers of their relief.

officers were both eventually assigned to further combat duties. Their greatest accomplishments, actually, were still ahead of them.

It took a while for them to find their new roles. Roosevelt, on leaving the 1st Division, was assigned to various odd jobs, including a stint as the liaison officer from Fifth Army in Italy to Juin's French Expeditionary Force. With the approach of D-day in Normandy, however, Roosevelt saw a chance for action. Exerting his formidable influence, he bludgeoned Bradley into assigning him to the 4th Infantry Division, which he knew was slated to make the landing at UTAH Beach.

Roosevelt was not the regularly assigned assistant division commander, but his lack of formal assignment to the 4th Division turned out to his advantage, because it allowed him to invent his own job. He made the most of his latitude. He approached the division commander, Major General Raymond O. Barton, with a unique request: he asked to accompany a lead infantry company as it came ashore on the beach. Barton at first denied the request; it was not the place, he contended, for a general to be with the lead troops.[34] But Roosevelt, in a handwritten note, pointed out that the 4th Division was new to battle: "It will steady the boys to know I am with them." Barton finally agreed, but very reluctantly. As he wrote later, "When I said goodbye to Ted in England, I never expected to see him alive again."[35]

The landing area of the 4th Division, at the base of the Cotentin Peninsula, was a tricky piece of terrain. The ultimate objective was the high ground around the town of Sainte-Mère-Église, a town about ten miles inland, the possession of which would protect the right flank of the invading OVERLORD force.[36] Between the beach and the town, however, lay a large marshy area, which the Germans had flooded, limiting routes of advance to four causeways leading across it. If all went well, the 4th Division would land, cross the causeways, and join up with elements of the 82d Airborne Division, dropped at Sainte-Mère-Église the night before. One infantry battalion was assigned to cross each causeway.

Roosevelt was scheduled to go ashore on D-day at Causeway #2, second from the left, in the 4th Division zone. As his battalion approached the beaches, all seemed well at first; the German defenses in the area were lightly manned. But suddenly Roosevelt noticed that something was wrong: wind, current, and inexperienced sailors had combined to land his battalion more than a mile to the south of the intended landing place.

34. Barton was correct about the unusual nature of Roosevelt's request. Roosevelt was the only general officer in the entire force who accompanied the lead elements.
35. Cornelius Ryan, *The Longest Day: June 6, 1944*, 231–32.
36. OVERLORD was the code name for the Normandy invasion.

Here was where Roosevelt's experience proved invaluable. He surveyed the area, debating in his mind whether to reembark to find the battalion's planned location. He did not hesitate long. "We'll start the war right here," he declared. Then, with his bad knee, arthritis, fibrillous heart, and fifty-seven years, he trudged up the beach to Causeway #2, ignoring the heavy incoming shells from German artillery. Somehow he made it through alive, and the 4th Division made its landing, traversed the inundated area, and joined up with the airborne troops.[37] For his action on D-day, Ted Roosevelt was awarded the Congressional Medal of Honor.

Regrettably, the nation's highest decoration was awarded posthumously; Ted Roosevelt's luck—or rather his body—had run out. On July 12, a little more than a month after his most heroic exploit, Roosevelt died of a heart attack. Bradley, the man who had previously relieved him, wrote, "Roosevelt had earned a division command as few have but we had waited too long. He braved death with an indifference that destroyed its terror for thousands upon thousands of younger men. I have never known a braver man nor a more devoted soldier."[38]

Terry Allen, hero of Tunisia and Sicily, returned to the United States on a high note. He was granted a month's leave to visit his wife and his adored son, Terry Jr., at El Paso. He was awarded numerous decorations, including the Distinguished Service Medal from the United States and two decorations from the French. Finally, on September 15, 1943, Allen was assigned to the command of the 104th Infantry Division in training for overseas duty.

The 104th was one of the last divisions to be organized. It was recruited largely in the Pacific Northwest, and its designation, "Timberwolves," was derived from the division shoulder patch, which portrayed the profile of a baying gray wolf. It was a good assignment, and it offered Allen a new challenge. In contrast to the 1st Division, whose ranks had included a large percentage of regulars, nearly everyone in the 104th was new. Allen was delighted, therefore, when wounded veterans of the 1st, on returning to active duty in the United States, made it a point to join him. Allen did everything he could to help them do so.

Over the course of a year, the Timberwolves trained under Allen's watchful eye. Fortunately, he had learned his lesson regarding military punctilio. He abandoned his informal ways of dressing and became somewhat of a martinet as regards neatness and military bearing. As in Tunisia and Sicily,

---

37. By then the troopers of the two divisions were intermingled, but their very scattering helped fool the Germans into thinking the Americans were stronger than they were.
38. Bradley, *A Soldier's Story*, 334.

he stressed the value of night attacks, conceivably with even more zeal than before. As one of his weary trainees put it, "[Allen] preached and preached and preached to us the need to inflict the greatest damage on the enemy with the fewest casualties possible to ourselves. He believed in night attacks. We night attacked all over the damned desert. We didn't spend a lot of time sleeping."[39]

Though Allen had always maintained that the 1st had been the greatest military formation of all time, he quickly adopted the idea that the 104th was at least the second best. At the risk of repeating himself, he insisted, "Nothing in hell can stop the 104th Timberwolf Division!" He may have been more anxious to go into action than his men, but his spirit caught on.

In the final weeks of August 1944, Allen's Timberwolves shipped out from Camp Kilmer, New Jersey, for the trip overseas to France. But much to Allen's disappointment, the division did not go immediately into combat: it was assigned to what was considered ignominious service details. Patton's Third Army was racing across France toward Germany, and his unexpected success had brought up a new problem: Third Army was running out of supply. To ease the delivery of gasoline, rations, and ammunition from Normandy to Paris, the Service of Supply had come up with an ingenious device called the Red Ball Express, a one-way loop of first-class roadway with trucks running twenty-four hours a day. Since maintenance of trucks took a higher priority than combat troops for the moment, the men of the 104th—such as were qualified—concentrated their time on keeping the trucks running.

It was at this time that Allen's staff benefited from his unconventional ways. On the trip over, he had called in his division ordnance officer: "You know what your job is. When I want my ammunition, I want it at the right place, the right time, and in the right quantity. I want the weapons repaired to the best extent of the ordnance company to do so. I want supplies maintained, weapons and vehicles also. If you do these things, I'll never ask questions."[40]

The officer took him at his word. A pool of 150 trucks had been assigned to the 104th to be put back in shape, and of these he kept the 60 best and returned only the other 90. "First Army," he reasoned, "is too screwed up to know the difference." He was right. The ordnance officer hid the trucks away and pulled one out whenever an organic 104th Division truck was destroyed. At the end of the war, the 104th had a full component of trucks. None of the replacement trucks the division had requested of First Army had ever arrived.

• • •

39. Astor, *Terrible Terry Allen*, 245.
40. Ibid., 252.

The first action of the Timberwolves occurred in October 1944, when the 413th Infantry Regiment was attached to a Canadian unit attacking to clear the north bank of the Scheldt estuary, to enable the Allies to use the all-important port of Antwerp. By fortunate coincidence, the operation involved a night attack, at which the division was expert. For the rest of the war, the division fought with distinction.

One day, during a visit of General Bradley to the 104th command post, Bradley was in an expansive mood. "Terry," he said, "I just want to tell you this 104th Division of yours, they're ranked with the 1st and 9th Divisions as the finest combat divisions in the ETO."

Terry Allen was not the kind to be flustered with praise. "Brad," he said lightly, "the 1st and 9th Divisions are in damn fast company."[41]

### Personal Afterthoughts

I never met either Teddy Roosevelt or Terry Allen, though I saw Allen once.[42] On about April 26, 1945, my duties took me to the front lines in the sector of the 104th Division. It had stopped at the town of Düben, on the Mülde River, the limit of the American drive in Germany. A day earlier a patrol from the 69th Infantry Division had crossed the no-man's-land between the Mülde and the Elbe, where they had made the first contact between American troops and the Russians coming from the East.

As I drove within a couple hundred yards of the river, I saw the unmistakable figure of Terry Allen, standing erect by the side of the road and grinning mischievously at something. I would have liked to stop, but I did not. Allen would have been cordial, as with any junior officer. But he would not have been interested, least of all by the fact that my father was Supreme Commander. I do not regret my decision not to bother him.

Unlike Roosevelt, Allen lived another twenty-three years after the end of the war. He was active in civil affairs in El Paso and died at age eighty-one, in 1969. His last two years were marred with tragedy. His son, Lieutenant Colonel Terry Allen Jr., was killed while leading his battalion in an attack in Vietnam. He was the general's only child, on whom he doted.

But even that blow could not defeat Terry Allen. He recovered quickly after hearing the news. He then stood up straight and declared, "There will be no tears here. You are in the house of an infantryman."

41. Ibid., 309.
42. I knew Roosevelt's son later, in Paoli, Pennsylvania.

General of the Army Douglas MacArthur (Library of Congress)

# 7

# Douglas MacArthur

## The Effect of Personality
## on Strategy

Tuesday, April 11, 1951, promised to be a quiet day in Tokyo, where General of the Army Douglas MacArthur was reigning as the American proconsul in occupied Japan. The Japanese government, under his supervision, was functioning well, so the main concern involved his role as the UN commander in the Korean War. There, after ten months of fighting, the situation was stabilizing; in fact, the North Koreans and Red Chinese were retreating under the blows being dealt by the United Nations Force, led by Lieutenant General Matthew B. Ridgway's Eighth U.S. Army. In Tokyo the main topic of conversation that morning revolved around the weather for Prime Minister Shigeru Yoshida's first garden party of the year. The afternoon threatened to bring some light showers, but Yoshida's party would go on.

MacArthur himself never attended such occasions. Much of his prestige depended on the aura of mystery he maintained, and mixing with the Japanese people had no place in that policy. Instead, he and his wife, Jean, entertained a senator and an industrial leader at lunch, after which the general retired for his usual siesta. He intended to return to his office, the Dai Ichi Building, at 3:00 p.m., as was his wont.

While MacArthur was resting, Colonel Sidney Huff, his aide, received a call from a newspaper friend that made him uncomfortable. The radio news from Washington announced that it would carry a press conference involving the general. While Huff was waiting for clarification, a messenger handed him a brown manila envelope addressed directly to MacArthur. Huff delivered it to the bedroom, where MacArthur opened it. The message, from Chairman of the Joint Chiefs of Staff Omar N. Bradley, was terse, even insulting, coming from one important general to another: "You will turn over your commands, effective at once, to Lieutenant General Matthew B. Ridgway. You are authorized to have issued such orders as are necessary to complete desired travel to such place as you select. My reasons for your replacement will be made concurrently to you of the foregoing message."[1] That was all. MacArthur turned to his wife and said, "Jeannie, we're going home at last." After eleven years away from the United States, in exciting and sometimes exotic circumstances, the MacArthurs were returning.[2]

Thus ended a spectacular military career. Almost from the day of his commissioning as a lieutenant in 1903, the charismatic Douglas MacArthur had presumed that he was a man of destiny. He presented a larger-than-life figure. By nature he was brilliant, bold, ambitious, and needful of personal admiration. Equally important, he had been lucky. But therein lay the seeds of his ultimate downfall. With every success he achieved, sometimes against remarkable odds, his self-assurance had grown. Like everything else he did, even his mistakes and misjudgments carried drama. Never mind that he could be paranoiac, that he could be devious in pursuit of what he was convinced was his destiny, that his superiors often distrusted him, and that those under him often resented his passion for personal aggrandizement. These were not the qualities the public saw.

Douglas MacArthur, given his heritage and upbringing, could never have been very different from what he was. He lived obsessed by the need to emulate or surpass the career of his distinguished father, General Arthur MacArthur, a national hero and recipient of the Congressional Medal of Honor for bravery at the Battle of Lookout Mountain in the Civil War. As military governor of the Philippines, General Arthur MacArthur had achieved such popularity among the Filipinos that he had developed a remarkable closeness to them. That emotional attachment had been inherited by the son.

Douglas MacArthur, born in 1880, was the third of three sons. The elder, Arthur, was liked and respected,[3] but for some reason the parents seemed to view Douglas, not Arthur, as the one to be cultivated and encouraged.

---

1. William Manchester, *American Caesar,* 642.

2. Despite the fact that most of the American public supported the president's relief of his outspoken general, it was obvious that the affair had been badly handled. After years of service, a top military leader was being dismissed without dignity. No trip home for "consultation," no chance for the general to address his troops or the Japanese people. Above all, no opportunity to retire voluntarily. President Harry Truman, in fact, had seen to that. "The son of a bitch isn't going to resign on me. I want him fired." Ibid., 643.

3. Arthur MacArthur III (1876–1923), who died young.

Perhaps Arthur's attending the Naval Academy rather than West Point was a factor. In any event, when Douglas was a cadet at West Point, his widowed mother, "Pinky," reportedly rented a room in the nearby Thayer Hotel, across the Plain from the cadet barracks. From her window she could see the lights of Douglas's barracks room.

If Mrs. MacArthur was checking on her son's diligence, she need not have bothered. He stood number one in the graduating class of 1903, and allegedly set an all-time record for high academic standing. He was also a varsity player on the West Point baseball team.[4] In his first-class (senior) year the Tactical Department made him the first captain—the highest-ranking cadet. Probably only Robert E. Lee ever rivaled his West Point record.

Though MacArthur graduated from West Point as the golden boy of the class of 1903, his early years of service involved nothing remarkable. Nevertheless, his tendency to perform flamboyant acts on his own volition surfaced during the U.S. occupation of the Mexican port of Veracruz in 1914. Apparently on his own volition, he conducted a dangerous reconnaissance into Mexican territory. Nevertheless, in a small army, he overcame the handicaps of being known as the son of one of its most noted generals. In 1917 Secretary of War Newton D. Baker called on him to be his own personal assistant, with special duties for the fledgling art of public relations.

Just how important an assistant MacArthur was is a matter of conjecture, but in his own mind he was influential indeed. His *Memoirs,* written many years later, tells a story, worth citing, that illustrates his recollection of his elevated status as Baker's assistant. As America was moving inexorably toward war against Germany, so MacArthur's account goes, President Woodrow Wilson and Secretary of War Baker were confronting the decision of what officer should head any army that America might send overseas. The leading contender for the post was Major General Frederick Funston, commanding the Southern Command in San Antonio, Texas. There was, however, another possibility, Brigadier General John J. Pershing, whose Punitive Expedition into Mexico in pursuit of the bandit Francisco (Pancho) Villa had recently been withdrawn in light of the growing European crisis.[5]

---

4. MacArthur's actual passion was football. He was too light for that sport, but never lost his zeal for West Point football throughout his life.

5. Another officer, Major General Leonard Wood, former chief of staff, had many supporters. His political activities against President Wilson's policies had, however, made him anathema to both Wilson and Baker.

On the night of February 17, 1917, Funston died unexpectedly of a heart attack. MacArthur, who happened to be duty officer for the General Staff that evening, lost no time in carrying the news to President Wilson and Secretary Baker. The two were attending a festive ceremonial dinner, and MacArthur was admitted to the gathering only after some difficulty.

The shock of Funston's death immediately broke up the party, and Wilson and Baker retired to a side room, with Baker beckoning MacArthur to join them. In the course of the discussion, according to MacArthur's recollection, Baker asked his opinion of whom the Army would favor for appointment in Funston's place. MacArthur answered that his personal choice would be General Pershing. Wilson and Baker agreed. MacArthur retained the impression that he, as a young major, had influenced Pershing's choice.

In all matters, Baker's confidence in MacArthur seemed unbounded. When the question arose as to how to raise an army of a half-million men, Baker considered that instituting a draft of all male citizens was necessary. But the decision would be politically unpopular, and Baker thought that Wilson would need convincing. So when Baker went to argue his case with the president, he took MacArthur with him. Surprisingly, Wilson readily agreed. Congress passed the Draft Act on May 19, 1917.

Another almost equally momentous problem faced by Baker was the question of how to employ the National Guard. The Army Chief of Staff, Major General Hugh Scott, opposed its use. Instead, he was in favor of leaving the Guard on the shelf and inducting all new draftees into the Regular Army. Such a plan, however, was sure to result in controversy; the politically influential National Guard would never stand for it. In addition, the recent call-up of National Guard units for service on the Mexican border meant that certain of its units were already somewhat organized, which was more than could be said for the spread-out Regular Army.

MacArthur is given much of the credit for helping Baker convince President Wilson to make full use of the National Guard, including the organization of a special Guard division to be composed of units from many states, a "Rainbow." Hence the birth of the famed 42d Rainbow Division. An emotional Baker intended to appoint MacArthur as its commander, but MacArthur wisely declined, accepting the post of chief of staff. Baker therefore selected Major General Charles Menoher, a strong admirer of MacArthur's. Perhaps MacArthur had a hand in that selection. Menoher always gave his subordinates great latitude and seemed to bear no resentment when the flamboyant MacArthur upstaged him.

Fortunately for MacArthur's ambitions, the Rainbow Division was one of the four divisions the United States was able to send to France during the year of 1917.[6] MacArthur started out as its chief of staff, but he had no intention of being confined to a desk. With General Menoher's forbearance, he mingled freely with the troops and took liberties in his uniform that any other man would have been court-martialed for. He eschewed the regular steel helmet and wore a service cap, with visor, but with the stiffener removed. Instead of the regulation officer's blouse, he wore his West Point sweater, with the large white *A* he had earned playing baseball at the academy. He carried a riding crop and draped around his neck a long muffler knitted for him by his mother. He was informal with the troops and was extremely popular with them. As William Manchester put it in *American Caesar,* "Difficult as it may be for Pacific veterans to credit, MacArthur's soldiers of 1918 idolized him. He was closer to their age than other senior officers, encouraged them to call him 'Buddy,' shared their discomforts and their dangers, and adored them in return."[7]

He also took great risks. On the night of February 26, 1918, for example, he joined a French unit making a raid on German positions near Lunéville. He avoided notifying General Menoher, who might have stopped him. On MacArthur's safe return, Menoher decorated him with a Silver Star. Promoted to the command of the 84th Infantry Brigade, he took over the Rainbow Division only a few days before the war's end, never discouraging the idea that he had been in command of the division throughout the war.

Not everyone adored him, however. His worst critics, for whom he developed a bitter enmity, were the staff of General John J. Pershing at Chaumont, whom he accused of downgrading a recommendation for a Congressional Medal of Honor to the lesser Distinguished Service Cross.[8] MacArthur apparently believed that the "Chaumont crowd" was jealous of him. He focused much of his resentment on Colonel George C. Marshall, Pershing's operations officer.

MacArthur returned home after the war as the most highly decorated officer in the AEF and next to Pershing probably the most noted.[9] It is

6. The others were the 1st Division (Regular), the 2d (Regular), and the 26th "Yankee" Division (National Guard).

7. Ibid., 55.

8. Actually, Pershing himself thought MacArthur's daring pure showmanship.

9. When considering MacArthur's list of lavish decorations, it should be remembered that such awards are frequently bestowed on high-ranking officers as a way of recognizing the risks that enlisted soldiers or company grade officers face every day. Nevertheless, General Pershing had his reservations as to how useful were the missions that MacArthur took upon himself.

not surprising, therefore, that when the Army was inevitably reduced to peacetime strength, he was one of the few officers who retained the star of a brigadier general. In 1919 he was assigned as superintendent of West Point, a prestigious assignment but also one where he was very much on the spot, given the intense interest that West Point graduates take in the fortunes of that institution.

MacArthur's task as superintendent was a daunting challenge. The Military Academy had been practically abolished during the war years as the Army—and the public—saw the need for young officers to fight in France. Academically, the normal four-year curriculum had been progressively shortened until one class had a course so short that its members were called back to complete their studies wearing the uniforms of second lieutenants. But MacArthur, drawing heavily on graduates of former years, was able to restore the institution to make it not too different from the old. He also introduced some innovations such as increased emphasis on liberal arts to modify the rigidly engineering school it had previously been. He codified the previously unwritten Cadet Honor System. He accomplished much, and his own prestige and visibility in the Army was increased.

Following his three-year term as superintendent of West Point, MacArthur's assignments became more routine. He served two terms in the Philippines during the next eight years, thus enhancing the close ties he held with the Filipino people, building on the reputation of his illustrious father. Then in 1930, he was jumped over the heads of many senior officers and appointed chief of staff, U.S. Army, at age fifty.

MacArthur was an unusually visible chief of staff, justifiably the most memorable of those who held the position between Pershing and George C. Marshall. He was conspicuous for the courage he showed when he urged Congress to increase the strength of the Army during the Great Depression. He established the Army Industrial College to broaden the professional horizons of future generals. He adjusted readily to the new Roosevelt administration when it replaced that of Herbert Hoover. His support of Roosevelt's Civilian Conservation Corps, anathema to more conventional officers, stood him in good stead. When MacArthur's normal term of four years was approaching its end, President Roosevelt asked him to stay an extra year. At the end of that year, in 1935, he finally left the post of chief of staff. He made no pretense that removing the extra two stars afforded him temporarily as chief did not cause him anguish.

MacArthur's tenure as chief of staff of the Army was marred by one severe blunder, however. In July 1932 a desperate but orderly mob of veterans of the Great War gathered from all over the country and marched on Washington. The Bonus Marchers, as they were called, intended to ask

Congress for the immediate payment of the bonuses promised for some years in the future. President Herbert Hoover ordered the Army to restore order, but he said nothing about how that task should be done. MacArthur, unable to restrain his weakness for taking personal charge, insisted on commanding the troops himself, even though the number was small. He appeared on the scene wearing full uniform, with decorations and polished boots.[10] The confrontation itself was relatively minor. Some of the veterans crossed the Anacostia River and entered the city, but they were removed bloodlessly by the troops. Not a shot was fired, but tear gas was rife and bayonets flashed. Worst of all, the troops set fire to the pitiful shanty village that the veterans, some with families, had constructed in Anacostia. The Bonus Army soon left, but it had made its point. The hearts of the public were with these pathetic people. MacArthur received a blemish to his image that he never quite lived down.

MacArthur was only fifty-five years old when he left Washington, nine years short of retirement age. He therefore remained on active duty and headed once more for the Philippines, encouraged by the fact that the president of the Philippine Commonwealth, Manuel Quezon y Molina, asked that he be sent to create a new Philippine Army, in preparation for Philippine independence in 1946. With him MacArthur took Major Dwight Eisenhower, who had been his assistant in the War Department. In certain respects the ensuing years made it a bad period for both men. On the official side, MacArthur missed the power he had wielded in Washington, relegated to a set of islands that, though considerably larger than Napoleon's Elba, represented almost as much of an exile. Eisenhower, for his part, itched to go back to troops with the American Army, and he had a wife who hated living in the tropics.

In addition, the mission assigned to MacArthur turned out to be frustrating if not hopeless. Neither the U.S. nor the Philippine government intended to spend enough money to develop a respectable Philippine Army, so budgets were cut time after time. As a result, neither MacArthur nor Eisenhower was at his best, and not surprisingly they clashed. The rift between the two, however, has always been exaggerated. They corresponded occasionally after Eisenhower's departure in 1939, but their subsequent careers took different paths.[11]

· · ·

10. Dwight Eisenhower, my father, was a personal assistant to MacArthur at the time, and Ike's pleas for the general to stay out of sight fell on deaf ears.

11. See D. Eisenhower, *At Ease.*

In July 1941 the relations between the United States and Japan had deteriorated seriously. President Roosevelt, concerned over the possibility of war, decided to call MacArthur back to active duty in the American Army. Given the rank of lieutenant general, MacArthur was placed in charge of all American and Filipino forces in the Philippines—Regular Army, Philippine Scouts,[12] and the Philippine Army.

Finally, the predicted blow came. On December 7, 1941, the Imperial Japanese Fleet, carrier-based planes, attacked the U.S. naval base at Pearl Harbor and Hickam Army Airfield at Hawaii. Automatically, the United States was at war with Japan, and a Japanese invasion of the Philippines logically followed. On December 10 the first Japanese landings on the island of Luzon occurred, three days after the Pearl Harbor attack. Mysteriously, MacArthur's air force of forty B-17 bombers and ninety P40 pursuit planes was caught on the ground at Clark Field and Nichols Field and was virtually destroyed. MacArthur declared Manila an open city.

MacArthur's actions to meet the threat to Luzon were essentially based on the plans that had been on the books throughout the years, ever since the United States had occupied the islands in 1901. The American defenders expected to be outnumbered, so the plans called for a retreat to a last-ditch position on the Bataan Peninsula and Corregidor Island in the mouth of Manila Bay. But MacArthur took a risk: he attempted to halt the Japanese landings at the Lingayan Gulf and up north at Apari on the basis that the best chance to defeat an invasion would be at the beaches.[13] The effort failed, and MacArthur's aggressiveness has been criticized. Nevertheless, the bulk of his troops was safely extricated and made it to Bataan.

It was probably here that MacArthur's mistrust of Washington, especially Marshall and Eisenhower, began to develop. He had never forgotten that Marshall had been a member of the "Chaumont crowd" from the First World War, and Eisenhower, his onetime assistant, was now on Marshall's staff, responsible for coping with the situation in the Philippines. MacArthur became convinced that Marshall and Eisenhower were purposely and maliciously withholding resources from him.

In the meantime, President Roosevelt decided to make use of MacArthur's status as the "man of the hour." To bolster public morale in the face of disastrous Allied defeats throughout Southeast Asia, the American gov-

---

12. The Philippine Scouts were Philippine troops, part of the American Army.

13. The reasoning for a forward defense, keeping little or no reserve, somewhat resembles that of Field Marshal Erwin Rommel when preparing to defend against the Allied invasion of Normandy in 1944. Realizing the capabilities of Allied airpower to restrict the mobility of his troops, Rommel attempted to stop the Allies on the beaches at the expense of his reserve.

ernment purposely set out to portray the beleaguered general as a symbol of American heroism in the face of impossible odds. MacArthur was promoted to the rank of four-star general, presented with the Congressional Medal of Honor he thought he had earned in 1918, and made the object of personal adulation.[14] The prominent correspondent Robert Considine published a book titled *MacArthur the Magnificent,* which sat noticeably on the desk of the Republican leader in the House of Representatives, Congressman Joseph Martin, of Massachusetts.[15]

MacArthur cooperated to the hilt. Of the 149 official communiqués that emanated from his headquarters before his departure for Corregidor, 109 carried MacArthur's name and no other.[16]

The Philippine-American position on the Bataan Peninsula held against the Japanese forces better than expected, due largely to superhuman exertions on the part of both Americans and Filipinos, aided by Japanese difficulties in supply. The handwriting, however, was on the wall: it was only a matter of time before Bataan, and later Corregidor, would fall to the Japanese. Washington was therefore faced with the prospect of having MacArthur, its superhero, captured and conceivably put in irons for public view. Unable to face that prospect, Roosevelt ordered him to turn over the Philippine command to Jonathan Wainwright, his second in command, and depart. MacArthur was authorized to take a few selected staff officers and his family. On leaving Corregidor, he was to take command in Australia.

MacArthur, of course, made the proper protests against leaving his men, but the president had left him no choice. In late March, therefore, MacArthur, with his wife, their son, Arthur (with nurse), and selected staff officers, began a hazardous trip by PT boat through Japanese-infested waters to Mindanao, which was still in American hands. There they transferred to a Boeing B-17 bomber and were flown to a point in northern Australia, near Darwin.

With an ordinary man, the flight might be seen as a humiliating departure, but MacArthur was able to dramatize the hazards of the trip from Corregidor, making it a triumph. On landing in Australia he declared grandly, "I have come through from Corregidor and I shall return." He ignored a War Department suggestion that he employ the term "*We* shall

14. Eisenhower, who was all too aware of MacArthur's penchant for self-dramatization, was dubious about building the general up too much. I remember my father snorting with disgust when some proper lady declared, "He [MacArthur] can put his shoes under my bed any time."

15. Other heroes also were extolled: Captain Colin Kelly was erroneously credited with sinking the Japanese battleship *Haruna.* Lieutenant Sandy Nininger, a recent West point graduate, was awarded the Congressional Medal of Honor posthumously.

16. Richard B. Frank, "The MacArthur No One Knew," 32.

return." MacArthur was well on his way to establishing himself as a larger-than-life personality.

The Australians greeted MacArthur and his entourage with enthusiasm. Fed up with sending large forces to defend British interests in the Mediterranean, the Australians now welcomed the Americans as their principal allies. MacArthur was given direct command of all American and Australian forces, plus all the surviving Netherlands troops from the Dutch East Indies. He established his headquarters in Brisbane, Queensland, and began to prepare for the long and arduous campaign to make good his promise to return to the Philippines.

By July 1942 the Japanese were no longer a threat to Australia, though not before they had taken Hong Kong, Singapore, the Dutch East Indies, and the Philippines. By then American naval power had recovered from Pearl Harbor to a large extent, and the Japanese advance had at least been halted at the Battle of the Coral Sea. Then, in June 1942, the American carrier fleet near Midway Island had delivered a crushing blow to a Japanese force heading toward Hawaii. The enemy never recovered from the loss of four carriers. Though it was not known at the time, the tide of war in the Pacific had turned.

MacArthur now felt that he could begin his planned offensive to retake the Philippines. To do so, he chose as subordinates a group that is interesting because together it reflected MacArthur's personality. As a vest-pocket operator, MacArthur did much of his planning in his own head. Accordingly, he amassed a weak staff, leading to the suspicion that they had been selected more for their loyalty to MacArthur than for their abilities. His commanders, however, were capable men. As his air commander he had Lieutenant General George Kenney, an aggressive believer in the Air Force role of ground support. His two armies were commanded by Robert L. Eichelberger and Walter Krueger, who both were strong commanders. He also received gratifying cooperation from Admiral William Halsey, whose naval forces were never placed in the formal chain of command. Unfortunately for the cause and his own future, MacArthur declined to give any subordinate commanders anything like the credit they were due. Commanders are touchy about such things, because feeling unappreciated is very damaging to the troops' morale.[17]

In preparation for his drive northward toward the Philippines, MacArthur was faced with a major terrain obstacle, a large island, New Guinea,

---

17. Eichelberger, a former superintendent of West Point, seemed particularly bitter about this neglect. He once also complained that, although in the Buna campaign MacArthur never set foot on that critical battlefield, his headquarters continued to claim that he was "leading" his troops.

heavily defended by the Japanese. Though New Guinea appears small on a map of the vast Pacific Ocean area, it spans east-west for fifteen hundred miles, the approximate distance from Brownsville, Texas, to the California border. MacArthur's tactic, therefore, was not to take the entire island, but to make use of the Allied superiority in naval power, which allowed him and Admiral William Halsey to pick and choose the strongholds they wished to take. Japanese resistance was fanatic, so during the rest of 1942 MacArthur's battles concentrated around the eastern end of New Guinea—Port Moresby (early taken by the Americans), Guadalcanal (under Admiral Chester Nimitz), and Rabaul (Japanese held). It then took the summer and fall of 1944, after the capture of Buna and Gona, for the forces of the Southwest Pacific Theater to hop their way across the northern shores of New Guinea. MacArthur could then turn his full attention toward the Philippines.

At that point the interplay between MacArthur and the Joint Chiefs of Staff in Washington came to the fore. In midsummer 1944, with the Western Allies under Eisenhower established in Normandy, the JCS approved MacArthur's plan for establishing a beachhead on Mindanao, the southernmost major island of the Philippines. When the time approached, however, Admiral Halsey brought word that the Japanese position in the Philippines was so weak that the objective could be switched farther northward to Leyte. On MacArthur's own order, therefore, Walter Krueger's Sixth Army, with four divisions, landed on September 17, 1944.

MacArthur made the most of the moment. His staff arranged for a photographer onshore to immortalize him wading through the breakers—a totally unnecessary gesture—followed by a miserable-looking but docile entourage. Once onshore, he announced to the public, "I have returned."

With his successful return, MacArthur's hubris seemed to grow. With it went a feeling of increased independence from the orders of the Joint Chiefs of Staff in Washington. Up to that time the JCS had set the objectives, and he, as the commander in the field, had executed them. But now MacArthur seemed to feel that his prestige with the public made him untouchable. So while the JCS pondered his next move—an attack on Formosa might have been a possibility—MacArthur set out, on his own volition, to clear the rest of the Philippine Islands. Those operations, consistent with his perceived destiny as the Philippine liberator, had little or nothing to do with the eventual downfall of Japan.

By early 1945 MacArthur had completed his liberation of Manila, and with the German surrender in Europe all eyes turned toward planning for the final assault on Japan. Here for the first time MacArthur came into direct conflict with the top admirals of the Navy, personified by Admiral

Ernest King, chief of naval operations in Washington, and Admiral Nimitz, MacArthur's counterpart in the Pacific. The admirals advocated besieging Japan with a naval blockade and air bombardment, to be commanded of course by Nimitz. MacArthur contended that Japan could be defeated only by a ground invasion commanded, of course, by himself. The Navy's plan had a great deal of merit, but MacArthur's prestige was such that the Joint Chiefs tentatively approved Operation DOWNFALL, to be executed in November 1945.

At the same time, a movement in Japan began for a negotiated peace, and the idea began to spread in various neutral capitals. Hope for such a move received a blow, however, in July 1945. The Big Three—Stalin, Truman, and Churchill-Atlee[18]—confirmed Roosevelt's "unconditional surrender" principle, announced Russia's entry in the war against Japan, and confirmed their intention that the Japanese emperor, Hirohito, would be replaced and treated as a war criminal. It stands to MacArthur's credit that he was "appalled" by those announcements, since he realized that now the Japanese would fight to the last to keep their emperor.[19] A million deaths could result.

The problem was soon averted, however. On August 6 and August 8, 1945, the United States dropped atomic bombs on Hiroshima and Nagasaki, presenting the Japanese with the face saving they needed to surrender. They insisted on only one stipulation: their emperor must retain his throne. The Allied powers and Russia accepted those terms, and on August 15, 1945, the Japanese announced their surrender. The Allies named MacArthur as Supreme Commander for the Allied powers, and American paratroops landed at an airfield on Honshu to begin the occupation of Japan.

Here was MacArthur at his most dramatic. He personally landed in Japan practically on the tails of the first battalion of paratroopers. On September 2, 1945, he staged an impressive formal surrender ceremony aboard the forward deck of the battleship *Missouri*. MacArthur then assumed the role of governor of Japan in Tokyo.

MacArthur's performance as Allied proconsul for the occupation of Japan constitutes the part of his service that has elicited the least criticism. He was sensitive to Japanese feelings and to the feelings of the emperor, who was now divested of his godlike attributes in the Japanese mind. MacArthur may have been given too much credit for the drafting of the new Japanese constitution, but it was done under his auspices

---

18. Clement Attlee defeated Churchill in the British election, held during the Potsdam Conference. He replaced the former prime minister at the table at Potsdam.

19. Manchester, *American Caesar*, 437.

and is generally regarded as a masterpiece. He was criticized occasionally for being too lenient on the Japanese imperial family, including Hirohito himself, but the criticism resulted in nothing. In one instance he defied orders from Washington by releasing stores of food supplies intended solely for military use to the population. Washington did nothing, and it is generally accepted that MacArthur, even if acting insubordinately, had done the right thing. He had prevented widespread starvation.

The peaceful occupation of Japan was shattered on the morning of June 25, 1950, when the Communist North Koreans invaded the Republic of Korea, an American protectorate. The United Nations, with the Soviet delegate absent, authorized intervention by UN Forces, and President Harry Truman appointed MacArthur to be UN commander. MacArthur did not move to Korea personally. He delegated ground command to the Eighth Army, under General Walton Walker, but kept General Edward Almond's X Corps temporarily in Japan, separate from Walker's, virtually under his own personal supervision. MacArthur could never completely delegate control.

The story of the Korean War is complicated, as the battle raged up and down the long Korean peninsula for a year and a half. At first, the Eighth Army was driven down to a bridgehead at the southern tip of the peninsula, based at the port of Pusan. There the Americans held on by their fingernails. Then, in September 1950, the arrival of reinforcements and a supply-stretched enemy permitted counterattacks. In conjunction with an attack by Eighth Army, MacArthur committed his X Corps in an amphibious landing behind enemy lines at Inchon. The North Koreans collapsed. This was MacArthur at his best; his subordinates had protested.

Following his success at Inchon, MacArthur moved the X Corps by sea to a point near Hamhung and Hungnam, on the east coast of North Korea. Against little opposition, the corps drove all the way to the Yalu River, the border between Korea and Manchuria.

Up to then the Communist Chinese had remained aloof, but now they were frightened, and they sent strong forces across the Yalu and lay out of sight in the mountains in the North. Shortly after Thanksgiving 1950, the Chinese attacked and drove the X Corps, with heavy losses, back to a point where it could be evacuated by sea and delivered around to Pusan to rejoin the Eighth Army.

This had been MacArthur at his worst. The Chinese had previously voiced their worries over a UN drive to the Yalu, and in early November, they had made a major attack on American troops on Korea's west coast, destroying a whole regiment of the 1st Cavalry Division. For some reason MacArthur ignored this action, which should have confirmed without a doubt that Chinese were present. Yet confident in his own illusions, he discounted these warnings. The blunder would have caused the relief from command of any lesser general, but so great was MacArthur's prestige that he remained in place and, to the best of my knowledge, was never rebuked.

It was MacArthur's ego rather than his tactical performance, however, that brought on his downfall. Refusing to admit a mistake in his conduct of operations, he claimed in public that he had "won" the Korean War and that the Communist Chinese had brought on a "brand-new" war. He raised his insubordination to a new height by making public speeches advocating measures that the JCS believed would have constituted acts of war against China. He even went so far as to send a letter to Representative Joseph Martin, the Republican minority leader and MacArthur's strong supporter.[20]

President Truman had now reached the limits of his patience. The message that arrived at the general's headquarters in Tokyo on April 11, 1951, was now inevitable.

MacArthur did not take his relief lying down. Aware that his removal had created a furor in the United States, he returned to New York, where he was accorded one of the greatest ticker-tape parades on record. He then accepted an invitation from Congress to address a joint session. He appeared before them on April 19, 1951, just a little more than a week after receiving his telegram of dismissal.

MacArthur's address to Congress turned out to be a sensation. It began mildly, paying lavish tribute to Congress and expressing the humility he felt in addressing that august body. He claimed unconvincingly to feel no rancor for his recent removal. He warned the nation of the global nature of its problems, a somewhat paradoxical statement given the reasons for his relief from command. He then reiterated the measures he had previously urged in public and that had been rejected.

MacArthur said very little about the Truman administration as such, but he repeated his claim that his forces had "won" the Korean War and that China had created a "new" one. He described the ensuing situation as one that "called for new decisions in the diplomatic sphere to permit the realistic adjustment of military strategy. Such decisions have not been forthcoming."

MacArthur's speech was defiant, but in the temper of the times he had nothing to fear from charges of insubordination. Regardless of substance, the part of the speech that was most noted was its closing:

20. See p. 239.

The world has turned over many times since I took the oath on the Plain at West Point, and the hopes and dreams have long vanished, but I still remember the refrain of one of the most popular barracks ballads of that day which proclaims most proudly that old soldiers never die, they just fade away.

And like the old soldier of that ballad, I now close my military career and just fade away, an old soldier who tried to do his duty as God gave him the light to see that duty. Good-bye.

Congress and the country went wild. It has reasonably been said that President Truman could not safely appear on the streets of Washington that day. What was probably Mr. Truman's most courageous act as president virtually destroyed what was left of the credibility of a waning administration.

MacArthur's declared intention to "fade away" was an appeal for sympathy and support, which he received. The sentiment, however, did not prevent him from accepting an invitation to address the 1952 Republican National Convention in Chicago as keynote speaker. Some pundits viewed this speech as an appeal for a draft as the party's presidential standard-bearer. If such was the case, he was doomed to disappointment. Fifteen months had passed since his dramatic address before Congress, and the temper of the public had cooled. MacArthur's last attempt at a comeback ended in a dud. He lived another dozen years in the Waldorf-Astoria Hotel in New York and died in 1964.

Douglas MacArthur was a man who evoked strong feelings, both positive and negative. Some observers admired him lavishly; to others, among them a great many of his former soldiers, he was anathema. It is interesting to conjecture how long and for what reason Douglas MacArthur will be remembered. What makes that answer imponderable is the fact that even successful soldiers are generally soon forgotten. Once a war is won, people lose interest and often underestimate the magnitude of their accomplishments.

With MacArthur it will probably be different. His days as "MacArthur the Magnificent" in 1942 have long been forgotten, as well as his spectacular escape from Corregidor to Australia. A few will remember his time as proconsul in Japan. Forgotten will be his most brilliant hour in risking the Inchon landing in Korea in September 1950, as well as his ignominious defeat two months later. Ironically, he will probably be recalled as our most prominent insubordinate. Like Samson and the Temple, his most remembered moment was his downfall.

General of the Army Omar N. Bradley (Library of Congress)

# 8

# Omar Nelson Bradley

Great military leaders come in all sizes and shapes. In stature they can range from the diminutive Napoleon to the gigantic Winfield Scott. Their uniforms can vary from the flamboyance of George Patton to the plain fatigues of Mao Tse-tung. Omar Nelson Bradley had his own style, that of neat, dignified simplicity. To the image makers in the press, he was typified as the Missouri schoolmaster, implying a prosaic man who had never left West Succotash. He did not look like a man who would ever be called on to make history.

They could not have been more wrong. Beneath that placid exterior was an intense, even touchy nature, capable at times of violent bursts of temper. But they were rare. His West Point classmates recognized the soldierly qualities that lay beneath Bradley's quiet, courteous manner. The 1915 *Howitzer,* the class yearbook, predicted that some day his classmates would be boasting, "Sure, General Bradley was a classmate of mine."

Part of that respect his classmates had for him probably stemmed from his athletic prowess. He was one of those athletes who played whatever varsity sport was in season. Baseball was his love. He was credited for having thrown the longest ball from the outfield in the West Point records.

Bradley's early Army career began inauspiciously. Like his friend and classmate Dwight Eisenhower, he was denied overseas service during the First World War, and for some years he was convinced that his career was thereby ruined. But also like Ike, his confidence was restored by his high standing at the Infantry School at Fort Benning, Georgia, in competition with combat-experienced officers. After that, "I never suffered a faint heart again."[1]

1. Bradley, *A Soldier's Story,* 19. Eisenhower's experience was at the Command and General Staff College, where he stood number 1.

Bradley's big break came in 1929 when he was assigned to the faculty at Fort Benning. Lieutenant Colonel George C. Marshall, the assistant commandant, noticed his stellar performance as the chief of the Weapons Section.[2] From that day on, Bradley would be on the list of those that Marshall regarded as "comers." When Marshall was promoted to the grade of brigadier general in 1936, Bradley sent his congratulations. Marshall's warm reply, given his habitual aloofness from personal relationships, was unusual: "I very much hope we will have the opportunity to serve together again. I can think of nothing more satisfactory to me."[3]

Marshall was as good as his word. In early 1941, even before the attack on Pearl Harbor, Marshall reached down the list of regular officers and assigned Bradley to be commandant of the Infantry School. Only six months later, Marshall put him in command of the 82d "All American" Infantry Division, then in training,[4] and later to the 28th Infantry Division, the National Guard of Pennsylvania. In these assignments Bradley faced problems that were unique to a training army, and he passed with flying colors.

During the two years that Bradley commanded those two divisions, the United States entered the war with the Allies against the Germans, Italians, and Japanese. During that period his classmate Dwight Eisenhower skyrocketed to the command of the Allied forces fighting in North Africa. Bradley received overseas orders in the spring of 1943, and he was hoping to command a division under Ike.[5] To his disappointment, however, he was given the much more important task of helping Eisenhower in his man-killing duties as Allied Force commander. Marshall had selected Bradley to serve Ike as his eyes and ears on the front.

Bradley arrived in Algiers just as the humiliating American defeat at Kasserine Pass, Tunisia, was drawing to a close. Patton had temporarily replaced Lloyd Fredendall as the commander of the II Corps, the largest American formation, and Bradley was sent to be Ike's "representative" with Patton. Patton, however, would have none of that: he objected to having a

---

2. At the service schools, it is generally the assistant commandant who actually runs the school. The commandant, usually a major general, is considered too much occupied with public relations and administrative matters to handle the day-to-day business of class supervision.

3. Ibid., 20.

4. The division later became the celebrated 82d Airborne.

5. Naturally, Bradley asked which way he was going, Europe or the Pacific. His informant only answered, "Remember your classmate? Well, you're going to join your classmate. I can't say anything more over the phone." The fact that Dwight Eisenhower and Omar Bradley had been classmates at West Point could hardly have been a secret from the enemy intelligence.

"spy" from higher headquarters. So Eisenhower appointed Bradley as Patton's deputy, where he could perform the same function. Bradley served under Patton throughout the El Guettar campaign, after which Patton was recalled to his Seventh Army command to plan the Sicily campaign. Bradley took over the U.S. II Corps.

Though Bradley's role at El Guettar was minor, he made a name in the latter stages of the Tunisian campaign. His II Corps performed the intricate logistical task of crossing through the lines of communication of the French on the Dorsal, and his Americans took Mateur and Bizerte. Thereafter Bradley was recognized as a preeminent American combat commander, slated to take his II Corps to Sicily.[6]

HUSKY, the Anglo-American invasion of Sicily, was launched on July 10, 1943, with the American Seventh and the British Eighth armies attacking abreast. General Sir Harold Alexander's Fifteenth Army Group was the senior ground command. Alex had not quite gotten over his distrust of the Americans, and just as he had done in North Africa, he chose to put his principal reliance on General Sir Bernard Montgomery's Eighth Army, which landed at Syracuse in the southeast corner of the triangular island. Monty was given the shortest and most direct leg of the triangle, a route that ran north from Syracuse to Messina. Patton's American Seventh Army, on the west, was essentially given the mission of protecting Montgomery's left flank. This arrangement, while reasonable, had drawbacks. Montgomery's route ran along a narrow stretch of land between the sea and Mount Etna, thus providing an ideal position for the German defenses. And the Americans felt strongly that they had been given an insufficient amount of resources.

A military campaign by coalition armies should not be regarded as a competition between the forces of the involved Allies, but Alexander's plan exacerbated the resentment the Americans already felt toward him. Patton, unusually motivated, even for him, took his Seventh Army around to the west to Palermo and then, turning eastward, drove it along the north coast and arrived in Messina a few hours before Monty, who stayed out of the city. This perceived triumph did much to enhance the pride of Patton and other Americans. Never mind the ferocity of the Germans who were desperate to hold the direct corridor from Syracuse.

It is difficult to assess the respective roles played by Patton and Bradley in Sicily, because the Seventh Army consisted of only Bradley's II Corps.

---

6. See chapter 6 for a description of the end of the Tunisian campaign and Bradley's role in it.

Both men, however, performed creditably, and Eisenhower's faith in both of them was enhanced.

At the end of the Sicilian campaign, the plans for OVERLORD, the invasion of Northwest Europe, were being formulated. General Marshall, who expected to command the operation, asked Eisenhower's opinion as to who the senior American commander should be. Ike recommended Bradley, and Marshall agreed.[7] Accordingly, Bradley left the Mediterranean theater for London shortly.

Bradley, as the senior American commander under Marshall, was given a say in selecting his own subordinates. Patton was an obvious choice, but he suffered from being Bradley's senior. In addition, he was under a severe cloud from the notorious "soldier-slapping incident," in which his conduct placed him in disgrace.[8] But when Ike replaced Marshall as commander of OVERLORD, he believed that Patton's talents in pursuing a beaten enemy were nearly unique. So when the soldier-slapping incident was explained to the public—and some time had passed—Eisenhower gave the wayward general the opportunity to command Third Army if he was willing to serve under his former subordinate, Bradley. Patton seized the opportunity, but Bradley had his doubts:

> My own feelings on George were mixed. He had not been my choice for Army commander and I was still wary of the grace with which he would accept our reversal in roles. For George was six years my senior and had been my Army commander when I fought II Corps in the Sicilian campaign. I was apprehensive in having George join my command, for I feared that too much of my time would be spent in curbing his impetuous habits. But at the same time I knew that with Patton there would be no need for my whipping Third Army to keep it in motion. We had only to keep him pointed in the direction we intended to go.

Bradley later changed his mind. "Patton," he later wrote, "not only bore me no ill will but he trooped for Twelfth Army Group with unbounded loyalty and eagerness." Further, he claimed, an officer from Third Army

---

7. D. Eisenhower, *Crusade in Europe*, 179.

8. During the Sicilian campaign, an exhausted Patton had committed the inexcusable mistake of losing his head and slapping a couple of soldiers he thought were malingering in an evacuation hospital. Having given Patton a stern castigation and forcing him to humiliate himself by apologizing to the troops, Eisenhower attempted to keep the matter quiet. It was an impossible effort, and word finally reached the American press. The public did not particularly like Patton at that stage of the war, and the furor was so great that it might become impossible for him to continue on duty. Even Eisenhower, in attempting to protect Patton, was taking some risk with his own future.

later told him that, though Patton had frequently excoriated his senior commanders, he never said an unkind word about Bradley.[9]

The period between early 1944 and the end of the war in May 1945 saw the really close relationship between Eisenhower and Bradley. Up to that time, another echelon of command had always been between them. Now, as soon as Bradley's Twelfth Army Group could be established, Bradley would report directly to Ike at Supreme Headquarters. They would then work hand in glove. It would be up to Bradley to make Eisenhower's ideas work. Ike felt utterly confident that he could rely on his friend.

A word about the Allied command setup for the OVERLORD invasion. To avoid an excessive number of command layers for a force fighting on a fifty-mile front, Eisenhower placed Montgomery temporarily in overall ground command for the landing and lodgment. Monty's Twenty-first Army Group consisted of two armies, Bradley's U.S. First Army on the right and Sir Miles Dempsey's Second British Army on the left. As soon as possible, Bradley would step up and assume Twelfth Army Group, coequal with Monty.

The beachhead was to comprise five independent landings, each about a division reinforced. Two of the landings were to be made by Bradley's First Army: UTAH Beach on the west and OMAHA Beach on the east. Of the two, OMAHA was the larger, and two divisions were to land on that beach. These divisions, the U.S. 1st and 29th, were under the direct command of V Corps, commanded by Major General Leonard T. Gerow.

D-day, the morning of June 6, 1944, witnessed the most important, certainly the most dramatic, action of Omar Bradley's long and distinguished career. Of the five Allied landings, he was present at OMAHA, the only one that ran into serious trouble.

Bradley was not included in the group that met on that stormy morning of June 4, 1944, at Portsmouth, where General Eisenhower launched OVERLORD with the simple words, "OK. We'll go." He was already at Plymouth, where he would leave with Vice Admiral Alan R. Kirk aboard the heavy cruiser USS *Augusta*. The weather was good at first, but the forecasts were frightening. They were forced to bide their time making calculations as to what time in the morning the landing should be made if the planned D-day, June 5, would have to be postponed. Fortunately, Bradley and Kirk had worked together before when Kirk had landed Bradley's II Corps in Sicily nearly a year earlier, and they were friends.

---

9. Bradley, *A Soldier's Story*, 355. At a small dinner in August 1945, I had reason to observe that General Bradley was being a bit optimistic in this passage.

Little to their surprise, word came in during the morning of June 4 that Eisenhower had delayed the invasion for a day. The two therefore went into the town of Plymouth that afternoon to meet their full staffs and make adjustments, especially since a second postponement to June 7 was possible. On the morning of June 5, however, the order came that the invasion was on. The *Augusta* slipped out of Plymouth Harbor that afternoon, easily keeping up with the main landing force for OMAHA Beach, where it would take station.

Early on the morning of June 6, Kirk and Bradley were on the bridge of the *Augusta* peering into the darkness. At about five o'clock it was light enough that the ship could begin firing its eight-inch guns on preplanned targets. A force of eighteen hundred heavy bombers dropped their loads ashore. But for the next seven hours word was indefinite. The Navy was able to pick up fragmentary reports, but Bradley's main source of information would be from Gerow's V Corps. But Gerow could make out nothing more than could Bradley.

The first news was good and bad. On the favorable side, word came that Colonel Earl Rudder's Rangers had made a successful scale of the cliff at Point du Hoc to the west. On the other hand, to nobody's surprise, most of the floating tanks had been swamped by the heavy seas. A party sent by Kirk and Bradley could ascertain only that the minefields on the beaches had been thicker than expected. Also, the enemy had placed more forces in the region than expected. The presence of the German 352d Infantry Division, a first-class unit, was not on the Allied planning charts.

Around noon came time for Bradley's critical decision. Since the landing force at OMAHA Beach was so far behind schedule, he had to decide where the reserve force, following up the assault force, should land. As he stood on the bridge of the *Augusta*, he pondered the situation. If the beach was not clear enough, the presence of the follow-up force would result in excessive crowding and confusion. But if he diverted the follow-up force to UTAH Beach or to somewhere in the British zone, the timetable for OVERLORD would be seriously thrown off. He decided to let the plan stand; the follow-up force should go across OMAHA as planned.

His decision was rewarded. Word came from Gerow at about one o'clock that the front-line units of the 1st Infantry Division and its attached 29th had broken through the first line and had moved inland. The OVERLORD plan was far from out of the woods, but it was now free to go ahead.

Bradley's decision was a simple one, but so fraught with dire possibilities that a less stable man might have faltered. Bradley did not.

It was a little more than two weeks after D-day that I met General Bradley for the first time. On June 24, 1944, a couple of days after our visit with Churchill,[10] we took a destroyer to Normandy. We transferred to a DUKW ("duck") for the few hundred yards to OMAHA Beach, where General Bradley was awaiting us. We traveled by jeep a few miles west-ward, through the ruined town of Isigny, and pulled off the road to the left to visit Bradley's First Army headquarters. He lived in a trailer amid a row of tents in a pleasant apple orchard, with the blue of the English Channel visible to our rear.

It was a surprisingly peaceful atmosphere. On hand was General Gerow, commanding the V Corps, Lieutenant General Henry D. G. Crerar, com-manding the Canadian Corps on Bradley's left, and others. Eisenhower, Bradley, and Gerow were lifelong friends, and Crerar was a pleasant gen-tleman. After lunch under a blue sky, we aides were sent out of earshot while the generals conferred. We were unaware—and indeed I cannot vouch for it—that the decision to shift the weight of the Allied Force at-tack from Monty on the east to Bradley on the west was made that day. The lunch in the apple orchard was an unspectacular event, but it was historic.

During July 1944 the Americans and British executed Operation CO-BRA, later known as the St. Lô breakout. Bradley played a central role.[11] COBRA was planned as a combined air-ground operation. First, the Al-lied air forces, using light and heavy bombers, were to pulverize that sec-tion of the German lines along the St. Lô–Périers road. Then Bradley's First Army, employing two corps, was to pour through the gap. Major General J. Lawton Collins's VII Corps would turn northwestward to seize the port of Cherbourg, while Gerow's V Corps would drive southward to Avranches, a town at the corner made by the juncture of the Cotentin (Cherbourg) and Brittany peninsulas. It was at that point, when the break-through was accomplished, that Bradley was to step up from First Army to the command of Twelfth Army Group. Under him, General Courtney Hodges would take over First Army, and Patton's Third Army would go into action. William Simpson's Ninth Army would soon arrive.

This change of command arrangement took place on August 1, 1944. On that same day, Patton's new Third Army began pouring through the Mortain–Avranches Gap and turned eastward with two of its three corps.

---

10. See chapter 1.

11. Generals' memoirs usually place the author in the center of any operation that suc-ceeds. The subordinate recommends, the author decides, and the superiors approve the author's action. *A Soldier's Story* shows the heavy hand of Bradley's aide, who drafted it. It does not sound like Bradley.

Patton drove his troops relentlessly, and Third Army hardly missed a step until it reached the German border.[12]

Turning Patton for a sudden drive to the German border was fraught with risk. Hitler, aware of the narrowness of the American corridor between Mortain and Avranches, attempted to cut Third Army off from the rear with a strong armored counterattack at Mortain. Eisenhower, at Bradley's headquarters, then had a decision to make. As of August 9, Bradley was holding four divisions near the corridor to counter Hitler's offensive if necessary. Ike and Brad, however, preferred to send three of those divisions ahead with Patton and retain only one, the 30th, at Mortain to hold the corridor open. The gamble succeeded, with much help from the air forces, and Hitler's offensive became a disaster. With so many heavy troops deployed to the west, the German *Seventh* and *Fifth Panzer* armies were nearly surrounded when one of Patton's corps moved northward to Falaise—acting under Bradley's orders. The result was the German disaster at the Falaise Gap.[13]

Critics have said that the great victory at Falaise should have been even more decisive[14] because, they argue, too large a portion of the German *Seventh* and *Fifth Panzer* armies escaped the trap. Field Marshal Walther Model therefore, was later able to establish a defense line along the borders of Germany. In fact, however, it was well-nigh impossible for the Allies to meet the Canadians coming down from Caen. Even Argentan was a dozen miles into Montgomery's territory.[15] Bradley had to order Patton to hold at Argentan and to pull back whatever troops had gone north.[16] Bradley, in writing of the episode, stated it somewhat apologetically: "I would rather have a strong shoulder at Argentan than the possibility of a broken neck at Falaise."[17]

---

12. The original plan called for all of Patton's army to be committed in Brittany. However, with the unexpected success at St. Lô, Eisenhower had changed his plan. If he could attack eastward with the bulk of Patton's army, he wrote to General Marshall, the "results will be incalculable."

13. As a matter of courtesy, Ike and Bradley made a phone call to Montgomery, who was formally in command of the ground operations. Monty, though reluctant, was in no position to say no. Had he so attempted, Ike would probably have overridden him.

14. Eisenhower estimated ten thousand bodies counted on the field, plus fifty thousand prisoners and untold numbers of German wounded.

15. Eisenhower, even though Bradley's army group was equal to Monty's in other respects, had still granted Monty the authority to set boundaries between them.

16. Patton took his time about reporting this success. Finally calling Bradley, who was still at Mortain, he declaimed, "We've got elements in Argentan. Let me go on to Falaise and we'll drive the British back into the sea for another Dunkirk!" In his rivalry with Montgomery, General Patton sometimes forgot who his enemy was.

17. There is an interesting parallel between Bradley's stopping at Argentan and Major General John Lucas's failure, at Anzio, to push inland after an unopposed landing and drive

Bradley was probably right. The initial attack by the Canadians on August 7 had been stopped by fierce German resistance, and a large portion of the German armor was still located at Caen. So perhaps J. Lawton Collins was being a bit harsh when, in later reviewing the situation with Montgomery, he said, "We only pushed them out of the bag."[18]

Contrary to Allied expectations, the Germans did not attempt to defend along the Seine River after Falaise. Instead, the survivors of the Normandy campaign fell all the way back to the Siegfried line, a strong position on the German border that Hitler had been repairing for such a contingency. In mid-September Montgomery, on the north, made his controversial attempt to secure a crossing of the Rhine by a combined airborne and armored assault in Holland. This was Operation MARKET-GARDEN, better known by the descriptive term *A Bridge Too Far.*[19]

At that point the Allied drive halted for lack of supplies. Nobody had expected a rapid advance. For the month of October, therefore, attacks all along the front were localized. The Allies, especially the Americans, had been the victims of too much success.

In late October the supply situation was improving, and Eisenhower had determined to keep pushing the attack against Germany through the winter. Second, he had decided to pursue what was termed the *broad front strategy:* one attack toward Berlin north of the Ardennes, and another south of that region. Mutual support between drives would be impossible. The Ardennes, a hilly, wooded, stream-cut region in eastern Belgium and northern Luxembourg, made movements between them arduous.[20] Of the two approaches, the North German Plain was wider and more direct, but even so it could handle only about twenty-four divisions, or three armies. The Frankfurt Corridor between Metz, the Saar, and Frankfurt, was also necessary to seal off the southern edge of the Ruhr Valley.[21] The Frankfurt

---

for the Alban Hills, just south of Rome. The British, especially Churchill, blamed Lucas for the fact that his own ill-conceived plan had not produced immediate, decisive results. Both men were criticized for excessive caution, but the bulk of opinion supports what they did. Lucas was later replaced for his chronic pessimism, but Bradley, who had a weaker case, was untouched.

18. John S. D. Eisenhower, *The Bitter Woods,* 352. Collins is listed as an interview in the bibliography, but I was unable to fix the exact date.

19. The title of the book *A Bridge Too Far,* by Cornelius Ryan.

20. Ironically, the Germans had gone through this "impassable" defense to defeat the French twice in the space of seventy-five years, once in 1870 and again in 1940.

21. Encircling the Ruhr had always been in the plans. The unexpected success in Normandy and the quick liberation of France had emboldened Montgomery to challenge it.

route could not carry the same number of divisions as could the North German Plain, but it was the "traditional" invasion route of history, from Attila the Hun to the émigrés attempting to overthrow the French Revolution in 1792. The 6th Army Group, under General Jacob Devers, fought in the South, at Colmar.

Monty's landing on the east automatically placed the Twenty-first Army Group on the North German Plain, but that corridor was capable of carrying more than his fifteen-division group, so the gap had to be filled with Americans. Bradley, therefore, was stretched from Aachen to Metz, forced to provide an army to support Monty. He thus made an adjustment to his front, switching his lineup of armies so that the Ninth, the latest and least experienced, would be located on the left, adjacent to Monty. Then when Monty, as expected, received the attachment of an American Army north of the Ardennes, it would be the Ninth, not the First, that would go.[22] Bradley was not by nature a conspirator, but he was already developing a hostility toward his counterpart.

With parts of his Twelfth Army Group fighting on two separate avenues, Bradley took a risk, which Eisenhower approved. He split his effort into two thrusts, one north of the Ardennes, largely in support of Montgomery, and the other south, from Metz up the Frankfurt Corridor. In between, the line was to be held by minimum forces. Since both men considered Patton's attack at Metz to be the main American effort, Bradley established his headquarters in a hotel in Luxembourg City. Hodges, of First Army, would give the priority of his attention to the area around Aachen in the North. It seemed to be a logical setup.

Given the length of Bradley's front, this deployment of Twelfth Army Group depended on a presumption that any German attack into the Ardennes would be minor and would not cut communications between Bradley's two lines of attack. But in war, things do not always turn out as expected.

On the December 16, 1944, Adolf Hitler launched his great Ardennes offensive that came to be known as the Battle of the Bulge. It so happened that Bradley was visiting Eisenhower at his headquarters at Versailles that evening, discussing other matters. Their conversation was abruptly interrupted by an alarming message: the Ardennes front had been penetrated in five different places by German attacks of unknown strength. Such a situation implied a major enemy effort. And since the Americans had sup-

---

22. Bradley later admitted that the move had no effect, because Ninth Army, under the very capable William Simpson, would soon become a first-class formation.

posedly placed no major supply dumps east of the Meuse River, Brad and Ike reasoned that the Germans could have no strategic objective short of driving to Antwerp or at least Liège.[23]

They made a quick map survey. It indicated that the Americans had two armored divisions out of the line: the 7th Armored in the zone of Simpson's Ninth Army on the north, and the 10th Armored in Patton's Third Army to the south. Eisenhower decided to send both of those divisions toward the zone of First Army's VIII Corps, the area of the penetrations. That meant a quick phone call to both Simpson and Patton. Eisenhower called Simpson personally and ordered the dispatch of the 7th. He did, however, leave it to Bradley to cope with an irate Patton, who called the German action merely an effort to interrupt his own attack toward the Saar.

During the next couple of days, the situation became clear. The German attack was indeed a major effort, which had been in planning ever since the previous September. Taking advantage of cloudy weather, which precluded detection and attack by the Allied air forces, the Germans had amassed a force of some twenty-four divisions under three separate armies, and by superb discipline had moved them undetected into the Eiffel, geographically the eastward extension of the Ardennes. By December 19 the time had come for the Americans to begin their counterattack. A meeting was set for the top commanders at Bradley's "main" headquarters, a dingy barracks at Verdun.

Bradley said little in that Verdun meeting because Eisenhower, the overall boss, and Patton, who would actually make the attack, held center stage. But the atmosphere, at Eisenhower's insistence, was positive. A great opportunity had appeared by virtue of the fact that the weakened German army had come out from behind its fixed defenses. At the end of the meeting, Eisenhower had directed Patton to cancel his attack toward the Saar and turn Third Army northward toward Bastogne, an important road hub that was now about to be surrounded. The Germans might keep driving westward for another week, but the turning point had actually been reached that morning of December 19.

One aspect of the situation, however, troubled Eisenhower. Though he said nothing of it at the Verdun meeting, he was becoming convinced that Bradley, with his headquarters so far south in Luxembourg, would be cut off from the main scene of the action in the North. The Germans had driven so far to the west that travel from Luxembourg to Liège required taking

23. This assumption later turned out to be erroneous. A major gasoline and oil depot was located at Francorchamps, south of Liège. When Eisenhower learned of this failure in communications, a certain mild unpleasantness occurred, which soon blew over.

a route west of the Meuse River. Bradley, Eisenhower concluded, could not direct both Patton and Hodges under those circumstances.

Eisenhower therefore decided to split the battlefield. That night of December 19 he drew a line on the map between the German town of Prüm on the east and the French town of Dinant on the west, with all American forces north of that line to be temporarily placed under the command of Montgomery. As a matter of courtesy he checked with Bradley, who, though he hated the idea, felt he had no right to protest. He feared, he later wrote, that his own reluctance was due too much to personal feelings.

Tactically, the arrangement functioned well, and had it not been for Monty's ego, it could have come off without a hitch. Actually, reports from Americans at First Army confirm that Monty handled the situation with tact and competence. But Monty, being Monty, could never avoid gloating in public, and the tone of a press conference he held on January 7, 1945, was vainglorious and strongly implied that he had come to the "rescue" of a failed American command. The British press, always hungry for such opportunities to take digs at the Yanks, touted his remarks. Bradley's reluctance had proved to be justified. He was now infuriated.

Bradley complained to Ike's headquarters and held his own press conference. To make matters worse, Monty had revived his ongoing campaign to make the changeover permanent, leaving Bradley with only one army, Patton's Third.

Bradley stood the perceived humiliation as long as he could. A short time after Montgomery renewed his campaign to be appointed overall ground commander for the European Theater, Bradley now feared that Eisenhower might give in to such an arrangement. As Bradley later reported their conversation,

> "You must know," I said, "after what has happened I cannot serve under Montgomery. If he is to be put in command of all ground forces, you must send me home, for if Montgomery goes in over me, I will have lost the confidence of my command."
> Ike flushed. He stiffened in his chair and eyed me hotly. "Well," he said. "I thought you were the one person I could count on for anything I asked you to."
> "You can, Ike," I said. "I've enjoyed every bit of my service with you. But this is one thing I cannot take."[24]

The tragedy of the confrontation was that it was unnecessary. Eisenhower had never even considered acceding to Montgomery's campaign.

24. Bradley, *A Soldier's Story,* 487–88.

He did, however, resent Bradley's ultimatum. I have the feeling that the relations thereafter between the two men, while still friendly and warm, were thereafter just a little bit less so than before.

Though I had met General Bradley before, including lunch in Normandy, my first extended contact with him began in early February 1945, when I reported for duty at Twelfth Army Group headquarters—EAGLE TAC— at Namur in northern Belgium. The Battle of the Bulge was a thing of the past, and preparations were under way for the spring offensive to clear the west bank of the Rhine. I was there because Bradley himself had removed me from my infantry unit to avoid adding to my father's worries.

Soon after arrival I was told to go up to Bradley's personal office. It was a modest room, and I found the general poring over a map of the Huertgen Forest area. He greeted me in a friendly way, and without delay he explained my situation. I was to be assigned to his headquarters temporarily. Following that, he said, "I can put you in one of two spots. I can assign you to the headquarters of an infantry regiment. That's safe enough. We won't have any more regimental headquarters overrun—not in this war."

Then, after a pause, the general went on. "But there is a unit that I am particularly interested in. It is modeled after the British Phantom, which is designed to keep higher headquarters aware of the situation at the front. The Phantom has done great service for us, and we are organizing the American version. I would like to have a regular officer with a knowledge of it. It's up to you as to the unit you want. You can go either way."

I did not think of it at the time, but I am sure that Bradley was easing my conscience of having been removed from my fellows by indicating that there was something he personally wanted done. I selected his unit, the SIAM unit, and he agreed.[25] Then, with a slight smile, he turned and said, "I guess I had better get back to those damn dams."

I spent the next few days fretting around Twelfth Army Group waiting for Captain Joe Ryan, the officer whom Bradley had designated to deliver me to the SIAM unit. During that time, I was able to observe Bradley and his staff at close hand. One day, for example, as the staff was gathered for lunch in the cheerful officers' mess, I watched Bradley talking to a small group in his quiet, chirpy voice. He was complaining about some little item that had appeared about him in the newspapers, even though it was

---

25. The name "Signal Information and Monitoring" is misleading. The "Phantom" mission had been to send tactical information from the front directly to higher headquarters, thus bypassing the cumbersome reporting procedures of the echelons of command. Not surprisingly, the SIAM patrol leader was not usually welcome when he reported to the local operations officer.

favorable. "I don't want that kind of publicity," he said. "Any day I can stay out of the papers is a day to the good." On a couple of occasions he sauntered over to me and, brightening up, asked, "When is Joe Ryan turning up?" I had no answer as to the location of my missing guide.

I have always noticed that Bradley appeared to develop favorites among young officers. As a rule they were highly competent, bright young men, with gregarious and outgoing personalities just the opposite of his own. I sometimes wonder if he tended to dote on the "sons he never had." One was his aide, Major Chet Hansen, a newspaperman in civilian life who played a major role in Bradley's later writings. And Bradley beamed whenever Joe Ryan's name came up.

I found it somewhat amusing that Bradley's headquarters, EAGLE TAC, was officially designated as the "rear of the combat zone," even though it was located about sixty miles behind the actual front lines. Uniform during duty hours was always battle jacket ("Ike" jacket), highly polished paratrooper boots, and shiny helmet liner. At dinner in the evenings, dress uniform was "blouse and pinks"! I was once a trifle annoyed by the smug look on the face of one of the aides as he sipped a martini before dinner. That, however, was not Bradley's fault: nothing was to be gained by keeping the hardworking staff uncomfortable.

By the end of the war in Europe, Bradley's Twelfth Army Group comprised forty-three divisions, extending from the Elbe River to Linz in Austria. He returned home soon after the end of hostilities, and since he was a figure so trusted by the soldiers, he was made the head of the Veterans Administration, charged with caring for literally millions of soldiers, many of whom he had commanded. The assignment was only temporary, however, and when Eisenhower retired as chief of staff in February 1948, Bradley succeeded him. When the position of Chairman of the Joint Chiefs of Staff was later established, in 1949, he was appointed to that position. At the same time, President Harry Truman promoted him to the rank of general of the Army—five stars—thus putting him on a level with Marshall, MacArthur, Eisenhower, and Arnold.[26]

Bradley's tenure as Chairman of the Joint Chiefs was not an easy time. The Department of Defense had been established in 1947, making the Air Force independent of the Army.[27] But the emotionally loaded matter of

26. I will not debate the wisdom or the motive of that appointment, of which I have vague doubts. Suffice it to say that the practice was discontinued.

27. For a short time the Department of Defense was designated the National Military Establishment.

control of airpower still remained. The Navy fiercely resisted every tightening of control over its naval aviation, and many concessions had to be granted to bring the admirals aboard.

Bradley was not ideally suited for the role of moderator. At one point, just after the Navy had protested the cancellation of the new carrier the *United States,* he became convinced that the testimony of the admirals was outright insubordination. In a meeting he let fly with a statement that has stuck with his name. "This is no time," he declared, "for fancy Dans who won't hit the line with all they have on every play unless they can call the signals." It was not so much the words, which were angry enough, but the way in which they were expressed. One witness, Captain Fitzhugh Lee, later described his demeanor: "I will never forget his speech. He started off quietly and gradually worked himself into an hysterical delivery in which his voice kept rising in pitch, and he was trembling. . . . I never dreamed that a four-star officer in the armed forces could so completely lose control of himself."[28]

Fitzhugh Lee may have been exaggerating, as he was on the other side. But a few days later Bradley rejected every one of the Navy's claims against "strategic bombing, the B-36, and the treatment of the Navy by the Pentagon high command."[29]

Bradley's remarks caused a great deal of eyebrow raising, but he was under great strain. His utter loyalty to President Truman and Secretary of Defense Louis Johnson only raised his standing with the president.

In June 1950 the Korean War broke out, and in April 1951, when President Truman fired General Douglas MacArthur as Supreme Commander in the Far East, he made the move with the military recommendation of Bradley, and Truman delegated to Bradley the onus of sending the message of dismissal. The wording of Bradley's message to MacArthur showed that he was cowed by nobody.

In late 1952 my father was elected president, and as president-elect, made his promised trip to Korea. Bradley was one of the party that accompanied him. I was recalled from my unit and spent three days in their presence. The atmosphere appeared to be as cordial as ever, even though they had had a couple of disagreements. At one point Bradley referred to the recent election with the words, "We were all hanging on the edges of our chairs." The implication, of course, was that Bradley had been rooting

28. Jeffrey Barlow, *The Revolt of the Admirals,* 262.
29. Ibid.

for Ike, but I analyzed the wording closely. I am not at all sure that such was the case. After all, Bradley had served Truman faithfully.

I saw General Bradley only rarely after that. One instance occurred in the early fall of 1953, when he and my father played golf at Burning Tree Club in Washington. When Bradley, still chairman, rode back to the city with my father, all was relaxed and informal. In 1965 I interviewed him in his Pentagon office in connection with my book *The Bitter Woods* and was struck by the virulence of the rancor he still held for Montgomery after the passage of more than twenty years.

I know very little about Bradley's years in retirement. I was sorry when he published his memoirs in 1951, because *A Soldier's Story* had to have been ghostwritten. It was a good account, but the braggadocio tone bore no resemblance to the modest Bradley I had known.[30] In the mid-1960s he signed on as a "technical adviser" in the filming of the celebrated motion picture *Patton.* I could never understand how he could allow himself to be portrayed in such a pathetic light as errand boy between Ike and Patton. Perhaps he was not sensitive to the way he appeared. I don't know.

During that filming, the widowed Bradley met his second wife, Kitty, who was many years younger than he. I personally joined with many others of Bradley's friends in regretting the way that the new Mrs. Bradley displayed the old general at public events in full resplendent uniform with all the medals he was authorized—and in a wheelchair, barely able to talk.

The last time I saw the "GI General," as Ernie Pyle had dubbed him, he was in that condition. The occasion was the inauguration of President Jimmy Carter on January 20, 1977. The two of us spotted each other in the crowd, and he beckoned me over. We had a short, quiet visit; one would have thought that we had seen each other the previous week. We talked a while about nothing in particular, probably mentioning the general's daughter, Lee, a friend from West Point. Despite the informality of the chat, a strange feeling came over me. Though I was in my fifty-fifth year and had also been the ambassador to Belgium for a couple of years, I felt like a first lieutenant reporting to him at Namur. I understand that the experience is common in the presence of such a venerable relic of World War II.

---

30. In 1978 he was coauthor with historian Clay Blair in writing *A Soldier's Life,* an even more controversial book than his first one more than a quarter century earlier.

General Bradley lived for another four years. He was not a colorful man, nor in my opinion a very broad one. But he was a good man and a highly qualified professional soldier. He handsomely justified the prediction of the unknown writer in the 1915 West Point *Howitzer,* "Sure, General Bradley was a classmate of mine."

General Matthew B. Ridgway (Library of Congress)

# 9

# Matthew B. Ridgway

## Mr. Airborne

On the evening of December 23, 1950, Lieutenant General Walton Walker, commanding the U.S. Eighth Army in Korea, was on his way in subzero weather at a point near the front north of Seoul. As usual, his jeep was traveling at a high speed. All of a sudden the vehicle hit a civilian truck head-on, killing Walker instantly. Eighth Army, on top of all its tribulations at that dark period of the Korean War, was without a leader. Walker would have to be replaced immediately.

Walker's loss was a real blow. He had been a distinguished soldier in the Second World War, the man whose XX Corps had spearheaded General George Patton's dash across France in August 1944.[1] But despite Walker's admirable qualities, Eighth Army, at the time of his death, was in a deplorable condition. The men were exhausted from heavy fighting, confused, and freezing with inadequate winter clothing. It had just sustained a crushing defeat at the hands of a large army of Communist Chinese in the North,[2] and the previously separate X Corps had been evacuated by sea and delivered back to Pusan to join the rest of Walker's command. The whole Eighth Army, including the portion that had gone up the west coast of the peninsula, was in the process of retreating back to the thirty-eighth parallel. It was uncertain whether the withdrawal would even stop there.

---

1. In his honor, the Army named its new light tank, the M-41, the "Walker Bulldog."
2. It seems probable that the Chinese involvement came about from fear that MacArthur's forces, having defeated the North Korean army that fall, would cross the Yalu River and continue their advance into Manchuria.

In these dire circumstances, President Harry S. Truman and the American Joint Chiefs of Staff scanned the list of candidates from which to name a successor to Walker and quickly settled on the name of Lieutenant General Matthew B. Ridgway, currently serving as the Army's deputy chief of staff for operations. Within a couple of days, Matt Ridgway was in the office of the Supreme Commander of the UN Forces in the Far East, General Douglas MacArthur. The two men had served together previously, and MacArthur gave his new Eighth Army commander a virtual blank check to run the Korean War as he saw fit, a rare gesture on the part of the authoritarian MacArthur.

On his arrival at Eighth Army, Ridgway found a spirit of defeatism. Colonel (later Major General) Frank Moorman, a member of the Eighth Army staff, found a staff study recommending that Eighth Army should withdraw from Korea and take the necessary steps leading to the departure. He initialed in the appropriate place and tossed the document into the "out" basket. Admonished that he was discarding without reading the views of the entire Eighth Army staff, he responded, "If these are the views of the entire Eighth Army staff, why then the entire Eighth Army staff knows little about its new commander. General Ridgway will neither approve the Conclusions nor carry out any of the Recommendations."[3] Moorman had his man right. Ridgway paid no attention to the staff study.

Ridgway's approach to rebuilding the Eighth Army was twofold. First, he replaced many of his staff and commanders with men he knew to be fighters. And aware that the authorities in Washington would never allow him to return far into North Korea, he invented a new mission, which he called "Operation KILLER." He announced that his objective would not be primarily to seize ground, but to kill Chinese. The idea caught on, and spirits among American troops rose.

Ridgway indulged also in a bit of personal showmanship by adorning his uniform with accoutrements that reflected his own philosophy.[4] He wore a steel helmet, chinstrap loose, with the three stars prominent, a field jacket, with harness, and on one harness strap he attached a hand grenade; on the other strap, he fastened a first aid kit. As such he made an impressive figure. Tall, rugged, erect, with a lined face and piercing eyes, he was

3. Frank Moorman, obituary of General Ridgway.
4. Ridgway always claimed that these accoutrements were not merely for show. In the latter weeks of World War II in Europe, he had been wounded by a German hand grenade. It might be argued that Ridgway had not been wise in exposing himself, but he sincerely believed that a commander should be up front.

the personification of command. It was the image by which the public re-members him, and which he emblazoned on the dust jacket of his later memoir.

Ridgway's positive leadership had an instant effect. Within a remarkably short time, Eighth Army was able to move northward from Seoul and drive the Communist Chinese northward to a line that ran roughly along the thirty-eighth parallel. He was then called to higher posts, just a little more than three months after taking command, to replace General MacArthur.

Though Ridgway's finest moment may have been the time in which his leadership turned Eighth Army around during the winter and early spring of 1950–1951, his career included such positions as Chief of Staff, United States Army; Commanding General of the famed 82d Airborne Division; Commander of the XVIII Airborne Corps, Supreme Commander of the Far East and United Nations Command; and Supreme Allied Commander, Europe, the military arm of the North Atlantic Treaty Organization.

During all this time, even though some of his assignments were of a diplomatic nature, he never departed from the mind-set of the "soldier's soldier." His military outlook had been established before he ever went to West Point; as an army brat—a term that those of us who qualify hold dear—his world was the Army. In accordance with the American Army's bent, he was an out-and-out professional, a true follower of the French military writer Antoine-Henri Jomini.[5] His troops swore by him. It was only in his last years of service, when he was called upon to adopt a broad-er national outlook, that he ran into difficulties. But more of that later.

For a man whose name would become legendary throughout the Army, Ridgway's career had an unusually inauspicious beginning. Like Eisen-hower and Bradley, he was denied overseas duty in the First World War, a circumstance that was generally thought to be fatal to his future military career. His plight was even worse than that of his two contemporaries, both of whom were assigned to tactical training units. Ridgway spent those years as a teacher of French up on the Hudson River.

After his six frustrating years as a language instructor at West Point, Ridgway finally received orders to attend the Company Officers' Course

5. In simplest terms, Jomini, a Napoleonic officer, advocated an army separate in out-look from the civilians of their country. As professionals, officers of the Jomini school gave their civilian leaders professional advice regardless of other considerations. Clausewitz, on the other hand, is best remembered for his doctrine that war is simply politics by different means.

at Fort Benning, Georgia. There, despite his lack of combat experience, he stood high in the class.[6] From there he was assigned to the 15th Infantry, at Tientsin, China, stationed to safeguard U.S. interests in that tumultuous region. In that routine but desirable assignment, he developed a friendship with Lieutenant Colonel George C. Marshall, a man sixteen years his senior, who retained an interest in the younger man throughout Marshall's long and illustrious years in the Army.

The 1930s saw Ridgway serving in routine peacetime jobs. After attending the Advanced Infantry Officers' Course at Fort Benning, he was sent, in 1932, to Manila as the military adviser to Governor-General Theodore Roosevelt Jr. There the two men, governor-general and major, made trips around the Southern Islands of the Philippines. Together they had adventures that Ridgway, never one to downplay the drama of a situation, told in his memoirs with relish.

In 1935 Ridgway's career began to take off. He was sought out by General Frank McCoy, commanding the Second Corps Area at Chicago, to plan a major maneuver to be conducted the next year. It was exhausting duty but rewarding, and it provided further contact with George Marshall, who was commanding a brigade. Soon he was assigned to the War Department General Staff in the prestigious War Plans Division under General Marshall, now Chief of Staff of the Army. When the Japanese Imperial Navy attacked Pearl Harbor and Hickam Army Air Base on December 7, 1941, Ridgway was still in War Plans.

By now Ridgway's reputation was secure. When War Plans was upgraded to Operations Division in April 1942, Eisenhower, as its chief, recognized him. As Ike later wrote, "Development of the Operations Division went so well that my key assistants and I gradually gained more time for thinking and study. We could safely leave routine operations in the hands of a group of outstanding young staff officers, supervised by Brigadier Generals Thomas T. Handy, Matthew B. Ridgway, and Robert W. Crawford . . . all of whom came into deserved Army prominence before the end of the war."[7]

No matter how good he was as a planner, however, Ridgway always believed that commanding combat troops was the highest form of military activity. General Marshall admired that quality and assigned him to

6. It is notable that three officers who remained in the United States during the First World War—Eisenhower, Bradley, and Ridgway—did remarkably well in the Army school system. Possibly they tried harder, knowing that their careers were at stake. They also had open minds—nothing to unlearn. In any case, the experience gave them much-needed confidence to continue their careers.

7. D. Eisenhower, *Crusade in Europe,* 41.

be assistant division commander of the 82d Division, under another of Marshall's protégés, Major General Omar N. Bradley.

With the Army growing so rapidly in mid-1942, General Marshall apparently decided that he could not afford to have two of his future leaders assigned to the same division, and he soon moved Bradley to take command of the 28th Infantry Division, with Ridgway taking over command of the 82d. Around August 1942, Ridgway learned that his new command was to become the Army's first airborne division, a new organization based on developments in Europe, especially the German capture of Crete in 1941 with airborne troops

The airborne division, as first organized, consisted of two paratrooper regiments and one glider regiment. The paratroopers considered themselves the elite of the Army, and they would probably have preferred to have three paratroop regiments. But the division needed a regiment of gliders for carrying jeeps, light artillery, and other equipment that could not be dropped by parachute. Still the division lacked the heavier weapons necessary for survival on the modern battlefield, especially antitank defense. Few people outside the airborne were aware of the vulnerability of the airborne division fighting alone. Ridgway, however, was well aware, and as a result was often unfairly accused during the war of being a naysayer.

Nevertheless, General Marshall and the War Department liked what they saw in the 82d Airborne, and they decided that the Army needed another such division. In order to do so, they decided to split the 82d in half, creating the 101st Airborne Division to be the 82d's counterpart. To command the 101st, Marshall chose the man known as the Father of the Airborne, Major General William C. (Bill) Lee, who had organized the first parachute platoon at Fort Benning in 1940.[8] Lee and Ridgway came up with a new scheme for dividing up the personnel of the 82d. The two commanders sat down together and selected two groups they deemed of equal quality. They then flipped a coin to determine which division received which group. It made for the fairest split-up possible.

Training went on for nearly a year. On the morning of May 10, 1943, Ridgway and his men, being transported to North Africa in three ships, saw the spires of Casablanca for the first time.

· · ·

8. Lee continued to command the 101st Airborne, which was not sent to the Mediterranean. He expected to jump into Normandy on D-day, June 6, 1944. Unfortunately, however, he was struck by a heart attack and evacuated home just before the jump. He retired that year and died in 1948 at the age of fifty-three.

The 82d Airborne did not have long to wait in Morocco before going into combat. Three days after its arrival, the German forces in Tunisia surrendered, and all efforts turned to preparation for the invasion of Sicily (HUSKY), only two months away. In the course of the planning, Ridgway ran afoul of Major General Frederick "Boy" Browning, the foremost British airborne officer, currently assigned as airborne technical adviser to General Eisenhower's Allied Force Headquarters. When Ridgway perceived that Browning was using his position to favor the 1st British Airborne Division over his own, he sent Browning a blunt note. Word reached Eisenhower, who as a matter of policy bent over backward to cement the alliance, sometimes at the expense of the Americans. As a result, Ridgway came close to having a short career in the Mediterranean. The incident represented only one instance in which Ridgway's standing up for his troops would put his own position in jeopardy.

Shortage of troop carrier transports dictated that the entire 82d Airborne could not be employed in the initial landing force on the southern coast of Sicily. Only one regiment, the 505th Parachute Infantry regiment under Colonel James Gavin, could go the first night. Ridgway, therefore, accompanied the Seventh Army commander, General George Patton, on D-day. The landings went satisfactorily for nearly everyone but the 505th, which was scattered by thirty-five-mile-per-hour winds over the large area in front of the 1st Infantry Division landing beach. On the second night tragedy struck. The 504th Parachute Infantry, carried by the 502 Troop Carrier Command, was mistaken for enemy aircraft, and naval forces shot several of the planes down. The 504th lost many men in that painful episode.

Ridgway, on the beach at Gela, had no idea where his troops were. He asked General Terry Allen, commanding the 1st Division, if he had seen any of his troopers. Allen had seen no evidence of them. Ridgway therefore took a jeep and drove forward ahead of the front through unoccupied territory. The first man he encountered was Brigadier General Theodore Roosevelt Jr., his old friend and onetime governor-general of the Philippines. A bit farther on, he finally encountered a member of the 505th, Captain Follmer, with a broken ankle. Eventually, Ridgway was able to find his two parachute regiments, and they organized once more as a division, fighting as light infantry for the rest of the Sicilian campaign.

Paradoxically for an aggressive soldier, Ridgway's most significant contribution in the Mediterranean was a negative one: his role in preventing the suicidal employment of the 82d Airborne Division in an airdrop in the vicinity of Rome. The Allied landing at Salerno was timed, as best it could be done, to coincide with the surrender of the Italian armed forces to the British and American Allies, and it was hoped that the Italians, with the encouragement of Americans in Rome, would overwhelm the vastly out-numbered Germans.

The scenario was complicated. Following the ouster and arrest of Italian dictator Benito Mussolini on July 26, 1943, Italian prime minister Pietro Badoglio announced on the air that Italy would continue to fight on Germany's side against the Allies. His broadcast, however, was obviously an empty gesture; everyone, both the Italians and the Allies, was aware that the Italian people wanted out of the war. Accordingly, clandestine negotiations between Badoglio and Eisenhower's headquarters soon began for Italy's exit from the war.

General Eisenhower, in his memoir of the war, described what followed: "Then began a series of negotiations. Secret communications, clandestine journeys by secret agents, and frequently meetings in hidden places that, if encountered in the fictional world, would have been scorned as incredible melodrama. Plots of various kinds were hatched, only to be abandoned because of changing circumstances. One of these plots involved the landing of a large airborne force. At the last moment either the fright of the Italian government or the movement of German reserves forced the cancellation of the project."[9]

Ridgway was not involved in these talks, but when he learned that his division was being considered for a drop near Rome, he was aghast, suspicious that higher commanders were unaware of the limitations of an airborne division. He was also aware that the Germans had amassed about six good divisions in the Rome vicinity. So disturbed was he by the prospect that, according to his account, he sat up all night at his headquarters in Sicily pondering the fate of his men. In the morning he sought out General Walter Bedell Smith, Eisenhower's chief of staff, who was in the vicinity.

Smith was impressed by Ridgway's dismay and recommended that he present his case to General Alexander, who was in direct charge of the tactics of the AVALANCHE operation. Alexander, however, brushed him off with reassuring words: "Don't give the matter a thought, Ridgway. Contact will be made with your division in three days—five at the most." Ridgway, defeated, returned to his own command post.[10]

But his arguments had made an impression. Alex went to Eisenhower, who decided to send two emissaries on a secret mission to Rome.[11] The two officers, disguised as prisoners of war in the custody of the Italians,

---

9. Ibid., 183.

10. Matthew B. Ridgway, *Soldier: The Memoirs of Matthew B. Ridgway*, 81.

11. They were Brigadier General Maxwell Taylor, artillery commander of the 82d Airborne, and Colonel William Gardner, of the Army Air Force.

were taken to Rome to consult with Marshal Badoglio himself, where they quickly ascertained that the Italians were too frightened to be of any help in assisting an Allied landing near Rome. When their report reached Eisenhower's headquarters. Operation GIANT II, as it was called, was canceled.

Ridgway contributed, if indirectly, to the decision. And as it turned out, he helped avert a disaster. When the Italian surrender was announced by Eisenhower on September 9, the Germans around Rome immediately disarmed the Italians, despite an Italian numerical superiority of about three to one. It had been assumed that the Anglo-Americans would relieve the 82d in Rome in a few days. As it turned out, it would take another six months, to June 5, 1944, for them to reach the Eternal City.

The 82d Airborne was one of four American divisions scheduled for redeployment to the United Kingdom for the Normandy invasion at the end of the Sicilian campaign.[12] On arrival in the UK, Ridgway was assigned a dual mission. Primarily, of course, he was the commanding general of the 82d Airborne. But he was also, as the senior American airborne commander, the chief American adviser to Supreme Headquarters for airborne matters.[13] The latter was no empty position, because the prospective airborne drop for OVERLORD was crucial. It was difficult because his recommendations involved his own command.

The success of OVERLORD, in Eisenhower's view, depended on quick seizure of Cherbourg, on the Cotentin Peninsula, the western end of the lodgment area. The five landing beaches across the Allied front could never support the entire force for a great length of time, especially after the anticipated breakout into the open. To that end the plan called for Major General J. Lawton Collins's VII Corps to land at the base of the peninsula (UTAH Beach) and swing westward and northward to seize the port.

The greatest danger to the UTAH Beach landing, as described in chapter 6 above, was the floodplain that had recently been inundated by the German defenders, the solution to which was the seizure of four causeways that traversed it.[14] While the 4th Infantry Division assaulted the beach, the 82d and the 101st Airborne Divisions were to seize the high ground north of the obstacle. The objective of the 82d would be the town of Sainte-Mère-Église, and the 101st was to seize nearby Carentan. All the Americans were satisfied with this operation.

---

12. The others were the 1st and 9th infantry divisions and the 2d Armored.

13. General William Lee, commander of the 101st, had been retired, his place taken by General Maxwell D. Taylor, Ridgway's former artillery commander.

14. One of these, incidentally, was being assaulted by Teddy Roosevelt Jr.

As D-day approached, however, Air Chief Marshal Sir Stafford Leigh-Mallory, the senior air commander for OVERLORD, began to develop serious doubts. With the threat of heavy winds and other bad weather, as well as German strength in the area, Leigh-Mallory felt it his duty to protest against the venture. He went to Eisenhower with his dismal prognostications only a very short time before D-day.

In the light of such somber advice from his top air commander, Eisenhower was forced to reconsider. He went over in his mind the entire landing concept and reluctantly concluded that success depended on the airborne drop. He consulted Ridgway and others, and all of them reassured him that Leigh-Mallory, with his estimate of unacceptable casualties, was overly pessimistic. If not, the risk had to be taken. The operation went ahead.[15]

Oddly, considering that Ridgway was considered "Mr. Airborne," the drop into Normandy would be his first combat jump. He had long been qualified as a paratrooper, and he had certainly been frequently at the front lines in combat, but he had never combined the two: both combat and a jump. He therefore went through all the emotions that beset others in his command, because for the first few hours, the two stars on his shoulders would be of no protection against enemy bullets: he was taking the same risk as any other soldier in his command.

As it turned out, Ridgway was one of the lucky ones. He landed with the usual jar, but collected his parachute and gear and set out to find his men. Until he could find enough to make a headquarters, he was not a commander; he was an individual. In due course, by eight in the morning, D-day, he had found his aide and his operations officer, the latter of whom acted as his chief of staff. It was the dawn of the third day before the 82d had made contact with elements of the 4th Infantry Division on one of the causeways. By chance Ridgway once more encountered his old friend Teddy Roosevelt Jr., whom he had previously met in front of the line of contact in Sicily.[16] The two airborne divisions had been so scattered by the winds that they were intermingled. As in Sicily, however, the lack of organization had its bright side; the Germans, reporting every landing, overestimated the actual size of the airborne attack.

---

15. D. Eisenhower, *Crusade in Europe*, 246–47.

16. By another incredible coincidence, the first man he ran across after his landing was Captain Follmer, the first man he met in Sicily. In Sicily Follmer had broken an ankle; in Normandy he feared it was his back. Ridgway does not tell us whether Follmer recovered completely from his second injury. Ridgway, *Soldier*, 6, 72.

The Germans still had plenty of fight in them. The 82d Airborne Division, dog tired, was given no respite. It was kept in the line for an incredible thirty-two days, in the meantime incurring 1,282 deaths and 2,373 serious wounds.[17]

Ridgway's time with the 82d soon came to a close after the Normandy fighting. The Allied High Command was organizing the First Allied Airborne Army, under Lieutenant General Lewis Brereton, and Ridgway was to command the XVIII Airborne Corps, the American component. He assumed command on August 27, 1944, two days after V Corps, of First Army, took Paris.

Though Ridgway was sad to leave the 82d, which he had now commanded for more than two years, he consoled himself by knowing that he would have three airborne divisions under him: the 82d, now under James Gavin; the 101st, under Maxwell Taylor; and the new 17th Airborne, under William H. Miley. And he viewed the duties of a corps commander as a particular challenge.

Ridgway took command of the XVIII Airborne Corps as Operation MARKET-GARDEN was being planned. It was Montgomery's effort to bypass the Siegfried line by an attack to cross the lower Rhine River at Arnhem, Holland. The British XXX Corps was to attack on the ground, and three river-crossing points were to be seized, each by an airborne division. Since two of the divisions were to be American, Ridgway had hopes that he might command the airborne phase. But the command went to his old nemesis General "Boy" Browning, and he was relegated to the role of observer. Ridgway could not, however, resist the role of critic, and he attributed the failure of the operation to the British ground elements, which he called "sluggish."[18] Almost the entire British 1st Airborne Division was lost, and Arnhem remained in German hands.

Operation MARKET-GARDEN ended unsuccessfully in late November, and the 82d and 101st Airborne Divisions went into reserve to refit and train near Rheims, France. Ridgway's XVIII Corps, with the 17th Airborne, remained in the Salisbury Plain area of southern England. On December 18, however, this rest period came to an end. A message from General Eisenhower's headquarters informed Ridgway that the Germans had bro-

17. Ibid., 15.
18. Ridgway's criticism of the armored elements of MARKET-GARDEN reflects the competition between the airborne and armored units that existed throughout the European campaign of 1944–1945. Too often did the airborne commanders plan an operation only to learn that their intended objectives had been taken before they had a chance to make their drop. Ibid., 111.

ken through the American First Army front in the Ardennes and he was needed at once. The 82d and 101st, not yet completely rehabilitated, were already being committed. When Ridgway reported to Major General Troy Middleton's command post at Bastogne, he learned to his disappointment that his two divisions were to be employed separately, the 101st at Bastogne and the 82d west of St. Vith. Ridgway's corps would take over a part of the line that included the 82d, but as a regular corps with no airborne function.

It was here in the Ardennes that Ridgway's command philosophy began to come under some criticism. He had always believed that a commander's place was at the very front line at the point of greatest crisis. In Sicily, Italy, and Normandy, that philosophy had served him well. In addition, he seemed to derive a certain satisfaction in personal combat. He roamed the front carrying a 1903 Springfield rifle, equipped with armor-piercing ammunition. In one instance, at least, he had a close call.[19] But at corps, in contrast to division level, that activity caused problems in that his front was much broader. In addition, his new staff lacked the confidence to take action without him.

In one instance, his lack of contact nearly caused catastrophe. In the early morning hours of December 22, 1944, Brigadier General Robert Hasbrouk, commanding the 7th Armored Division at St. Vith, sent a message to Ridgway's headquarters advising that his division and the remnants of the ill-fated 106th Infantry Division were in danger of being cut off and surrounded. That prospect did not seem to disturb Ridgway, who noted that airborne troops were accustomed to fighting surrounded. Brigadier General Bruce C. Clarke, however, was not convinced. A tanker who held Ridgway in no awe, he referred to Ridgway's decision to hold in place as "Custer's Last Stand."[20] An urgent message from Hasbrouk failed to reach Ridgway, who was away from his command post. In his absence, General Montgomery himself, who was now temporarily commanding all troops in the northern half of the Allied line, decided to withdraw them. Once notified of Monty's decision, Ridgway pitched in to help with the with-

---

19. "I was moving along through the woods, headed for one of the assault platoons [of the 30th Infantry Division] where I had been told I could find the battalion commander. All of a sudden I heard a tremendous clatter and saw something that looked like a light tank, with a big swastika on its side, coming at me from my left rear. It was only about fifteen yards away. I was alone then and I knew I would have to do something pretty drastic. I'd be dead there in the snow in another two seconds. So I swung around, firing my Springfield, and got five shots in, fast, at the swastika. The tank moved along, veering crazily, for another fifteen yards or so, and then came to a halt. I dropped in the snow and crawled away fast, thanking God for my old Springfield." Ibid., 116.

20. J. Eisenhower, *The Bitter Woods*, 299.

drawal across the Salm River. But he had not been in the picture when the decision had been made.[21]

The German attack in the Bulge hit its high-water mark on December 26, 1944, and on that day Patton's Third Army, driving up from the south, relieved the beleaguered 101st Airborne at Bastogne. It was not until January 3, 1945, however, that Montgomery began his attack southward from Elsenborn to meet up with Patton at Houffalize. Ridgway's XVIII Corps participated, with Gerow's V Corps on his left and Collins's VII Corps on his right. XVIII Corps, though still designated as "airborne," consisted of four veteran divisions, the 1st, 82d, 30th, and 84th, only one of which, the 82d, was an airborne division.

On March 24, 1945, Ridgway's corps again went into its designated role, but with only the British 6th Airborne and the new 17th Airborne Divisions. Early in the morning the Allied guns on the west bank of the Rhine River went silent as these two airborne divisions were carried across and dropped. Ridgway and his command group of five crossed the Rhine in a small British vessel and, as in Sicily and Normandy, set out to find their troops. Eventually, they found both divisions. With troops so scattered, however, no road could be considered cleared, and Ridgway's jeep ran into a cluster of an unknown number of Germans. In the resulting firefight, Ridgway found himself on the ground next to the front wheel of his jeep. A German hand grenade went off on the other side of the front wheel, saving him from certain death but nicking his shoulder. From that time on, Matt Ridgway was never without a hand grenade of his own, strapped on the front of his harness. It became, as noted, his trademark.

Ridgway's last assignment in Europe was to assist Montgomery in his final British drive to Lübeck in the final days of the war. His XVIII Airborne Corps was to protect the right flank of the Second British Army, commanded by Ridgway's friend General Sir Miles Dempsey.[22] It was an important mission. Though by prior agreement a defeated Germany would be occupied by four powers in predesignated zones, no such arrangements had been made in either Austria or Denmark. Therefore, if the Russians reached Denmark ahead of the British and Americans, that country would fall under their sway. To avoid that catastrophe, Eisenhower had attached Ridgway's corps to Montgomery to ensure that it did not happen.

The drive was successful, and Dempsey's army reached Lübeck on May 2, a couple of days before the Russians' arrival. Dempsey and Ridg-

---

21. See ibid., 299–304, for a complete account of this action.

22. Ridgway, it should be noted, did not share the animosity toward the British to which many other American officers fell victim—Bradley and Patton most noticeably.

way operated in mutual courtesy, and at one point Dempsey asked Ridgway to hold back to allow a British unit to take a town for purposes of British "prestige." Ridgway explained why such a holdback would be inadvisable, and Dempsey accepted his reasoning without murmur. Ridgway then reconsidered and held back, allowing British troops to take the town. Dempsey was grateful.[23]

Ridgway's next five years were filled with high-level but relatively routine assignments—in Panama, the Philippines, on a high-level commission. On the evening of December 22, 1950, Ridgway and his wife were visiting old friends, anticipating a happy Christmas. At about midnight he received a telephone call from General J. Lawton Collins, Army Chief of Staff. Walton Walker, Collins said, had been killed in Korea, and Ridgway was to leave at once to replace him as commanding general of Eighth Army. He was an ambitious man, deputy chief of staff at the time, and he would ordinarily have welcomed such a command. But the combination of grief for his friend Walker and the prospect of leaving his tiny family at Christmas was enough to make it a sad occasion. He refrained from telling his wife the news until coffee the next morning. After a quick and informal Christmas celebration with his wife and son, he was off across the Pacific immediately.

Ridgway's role as commander of Eighth Army has been told above. It came to an end in April 1951. At the front inspecting troop dispositions, word came in that MacArthur had been removed as Far East commander and that he, Ridgway, had been nominated to replace him. It was a gigantic move for an essentially combat general. He left Eighth Army, to be replaced by General James A. Van Fleet, with the usual nostalgia and admiration for the fighting quality of his troops. He could take satisfaction in the great contribution he had made during that short time, but it was daunting to be replacing one of the icons of the Second World War, MacArthur.

Despite the big shoes he was stepping into, Ridgway did not need to fill them completely. His functions as governor of Japan had ceased to be a large part of his duties. President Truman's emissary John Foster Dulles visited him twice (partly to size him up, Ridgway thought), and soon after Ridgway's arrival, the United States and Japan signed the peace treaty that ended the war between the countries. The United States was therefore sending an ambassador. But bigger things were calling. He was reassigned to replace General Eisenhower as Supreme Commander, Europe, the military

23. Ridgway, *Soldier*, 145.

arm of the North Atlantic Treaty Organization, the shield to protect Western Europe from the real and perceived threat from Soviet Russia.

In the late spring of 1952, Eisenhower had become convinced, in the light of overwhelming public support in the American electorate, that he should return from Paris to the United States to run for president. Truman, the incumbent, may not have been pleased with Ike's decision, but he was in no position to disapprove the general's request for relief of command. One hitch, however, occurred in the proceedings. Eisenhower, without consulting Truman, had decided that his chief of staff, General Alfred Gruenther, should succeed him. In preparation for the turnover, therefore, he took Gruenther along with him to introduce him to the many heads of state and government that he was supposedly to serve. Truman was apparently displeased with the general's temerity; at least he disapproved of it. Instead of Gruenther, the president appointed Ridgway.

Once more Ridgway was replacing one of the most celebrated five-star generals of the Second World War. His problems, however, were more serious than that. Lacking the popularity of Eisenhower in Western Europe, he was greeted with derision by the Communists, who commanded one-third of the vote in France, with vicious attacks. They invented rumors that in Korea Ridgway had authorized the use of germ warfare against the enemy. Large posters calling him "General Microbe" sprang up everywhere. Ridgway properly noted that one person with a bucket of paint could make a great deal of graffiti.

His role was made more exacting also by the fact that when Truman had appointed Eisenhower as SACEUR he had given Ike full command of all services—Army, Navy, Air Force—essentially reporting to nobody except the fourteen heads of government that he served. Just before Eisenhower's departure, the NATO powers had taken the step of establishing the NATO Council, the political body that Ridgway would report to. He adapted to that arrangement, however, with no difficulty. In addition, the rest of the six "equivalent" divisions America was sending to the NATO command were now arriving. NATO had been sold to the European governments by Eisenhower, and it was now up to Ridgway to make it work, to make military and command arrangements for the long-term future. Each man had performed a legitimate service.

Ridgway's tour as SACEUR was less than a howling success. Outside of his forte, combat leadership, he lacked the art of diplomacy, and by many reports was not particularly popular.[24] Dedicated to telling the facts as he

24. I have no documentation for this allegation, other than a confidential estimate made by Brigadier Sir James Gault, Eisenhower's British assistant during World War II. Gault was, however, quite positive in his views.

knew them, he quickly recognized that the NATO forces were in no position to fight the Russians and their allies. He made that estimate clear. He was premature; the European nations were having certain second thoughts about the whole project. He did, however, perform his job until Eisenhower, now president, recalled him to be Army Chief of Staff, putting his own first choice, Gruenther, in the position of SACEUR.

In the late summer of 1953, Matthew Ridgway assumed the post of Chief of Staff of the Army, theoretically, at least, the zenith of a military career. Unfortunately, the two years he served in that post turned out to be an anticlimax. Many factors were involved in this unhappy situation, but one of them, I believe, was simply that he was out of his field of competence. With all his soldierly virtues, he was not fully equipped to face his new duties on the Washington scene.

From the outset it was obvious that Ridgway was taking over the reins of the Army at an unfortunate time. The end of the Korean War in late July would have called for a drastic reduction of the Army under any circumstances. But almost coincident with that event was the Soviet Union's successful test of the hydrogen bomb, and soon thereafter they had developed long-range bombers. The United States, for the first time in its history, was vulnerable to instant devastating attack from outside its borders. The Air Force was the service responsible for the answer to this threat. Not even the Navy could contribute much to deterrence, and certainly not the Army. Nobody questioned the priority of building the Strategic Air Command and directing the bulk of the defense budget to nuclear deterrence, but the question was, to what degree must this be done?

Unfortunately for the Army in general and Ridgway in particular, personalities entered the equation. Secretary of Defense Charles E. Wilson, former president of General Motors Corporation, was a congenial man and doubtless a competent automobile man, but he lacked the slightest idea of government in general and the Defense Department in particular. He did, for example, demonstrate that he regarded the members of the Joint Chiefs of Staff as "recalcitrant union bosses," people to contend with in contrast to working hand in glove with.[25] The matter was exacerbated by the personality of Admiral Arthur Radford, who succeeded Ridgway's old friend Omar Bradley at about this time. Radford, who was something less than ecumenical with regard to the Army, gave every impression of leading Wilson in his actions, instead of the other way around.

---

25. The author, present at a cabinet meeting in 1954, heard Wilson say, in a sneering tone of voice, "If the Joint Chiefs are going according to form . . ."

Part of the problem, it must be admitted, resulted in a lack of rapport between Ridgway and the president himself. Though they started out with mutual respect—I once heard my father refer to Ridgway as "one of our most capable officers"—they were not close, and it is possible that Ike, who hated desk pounders, may have found Ridgway difficult. They differed in their views as to the role of the members of the Joint Chiefs of Staff. Eisenhower expected the military chiefs to be a part of the decision-making process in the matter of how to finance the defense budget. He expected the military, therefore, to be part of the national budgetary process.

Ridgway would have none of that. In his philosophy, the military should advise the political leaders what they deemed the country needed to fulfill its military needs, and then it was the business of the president and his cabinet to decide to what extent to provide it. In any case, Eisenhower's and Ridgway's positions were far apart, and neither man ever relented.

Ridgway's greatest contribution as Army Chief of Staff—one for which he was given little credit in higher quarters—was his advising against American involvement in the ongoing war in Indochina, which in 1954 was still occupied by the French but under very heavy siege from the Vietminh insurgents.

The French, apparently underestimating the capabilities of the Indochinese, occupied a position in North Vietnam at a place called Dien Bien Phu, a relatively defenseless position but selected, apparently, to lend encouragement to the Laotians, whose country, together with Cambodia and Vietnam, constituted Indochina. As the nations of the West watched in grief, Ho Chi Minh's troops gradually reduced the dwindling Dien Bien Phu position, manned almost entirely by members of the Foreign Legion, as it lost ground every day. Finally it fell, and negotiations began between the French and the Vietnamese that resulted in the truce of 1954 that lasted about a decade afterward.

While this was going on, pressures mounted from some quarters for the United States to come to the rescue of the Dien Bien Phu garrison. Admiral Radford reportedly advocated the use of an atomic bomb to destroy the besieging Vietnamese. At that time Ridgway sent a team of experts to evaluate the conditions under which U.S. troops might be employed, if unwillingly so ordered, to intervene on the ground. Terrain, port facilities, and the road net were among the features the team studied. When its members reported back, their findings were negative in the extreme. As Eisenhower himself later stated, war in Indochina would be a "nightmare."

Ridgway reported his findings to the Joint Chiefs, but he never saw Eisenhower personally on the matter. Eisenhower, as aware as Ridgway of the military considerations, refused to intervene in Vietnam on the side of the French. Ridgway never knew the extent of his influence in this important matter, because in the first volume of Eisenhower's memoirs of the White House, he never mentions Ridgway's role. But Ridgway liked to think that, as in his protests against the airborne landing in September 1943, he had exerted an influence.[26]

In 1955, at the end of Ridgway's supposedly first two-year term in office, President Eisenhower did not reappoint him. In his memoirs, *Soldier*, Ridgway claims that before assuming his post as chief of staff, he had already decided to retire from the Army when he reached the age of sixty, which was that year. Would he have accepted a second two years if urged? My guess is definitely yes. As it was, Eisenhower, having received complaints from Radford and Wilson, did not make the offer. Ridgway, with his wife and son, retired to the vicinity of Pittsburgh, where he lived an incredible thirty-eight years more, the same length of time as his entire military career.

It was after his retirement, when he was living in the suburbs of Pittsburgh, that I had my only extensive conversation with the general. It was in the form of an interview for *The Bitter Woods*, the story of the Battle of the Bulge, 1944–1945. Ridgway had played a prominent part in it, and he had granted my request for an interview. We were to meet at his home, which stood atop a ridge overlooking the river a few miles east of the city.

I did not know what to expect by way of a reception. Ridgway and my father had parted on less than warm terms, and Ridgway had been circumspect regarding Ike in his book *Soldier*, we were both aware of the facts. I was not, however, particularly concerned. I was doing the reporting, a fact that made my position secure.

To my mild surprise, the general gave no indication of knowing who I was, even though we had met some years earlier in the White House. Nor was the Eisenhower name even mentioned. In the back hall I could hear someone moving around, probably Mrs. Ridgway, but she never appeared.

He seemed to have one particular interest: to impress me with the size and strength of the XVIII Airborne Corps, which he had commanded in the Ardennes. It was, admittedly, a large formation, of which only three

---

26. In 1962, assisting my father as he wrote his White House memoirs, I researched the Indochina matter thoroughly. In all the National Security Council and personal papers, I never found his name. What influence Ridgway had within the Pentagon, however, may have been significant.

divisions were airborne.[27] He was intense but neither friendly nor un-
friendly. But I was struck by his eyes, which bore an unexpected sadness.
I also noted a very slight, soft southern accent in his speech. In common
with most such interviews, I gained very little information that was new.

My most vivid recollection, strangely, was my departure. The snow was
beginning to fall and had accumulated only about a quarter of an inch.
Over my protests, the general picked up a snow shovel and scraped a narrow passageway out to the door of my car. I have no idea why he made
this gesture; I just write it off to exceptionally good manners.

If Ridgway had a sad look, I wince to think of the anguish he and his
wife must have endured when, about five years after my visit, his son,
Matty Jr., was killed in a freak train accident. Ridgway had many years left
to live with that tragedy.

Ridgway was a great soldier, and it is to be regretted, in my mind, that
he was ever involved with Washington politics, for which he had little
aptitude. The apotheosis of his career occurred during the three months in
1951 when he commanded Eighth Army in Korea.

---

27. "Twenty-two divisions, all told, were under my command at one time or another."
Ridgway, *Soldier*, 107.

# Appendix

## Home Movies

### Incident in a Tailor Shop

In his retirement in Gettysburg, my father wrote *At Ease: Stories I Tell to Friends,* an informal story of his life. One meaningful passage described his first day at West Point. After a short reference to the confusion and rapid adjustment of the day, he described his feelings when he was sworn in as a "new cadet": "When we raised our right hands and repeated the official oath, there was no confusion. A feeling came over me that the expression "The United States of America' would now and henceforth mean something different than it ever had before. From here on it would be the nation I was serving, not myself. Across half a century, I can look back and see a raw-boned, gawky Kansas boy from the farm country, earnestly repeating the words that would make him a cadet."[1]

Thirty years later, I shared much the same experience, as the flag went down at the first retreat ceremony. As an army brat, I had witnessed many such ceremonies. Now, for the first time, I was a full-fledged participant. My memory, however, goes back even more to another, rather mundane, experience in (of all places) the cadet tailor shop.

To me, my father's account was highly understated. The Beast Detail in the areas of barracks had done a miraculous job in a single day of transforming a group of civilian boys, some of us utterly bewildered, into a body of men somewhat resembling soldiers.[2] After the first greeting—a sort of shock treatment by smartly uniformed upperclassmen—we were sent to the barbershop to have our locks shorn. We were issued uniforms—white short-sleeved shirts, uniform caps, black shoes, and lightweight gray slacks, called "plebe skins." Immaculately uniformed upperclassmen

---

1. D. Eisenhower, *At Ease,* 4–5.
2. A "new cadet"—an official term—was informally called a "beast." The first classmen (seniors) assigned the job of receiving and processing them were therefore referred to as the "Beast Detail."

taught us enough rudiments of close-order drill to enable us to at least keep in step. That accomplished, we were sworn in at an impressive ceremony on Trophy Point.

Throughout this period, the new cadets were treated harshly and impersonally, even by former friends. It was therefore with a great sense of relief that sometime during that first week I was assigned to a group that was marched to the tailor shop to be fitted for our real cadet uniforms. There was nothing casual about the process. Standing single file, savoring a few moments of temporary relaxation, each individual was called by name and stepped forward. It was in a bright room over the west end of Central Barracks, where Major King, a tactical officer, inspected each cadet's fit with a careful eye, sometimes stroking his chin. His concentration on his job was remarkable. He never looked anyone in the face; his whole being was absorbed in inspecting the fit of the trousers, in every detail.

Major King gave his orders to a civilian tailor, and behind them were a few other tailors awaiting their turns. One of them spoke quietly, the first friendly word I had heard in days: "Your name's Eisenhower, isn't it?"

I looked over to see a slightly chubby, balding, middle-aged man with his tape measure dangling around his neck. "Yes, it is," I answered.

"I remember your father," the little man said. "Class of 1915."

"Yes, that's right."

A distant look came over the little man's face as he stared off into space, obviously enjoying pleasant memories. He had already forgotten about me. "Yes, sir," he repeated with a slight smile, "Ikey Eisenhower."

At that point I enjoyed a moment of quiet relief from all the harassment. I realized that after all I had joined a fraternity called the "Long Gray Line." That middle-aged tailor, remembering my father over a space of thirty years, gave me a feeling that I belonged.

### Incident on a Hill at Benning

One evening in late November or early December 1944, the forty-four men of 2d Platoon, Company "B," 14th Infantry Regiment, were looking forward to the end of their exhausting day of marching. We had been on a three-day maneuver through the area of Fort Benning known as Sand Hill, part of an intensive training program instituted by the new commander of the 71st Infantry Division, Brigadier General Willard G. Wyman. Wyman had been the assistant division commander of the 1st Division on OMAHA Beach on D-day, but even so distinguished an officer was of little interest to the GIs of the 2d Platoon. We were interested only in getting some rest.

When we reached our assigned position near the point where Moye Road crossed St. Mary's Road, the men heaved a sigh of relief: on the forward slope of the hillock assigned the platoon was a row of recently dug foxholes, just made to order for our occupation. We would be spared digging in. As the platoon leader, I readily gave the squad leaders permission to occupy these welcome comforts.

Our joy was short-lived. Hardly had I settled into my own foxhole when I heard a noise behind me, and I quickly perceived a group of officers led by no less than the division commander himself. This can't be so, I thought. None of the previous division commanders had ever been seen out of their comfortable, warm headquarters in the center of our cantonment. But there was no doubt about it; General Wyman quickly motioned for me to come over to him.

"Lieutenant," he said quietly, "your position here is all wrong. Your men can be picked off one by one if they are spread out like that. I want you to place two of your squads, one at each end of this knoll, keeping them together as units. Cover the space between them by fire. The third squad should be placed in support on that lump back there." Once the general was sure that I understood his order, he departed, leaving me to rouse my men and put them to work in their new positions. Bone-weary though we were, we had come to expect such disruptions in those intense days. We gave the matter no further thought.

A few days later an order arrived for all the officers of the division to assemble at the Sand Hill theater to be addressed by General Wyman himself. When the general made his appearance and gave a short talk, a couple of soldiers carried in an easel on which was fastened a watercolor terrain map. I was astonished to see that it was a drawing of our Moye Road position. Wyman had found an artist in the division who could paint such maps, and he had several of them. Then he explained the error that "this lieutenant" had made, repeating the circumstances and the instructions he had given me that evening a few days before. A good many officers doubtless learned something from all this—I certainly did—and though he did not mention my name, the six officers of "B" Company had no doubts who the goat had been. It was a cause of considerable mirth.

A few days later a package was delivered to me at "B" Company. When I opened it, I was astonished to find a present from General Wyman, the watercolor drawing he had used in my lesson. Instead of embarrassment over the episode, I felt elation.

In all this, no mention was ever made that General Wyman, as a major, had been my next-door neighbor at Fort Lewis three years earlier, that he had been my father's warm friend at IX Corps during that time, that I had once tried to sell him our family car, or that I had often casually dated his very attractive daughter Patricia. Training a division was far too important to recall such details.

## The Bull

It has been many years since I wore the uniform of the U.S. Army, and the institution has undergone many dramatic changes since I left. But one of my fondest memories of the Army in which I served is the tolerance for individual eccentricities.[3] During my time I encountered many talented people with foibles, and as a result I have always been careful to avoid allowing an individual's mannerisms to overly affect my judgment of him. After all, if the world had dispensed with Churchill, Patton, or Orde Wingate for their unconventional ways, a great deal of talent would have been lost.

One officer who struck me as on the eccentric side was Lieutenant General Paul W. Kendall, who had been an effective commander of an infantry division in Italy during the Second World War. My encounter with him came later, in 1952, during the Korean War. He was commanding general of I Corps. I was a major, assigned as the operations officer of the 1st Battalion, 15th Infantry, 3d Infantry Division.

The circumstances of that encounter were somewhat unusual. Around September 1, the 15th Infantry had been pulled off the Kelly Hill line on the Double Bend of the Imjin. Its 2d and 3d Battalions were sent to Camp Casey for rest and training, but the 1st Battalion, much to our joy, was attached to one of the regiments of the 1st Marine Division on the Han River as a regimental reserve battalion. Though the Han River is a formidable defensive obstacle at that point, the position, including the reserve battalion, was designated as being "in contact with the enemy," thus authorizing its members the coveted four "rotation points" per month, a big hunk out of the thirty-six points necessary to send an individual home. So we of the 1st Battalion had it both ways—a relatively quiet sector but one that authorized four rotation points.[4]

As an added bonus, we were comfortable. The men were luxuriating in tents rather than bunkers, and our area included a small flattop hill that served as a helicopter pad and doubled as an outdoor sitting room. Carpenters had furnished it with crude wooden tables, chairs, and sofas. Nothing plush, but we didn't need cushions; we were unspoiled.

---

3. I once heard my father complain to a colleague that if you wanted to get rid of an officer in peacetime, you would find it very difficult. "An officer can be crazy as hell and they'll keep him," he said—or words to that effect.

4. The staff of the Marine regiment had greeted us cordially but looked askance at our ambitious training program. They felt that it might jeopardize their status as being in contact with the enemy. Nevertheless, they tolerated it.

The morning in question promised to be routine. The troops went out into the field for training, and the sole excitement promised to be a visit from our regimental commander, Colonel Carl Herndon. The battalion commander, Gene Welch, had driven down the hill to escort him up to the battalion command post. I had been left behind in temporary command of the camp.

At about midmorning, I heard the sputter of an incoming helicopter. It had to be someone important, so I left the operations tent and ran up the hill to the spot where the chopper was coming in.

It was instantly obvious who the visitor was, though I had never seen him before. Dismounting slowly, carrying a long walking stick, was a stooped, heavy-set, graying man, with light-blue eyes. His three stars and his I Corps shoulder patch identified him as the corps commander beyond a doubt.

General Kendall glanced around the area with a look of mild disapproval. His eye fixed briefly but impassively on me, and he demanded loudly, "Who are you?" I identified myself as the operations officer. "Where's the battalion commander?"

"He's gone down the hill to meet the regimental commander, sir."

The Bull turned red. "He's gone to meet the regimental commander rather than the corps commander?"

"He didn't know you were coming, sir."

"Humph."

The general then asked where the troops were, and I answered that they were out training. He asked on what subject. "Fire and maneuver, sir," I said.

For the first time the general's ominous scowl brightened. "Ah, fire and maneuver!" he exclaimed. "That's good. That's fundamental. Good."

A transformation then descended on the general. While I watched in bewilderment, he seemed to pass into a trance. He stared straight ahead, his walking stick clutched under his arm, and stepped forward slowly. Right foot and right fist forward. Left foot and left fist forward. All the time he kept mumbling to himself, "One man shoots; the other man moves. That man shoots; the other man moves." He kept this up for what was probably ten or twelve feet, always staring straight ahead, while I followed him as if witnessing an extremely slow tennis game.

Suddenly, he stopped and looked around, casting his eye on the rows of tents. Some of the tent flaps were rolled up; others were rolled down. Somehow that scene struck the general as hilarious. Noticing me as a human being for the first time, he pointed out the inconsistency as if sharing a joke. He even gave me a slight nudge, as if we had a secret in common. Then he got serious. "That will never do! When the battalion commander returns, you tell him that when your troops leave for drill in the morning, make your decision: is it going to rain or isn't it? Then if you order the tent flaps rolled up and it rains, you know you've made the wrong decision."

Before I could answer, I was rescued by the arrival of Colonel Welch and Colonel Herndon, who identified themselves and spent a few moments describing the battalion setup to the general. Kendall seemed satisfied. "Is there anything I can do for you?"

"Yes, sir," Welch said. "We're scheduled to leave here in ten days and would like to spend the rest of the reserve time here."

Kendall paused for a moment and then, sticking his shillelagh into the ground in front of his feet, spoke slowly. "I hereby decree that the 1st Battalion, 15th Infantry, will remain attached to the 1st Marine Division for the remainder of its time in reserve."

Welch was delighted. "It would be wonderful if you could do that, sir."

Kendall turned on him fiercely. "Do it?" he roared. "I just did it!" Then, apparently not overly impressed by what he had seen, Lieutenant General Bull Kendall climbed back in his helicopter and was off.

I shrugged. Later it crossed my mind that the Bull was checking on me personally. I was the biggest liability in Korea.

Some months after that encounter I saw General Kendall again. The circumstances were quite different.

In November 1952, my father, as president-elect, made good on his campaign pledge to visit Korea. He arrived at Eighth Army Headquarters in early December, and his itinerary called for a briefing at I Corps Headquarters, a few miles north of Seoul, at Uijeongbu. There in a crowded squad tent full of maps, he had a slight brush with—who else?—Bull Kendall.

The subject was the employment of minefields. Kendall explained our dislike for the minefields that had periodically been sown in front of the corps position; they were, he declared, worse than nothing. With the rotation of units in the front-line positions and with mine charts long lost, we had no idea where the mines were. We were therefore restricted in our movements to the safe lanes in front of our main line. The Chinese, on the other hand, were indifferent to loss of life, and they roamed freely. Kendall wished that we had never laid them.

My father demurred, harking back to his experience in the Second World War. In that situation, on the attack, "strewing a few mines around when you stop for the night can protect your flank."

To his credit, Kendall stood his ground, and I agreed with him—for our situation. Actually, both men had a point, for different situations. Kendall's was right for ours.

• • •

I never saw General Kendall again, but I heard his name mentioned indirectly. Just after the Korean Armistice of July 27, 1953, I visited a friend, Colonel Shelby, the deputy intelligence officer of Eighth Army at Seoul. While we were conversing in his office, the clock struck twelve noon. Hastily, Shelby ran outside, studied the weather, and scribbled something. I asked what in the world that was all about.

Shelby explained. "General Kendall has been transferred to theater headquarters in Tokyo," he said, "and he has developed a feud with the Air Force. So every intelligence officer in Korea, down to corps level, has been instructed to scrutinize the skies every noon and send him a report of the findings. He compares those reports with the Air Force weather forecasts, and when the forecasts are wrong, he gives them hell."

"Unconventional" Bull Kendall may have been, but I still hold a nostalgia for people like him, the eccentrics of the Old Army.

### The Topkick and the Guardhouse Lawyer

During the time I commanded an infantry company in Vienna after the war, I ran across many memorable soldiers. But the two that stuck out in my memory were two men who lived at the opposite ends of the personnel spectrum: First Sergeant Howard Griggs and Private Nathaniel Palmer. No two men could be more different.

I can still remember my first glimpse of Sergeant Griggs. I was a young captain, commanding Company "D," 1st Battalion, 5th Infantry. It was the summer of 1946, and never did a company need a first sergeant as much as this one.

I had been expecting a new first sergeant for some time, and I was anxious for him to arrive, so I was glad when I looked up from my desk one morning and saw the stripes of a first sergeant in the adjacent orderly room. Griggs was already issuing orders, even before reporting in to me. There was no question that he expected those orders to be obeyed.

Oddly, I have no recollection of our formal meeting, but when I got a close look at the new topkick, I was both surprised and pleased. Instead of a graying old soldier that fitted the usual image of a first sergeant, I saw a man less than thirty years old. He was of medium size, muscular, with a thick shock of auburn hair. His jaw was firm, and his small mustache was full but neatly trimmed. He was formal and impersonal. Above all, he had a look of high intensity.

As time went on, I learned a little bit about Griggs, but not much. The patch he wore on his right shoulder was that of the 94th Infantry Division, an outfit that had seen its share of combat. I also learned that he was a victim of what is now called "post-traumatic stress disorder," which in simpler days we called "battle rattled." It was an accepted condition among those who had been under too much artillery and small-arms fire. In an off moment, he admitted to me that every time a vehicle backfired—which was often in those days—his stomach knotted up.

Sergeant Griggs spent no time worrying about his condition. Instead, whether wittingly or not, he put it to good use. Totally dedicated to his job, he was disgusted and angry at the chronic misconduct of the young soldiers who had arrived in Germany and Austria after the fighting had ended. Trained for combat but arriving in peacetime, many sought to emulate battle veterans by taking out their frustrations on Austrian civilians. I can still hear Griggs's voice reverberating through the door as he berated a young man for "dishonoring the guys who fought and died to make this here occupation possible." A crack in his voice added emphasis to his words.

Occasionally, I heard things not intended for my ears. "That's the way it is," he once announced, "and that's the way it's gonna be as long as I'm running this company." Then, noticing that the door was open, he caught himself: "As long as I'm first sergeant of this company."

With a topkick like that, I had no occasion to interfere much with the day-to-day running of the company. I had my hands full inspecting guardposts and coping with higher authorities. On rare occasions, however, Griggs went a little too far. One day I noticed that certain men were always being assigned to the most difficult guardposts, such as those far out in the Russian Zone surrounding Vienna. I called it to the sergeant's attention.

"Yes, sir, that's what I'm doing," he admitted. "I'm putting them eight balls on the tough posts."

"We can't do it that way," I cautioned him. "Punish them for messing up, but we have to keep the guard roster fair."

Griggs stiffened up. He stood at attention and looked straight ahead. "If that's the way the captain wants it," he said in measured tones, "that's the way it's gonna be."

Griggs was not, however, an automaton. At one point he came up with a scheme to combat the epidemic of venereal disease that blighted all American troops in Vienna. He went to a local hospital that specialized in such diseases and made a bargain with the doctors. He then collected a candy bar from each man in the company and gave his treasures to patients willing to walk up and down the aisles of the hospital amphitheater exposing their diseased parts. He and I then marched all available men of the company to the auditorium of the hospital. The men were shocked at what they saw. A few got sick. Many of the rest apparently mended their ways temporarily. Company "D" went an unheard-of seventy-three days without a case of venereal disease.

The soldiers of "D" Company held Griggs in fear but not in awe. One day, as I was returning to the company in my jeep, Griggs was standing by a pile of lumber, scratching his head, apparently figuring out how to move it into barracks. My irreverent driver leaned out and shouted, "Call it to attention, Sarge, and march it up the stairs."

Our time together lasted only a few months. In October 1946 I was called away for three weeks of temporary duty, and on my return I discovered that the 1st Battalion, 5th Infantry, had been absorbed into the 1st Battalion, 16th Infantry, 1st Division. I was to remain in command of the company, but Griggs had been replaced by an older, gentler, graying man. Nothing I could do could change this arrangement; the authorities dictated that seniority predominated. I saw Griggs only once or twice, disconsolate but resigned. It was of little matter; he rotated home for discharge very soon thereafter.

I had the greatest respect for First Sergeant Griggs, and I hope he reciprocated to some degree. But I doubt that he gave me much thought. To him, I believe, Captain Eisenhower was only the cardboard cutout in whose name he was doing his duty. No matter; we never served together again.

The memory of Griggs has made me ponder at times. If given an education, would he have made a good officer? Perhaps so, even a four-star general. On the other hand, perhaps he was just where he belonged; becoming an officer might have violated the Peter Principle.

I'll never know.

Private Nathaniel Palmer, one of those soldiers who were such headaches to Sergeant Griggs, was also by all odds a tragic figure—an alcoholic with an unfortunate tendency to become belligerent when drunk. When sober he was a quiet, even somewhat cheerful man, small in stature and docile, but his eye carried a look that implied demons underneath. To the observer he showed nothing to compensate for this dreadful affliction. Yet I sometimes think of Palmer, and for some reason I smile.

Why I remember Palmer with fondness is a mystery. Perhaps I am amused by the contrast between Palmer's disorderly conduct and his dignified name. He would have been less noticeable had his name been "Billy Bob Jones," but the name "Nathaniel" carries dignity; it could have belonged to a signer of the Declaration of Independence. Another factor may be that in spite of his unspeakable conduct and that haunted look in his eye, he was, as mentioned, somewhat friendly and respectful when sober.

But the thing I found amusing about him was his attitude toward military law. He was the epitome of what we used to call a "guardhouse lawyer." Palmer seemed to carry a sort of twisted pride in his sorry disciplinary record. It gave him distinction.

Palmer was not alone in his misconduct, perhaps not even the first among equals in the battalion. As Griggs and I were well aware, there were many soldiers in the battalion who were repeating cases of drunkenness and venereal disease. It is difficult to condemn these young men, however, because the conditions under which they served were the worst I have ever witnessed in peacetime. The mission of our battalion was pure and simple: guard duty, protecting targets that Vienna Area Command thought important, based on requests from American and Austrian businesses. Some of these targets were located miles out in the Russian Zone, across the Danube.[5] We were vastly understrength, with corporals and sergeants joining privates in walking three hours on, three hours off. And they performed this duty three days out of four. Add to that the lack of winter equipment in the record-breaking cold, plus austere stone barracks in the middle of the city, and you have every reason to expect disorderly conduct, perhaps more than occurred.[6]

Palmer and a couple of companions, however, were outstanding even in the company. Today they would probably be hospitalized. But in those days they pulled their regular duty fairly well but went on a rampage off duty. The Army unwisely exacerbated the situation by issuing every soldier a fifth of whiskey every week, which a young soldier might well drink in one evening. It was impossible for the Army to court-martial all these men who went on binges; there would have been no battalion to stand guard over the targets specified by a comfortable Vienna Area Command Headquarters.

But to the serious cases such as Palmer, a fifth of bourbon a week was trivial. He and his fellow addicts bought cognac and schnapps on the civilian market, and when confined to quarters as punishment for their misconduct, they even resorted to swigging shaving lotion. One day I confronted one of these victims and warned him that he would kill himself. "Yes, sir," he answered respectfully, "that's what I'm trying to do."

But back to Nathaniel Palmer. After I had put him up for court-martial several times, he seemed to develop a mysterious friendship for me. One time, after I had drawn up charges against him and an accomplice for

---

5. One guardpost protected an American Esso Station, a one-room shack about a dozen miles into the 21st Beserk, in the Russian Zone.
6. Griggs departed before the winter set in.

assaulting an Austrian civilian, the two accused were tried separately, Palmer's friend first. During the first trial, Palmer and I waited in a small side room. He sat, ear to the door, critiquing the progress of the trial. He thought the trial was being conducted badly. Occasionally, he would turn and tell me indignantly, "They can't do that!" Finally, his patience completely broke, and he turned and looked me in the eye: "This is the most—ed-up trial I ever heard!" But soon it was Palmer's turn, and he received the same sentence as his friend.

Finally, the battalion commander and all the rest of us had had enough of Palmer, and despite our shortage of soldiers, we decided that it was time to get rid of him by a procedure called a "Section 8." I was assigned as prosecuting officer.

It was not a difficult task; no preparation was necessary. My main duty was to stand before the board and read the charge, as Palmer sat at a small camp desk to my left. I duly went down the list of offenses, specifying the number of each Article of War that had been violated. Having finished reading the list of perhaps twenty or so, I turned to Palmer and asked, as required, "Is this correct?"

Palmer was agitated. "No, sir!" he shouted. I asked for his objection, and he answered that one of the Articles of War was incorrectly listed. He provided me the proper number, and I accepted it. When I repeated the question, Palmer settled back contentedly, "Yes, sir."

It was an open-and-shut case. Palmer, among others, was to be sent home and given a less-than-honorable discharge from the United States Army. The scourge was out of my life.

But not quite. Four or five months later, in May 1947, my time had come to rotate home, my period of occupation duty in Vienna over. While awaiting embarkation at the port of Bremerhaven, I strolled down the pier one day and heard my name shouted wildly, "Captain Eisenhower! Captain Eisenhower!" As I turned I saw a contingent of marching men, in the middle of which was none other than Nathaniel Palmer, waving wildly and grinning from ear to ear.

I can say one thing for Nathaniel Palmer. He didn't bear a grudge.

## The Close Shave of Private Pataki

With the passage of years, I remember few names from the days of "D" Company, 5th Infantry, in the summer of 1946. Private Pataki, however, remains vivid in my memory along with First Sergeant Howard Griggs and Private Nathaniel Palmer. Unlike Palmer, however, Pataki was generally a good soldier. He did not present a military appearance—tall, scrawny, slightly bent, with a shock of tousled coal-black hair. But he kept out of trouble. I never had to discipline him. As company commander I would settle for that.

Pataki was noted for an attribute that set him aside from the other young soldiers: he was a first-generation Hungarian and was able, I was told, to communicate with the Russians, who along with the Americans, British, and French were occupying Vienna. Because of his language ability, we placed him on a special assignment. He was to make the nightly supply run out to a company outpost located in the Russian Zone across the Danube from the main part of the city. Theoretically, at least, if Pataki ran afoul of the Russian authorities, he would be able to explain what he was doing there.

We hated that guardpost. Situated about ten miles up the left bank of the river, it consisted of a shack with a single Esso gas pump, probably used as a refueling station for river traffic in happier days. We considered it outrageous, because it stood very near a Russian club, where the festivities at night often entailed a certain amount of lighthearted small-arms fire zinging around the neighborhood. Our half-dozen unhappy guards were forced to keep their heads down between dusk and whenever the ruckus toned down, around midnight. I had tried to get rid of it, but the powers in the U.S. Vienna Command were more concerned with public relations than they were with the safety of the men of the 5th Infantry. Pataki, however, did not seem to mind driving his jeep out there. The chore was easier than walking guard under the nearly unthinkable conditions forced on the rest of the men. For a while the arrangement worked.

One morning in September, as I arrived at the company, Sergeant Griggs stopped me before I reached my desk. The topkick always wore a look of mild concern, but this morning he seemed a little more perturbed than usual. "Captain," he said, "I think you better come down and take a look at what them Russkies did to one of our jeeps last night." So the two of us went down the stone stairway and out to the yard, where a lone jeep was waiting for us, with Pataki standing next to it.

Pataki was visibly rattled. On his run in the wee hours of the morning, a rifle shot had hit his vehicle, barely missing him. The damage to the jeep was only minor, and Pataki had experienced no trouble making it back to the company, but he had not enjoyed the episode.

Griggs and I took a close look at the jeep. We found that the canvas top had a hole in the rear, and the metal frame of the front windshield had been hit by a bullet without breaking the glass. To see how close Pataki had come to eternity, we put him in the driver's seat, ran a string through the two bullet holes, and drew the string taut. We concluded that the bullet had passed by his right ear, missing his head by only about an inch. For some strange reason, the crowd that had gathered found the event amusing, some hilarious—so long as Pataki was not hurt. We gave the matter little thought; crazy things were always happening in Vienna.

We finished our examination just in time for the daily company commanders' meeting. I reminded Griggs—as if such were necessary—to begin writing up the document required routinely in the event of damage to equipment, explaining the reason for the damage and requesting repair or replacement. I then climbed the steps to the office of the battalion commander, Colonel John C. F. Tillson III.

The meeting was, as usual, fairly relaxed, and at the end, almost as an afterthought, I turned to Tillson and mentioned the damaged jeep. Colonel Tillson chuckled absently. "That reminds me of a story," he began. Then he stopped in the middle of his sentence and asked abruptly, "They did what?!" I told him the circumstances. Immediately, he was on the telephone to the provost marshal of Vienna Area Command, and soon thereafter I was headed down the street to report to the provost marshal, Colonel William P. Yarborough.

Yarborough was an impressive man under any circumstances. A member of the class of 1936 at West Point, he was large and handsome. He had been a paratrooper who had distinguished himself in North Africa, Sicily, and Anzio, and later in his career would reach the impressive grade of lieutenant general.

As I anticipated, Bill Yarborough was not in a happy mood—far from it. He had just been humiliated in a meeting with his Russian counterpart, and in a testy confrontation had come out second best. Our relations with the Russians in Vienna were formal and correct, but there was always a competition as to whose troops were better disciplined and which were troublemakers. During the previous night, he told me, an American had attacked a Russian with a beer bottle or some other nonlethal weapon. Some injury may have been involved, but no fatality. The important thing was that the American was the aggressor. So Yarborough had been forced to listen to a lecture, something that did not sit well with him. Had he known of the incident of Pataki's jeep at the time of the meeting, it would have been Yarborough, not his adversary, who could have been the accuser.

Quite obviously, Captain Eisenhower was made to appreciate the results of his negligence in failing to realize what was at stake. I must give the colonel credit, however; he was stern but did not ask the battalion to take action. From that time on, needless to say, I reported in detail every small incident that occurred.

It was a small matter, soon forgotten. Only one winner emerged from it all. At his own request, and to his immense joy, Private Pataki was excused from ever driving across the Danube again.

## The Auk: Field Marshal Sir Claude Auchinleck

One early morning in the summer of 1978, Major General Woodrow W. (Woody) Stromberg and I took a car and driver down a narrow street in Marrakech, Morocco. We pulled up to a small stucco row house and were greeted at the door by a grizzled old British sergeant, who conducted us up a narrow staircase to the second floor. Waiting for us on a small balcony was a lonely, spare figure, who greeted us quietly, with perfect manners but little enthusiasm. Field Marshal Sir Claude Auchinleck, the vaunted "Auk" of the Second World War, had seen many visitors. He was receiving us as a courtesy.

As we were sitting in the lengthening shadows, it was difficult to see the old gentleman clearly. Though he was ninety-four years old, his close-cropped hair showed no sign of turning white. His face was gaunt, and his speech seemed a little vague. He spoke into space, without looking directly at us, though his demeanor was correct and reasonably friendly. For a moment he perked up when told that my father was General Dwight D. Eisenhower, but the interest quickly faded. Auchinleck and Eisenhower had never served together in the war.

Woody and I had not come to Marrakech for the sole purpose of this visit. I was writing a book about the Anglo-American alliance of the Second World War,[7] and our purpose was primarily to view the Taylor House, where Roosevelt and Churchill had rested up for a couple of days after the Casablanca Conference of January and February 1943. We were staying at the Hotel Mamounia, where Churchill had spent a good bit of vacation time painting during his years in the wilderness in the 1930s. But on arrival in town, Woody learned from his connections—in retirement he had joined a French aviation company in Paris—that Auchinleck was available. So immediately Woody had arranged the visit.

Auchinleck's record of service to the British Empire had been distinguished. In contrast to American practice, which gives an officer only one chance, he had seen his ups and downs. In August 1943 Churchill had relieved him as commander of the British Eighth Army and the Middle East. It had been an agonizing decision for Churchill. The Auk was a highly respected man, and in order to save Auchinleck's pride, the prime minister had invented a new theater of war and had offered it to him. The Auk, however, had refused the offer and was sent back to his previous post as commander of the Indian Army.

7. J. Eisenhower, *Allies*.

Fortunately, his relief constituted only one episode. He had not come from a wealthy background, as did most British officers. He came from a poor Scottish family, and he had worked hard to scrape together enough cash to enroll in the Royal Military College at Sandhurst. On graduation, he had asked to be commissioned in the Indian Army rather than the British because the Indian establishment did not require the money necessary to maintain an acceptable social standard in Britain. There was nothing unusual about that—Montgomery had done the same—but in contrast to other British officers, who transferred to the regular establishment as soon as they could afford to do so, Auchinleck had devoted himself to the Indian Army.

Auchinleck's "regular" regiment in the Indian Army was the 62d Punjab Regiment, where he learned to speak the language fluently. He served with the 62d in Mesopotamia during the First World War, where he developed a great deal of practical experience (call it realism). Between the world wars, he resumed his service in India. At the beginning of the Second World War, he was finally placed in command of an entirely British corps, an unusual thing for an officer of the Indian Army in those days.

In July 1941, his talents now fully recognized, Auchinleck was assigned as Commander in-Chief, Middle East, replacing Sir Archibald Wavell, a national idol who had fallen down on his luck as resources had been taken from him. Then, after one highly successful offensive against Rommel in North Africa, which had taken Eighth Army from the border of Egypt all the way to western Libya, Auchinleck's luck, like Wavell's, had also run out. Driven back to the area of El Alamein, near the Egyptian-Libyan border, he had fought hard to hold his position. This he had done competently, but Churchill had finally decided that the Auk was worn out. His successors' names are household words: Alexander and Montgomery.

Auchinleck did, however, have many important services still ahead of him. Having been fighting so long, a good general could become temporarily worn out without losing his long-term usefulness, as the British had come to realize. Churchill was wise in sending Auchinleck back to India to command the Fourteenth Army and later the entire Indian theater. There Field Marshal Sir John Slim, commanding in Burma, wrote of him, "It was a good day for us when [Auchinleck] took command of India, our main base, recruiting area, and training ground. The Fourteenth Army, from its birth to its final victory, owed much to his unselfish support and never-failing understanding. Without him, and what the Army of India did for us, we could never have existed, let alone conquered."[8] Churchill

---

8. Field Marshal Sir John Slim, *Defeat into Victory*, 176. Quoted in Wikipedia.

apparently felt the same way, because in 1946 Auchinleck was promoted to the grade of field marshal, the highest rank in the British Army.

But the Auk had been given one assignment too many. When India and Pakistan broke up in 1947–1948, he was placed in charge of establishing both their armies. Personally, he disapproved of the breakup between the two countries and considered it dishonorable of Britain (and Lord Louis Mountbatten) to accede to it. When he retired from the Army, therefore, he refused the peerage that all the other top generals had accepted. His wife having left him, he retired to Marrakech and lived alone for twenty-three years. Around the town he was known with respect as *Le Marechal*, but he was so low on resources that a wealthy American military history buff and philanthropist personally contributed much to his upkeep.[9]

After a short time, Woody and I decided that we were overstaying. The field marshal made no protest at our leaving. The visit provided me with nothing to contribute to my book, but I considered it a privilege just to visit this great man. It started me thinking about the wisdom of the British government in making the most of the services of a remarkable man such as Auchinleck. But I could not understand how the government could allow one of its best and most principled commanders to wind up in such hard circumstances. To me the Auk personified what Rudyard Kipling had meant in his celebrated poem "If." Auchinleck certainly achieved Kipling's ideal: "If you can meet with Triumph and Disaster / And treat these two impostors just the same."

## The Diamond in the Rough:
## Lieutenant General Reuben E. Jenkins

Soldiers in combat who are recovering from the shock of losing comrades tend to be touchy. It is not surprising, therefore, that troops of the 7th Infantry Division greeted the commanding general of IX Corps, Lieutenant General Reuben E. Jenkins, coolly. They were dismayed when the general dismounted from his helicopter carrying the body of a fox he had shot from his chopper. Expecting admiration, he found it hardly forthcoming. He did not realize that the unit was mourning the loss of a couple of men. That story, whether accurate or not, spread around, and Jenkins was for a while an unpopular man.

Shortly thereafter, the staff of the 3d Infantry Division, located at Kumwha, on the eastern shoulder of the Chorwon Valley, was notified that the

9. When Woody made the appointment the day before, the sergeant intimated that a gift of a bottle of scotch was always welcome from visitors.

corps commander was coming for a visit and a briefing. Despite the general's reputation, we gave the matter little thought.

It was about April, as I recall, and we had a small piece of good news to give. The Chinese Communist Forces had hit a battalion of the 7th Infantry on a position we called the "Boomerang," which lay beneath the Chinese-occupied Papa-San, or, more formally, Hill 1062. The attack had been handily repulsed, and as briefing officer, I may have gloated a bit that it had been a "good action."

To my surprise, my presentation was interrupted sharply by Jenkins. "Many get away?" he roared. I could not answer; I did not know. "Did ANYBODY get away?" he continued. Again, I had no idea.

"How many artillery rounds did you shoot at them?" I knew the answer to that one: eleven hundred artillery rounds, a mixture of light and medium.

"Your men were hit by a Chinese battalion, and you fired only eleven hundred rounds?"

"Our available supply rate [ASR]," I replied, "is eleven hundred rounds."[10]

Jenkins stood up abruptly. Turning on the division artillery commander, he shouted, "Don't talk to me about ASRs when you're attacked! If you get hit in battalion strength, call for all the goddamn artillery the Corps will give you, and NOBODY gets away!" With those words Jenkins stomped out of the tent and left, the briefing over.[11]

It was a minor episode. It was, however, significant. Rube Jenkins kept his word. From then on, when our front was attacked, we called for all the artillery that the corps would give us, and we thought it was noticeable that attacks on the 3d Division position became less and less frequent.

We heard little from General Jenkins for quite a while, but when we did, it was in connection with an episode that I will never forget.

As the spring of 1953 moved into summer, the new Eisenhower administration in Washington was experiencing success in bringing the Korean War to an end. By June it appeared that a truce was about to be signed. This situation suited everyone except Syngman Rhee, the president of South Korea, who was violently opposed to any such truce. To prevent its consummation, Rhee released twenty-five thousand Chinese and North Korean prisoners and turned them out onto the streets of Seoul. Such an

10. The available supply rate was an arbitrary figure designed by Division Artillery to conserve artillery ammunition when times were considered relatively quiet.

11. The 3d Division staff was resentful, but principally for an odd reason. We thought that Jenkins should have turned his wrath on George W. Smythe, the division commander, not on Osborne, the artillery commander. Smythe was responsible.

act was in violation of our understandings with the Communists, who dearly wanted those prisoners back. So there went prospects of an immediate truce. In the meantime, it became apparent that any attacks the Communists made on UN Forces were concentrated on ROK divisions, supposedly as punishment to Rhee, rather than on American.

On the morning of July 13, this situation came to a head. Word came to us at 3d Division that the UN front had been ruptured by an all-out Chinese attack at Kumsong, about thirty miles to our east. Just by chance the division was preparing to turn over our sector at Kumwha to the 2d Division; in fact, two regiments, the 15th and 65th, were already loaded up on trucks. But this was a true emergency. Several Chinese armies had broken through the Capitol ROK Division, Rhee's best, temporarily destroying it as a fighting unit and blasting a big hole in the front. This was in Jenkins's territory, and he sent us a message that morning that the 3d Division would be going to Kumsong, not into reserve.

The Capitol ROK sector had been in an uncomfortable area. No roads ran up from the rear to the position. The sector consisted of cross-compartments: three roads started out from the division left flank and then ran east-west, parallel to each other, at about six thousand yards apart. The northernmost road (call it "A") had been the line of contact. Along the next road, "B," were stretched the regimental command posts and some light artillery. The southernmost road, "C," held the Cap ROK command post and some batteries of medium artillery (or so I recall it).

Major General Eugene Ridings, division commander, was forced to give his regimental commanders a simple order. They were to keep the trucks and head for Kumsong. At Hill 604 they were to take the right branch onto Road "C." At points of their own choosing, the two regiments were to dismount and start climbing the precipitous hills northward and occupy positions on Road B—if the Communists did not get in the way. Ridings drew three X's on the map. The 15th Infantry was to occupy the right position between the middle and the most distant X. The 65th was to occupy positions between the middle X and the division west flank. That was all. "Move out."

As division intelligence officer, charged with finding out what was going on, I easily secured the permission of the division chief of staff, Edwin Burba, and headed eastward by helicopter. Making sure that I followed Road C, I soon located the command post of the Cap ROK Division and on entering was surprised to see that both General Maxwell Taylor, commanding Eighth Army, and Reuben Jenkins, of IX Corps, had preceded me. They were in close conference, but when we talked we could tell each other little; I did not know how soon the two regiments of the 3d Division would arrive, and they did not know the location of the front lines. It appeared, however, that the Communist attack had slowed.

In the early afternoon, General Ridings and a couple of staff officers arrived on the scene, and the headquarters commandant set up a small tactical command post. About dusk, as I recall, the first elements of the 15th Infantry arrived, dismounted, and headed north up the hills in a pouring rainstorm. General Taylor left for Eighth Army headquarters, but Rube Jenkins stayed for the night.

That was the only night in a year in Korea that I slept with my boots on. However, by about three in the morning we began to receive word that the infantry was meeting no resistance as the various battalions approached Road B, and many were making contact between them. By morning it was established that the Communists had stopped at Road B. They had been halted, we surmised, by paucity of supplies in that roadless country. They may also have been discouraged by the actions of our 64th Tank Battalion, which found itself facing an enemy lacking any antitank protection. (The commander later termed it a "turkey shoot.") By midmorning we knew we were safe. We settled into defensive positions, and less than two weeks later, on July 27, 1955, a truce was signed at Panmunjom, a truce that has lasted fifty-five years.

The episode was frightening, but it was over quickly. One thing I was aware of, however: Rube Jenkins had spent the whole night in that exposed position at the Cap ROK CP. It was an act of bravery that was totally unnecessary. My admiration for him grew by leaps and bounds.

The war over, those of us who had enough rotation points returned home. In September 1953 I assumed command of the 1st Battalion, 30th Infantry, located at Fort Benning, Georgia. One day in the spring of 1954, word came that my battalion would participate in the retirement parade of Lieutenant General Reuben E. Jenkins. The evening before the parade, a group gathered at the Officers Club for a send-off dinner. This was my only chance ever to talk to the general personally. I finally admitted, "You know, General, I didn't expect to survive that night of July 14 at Kumsong."

He did not hesitate. "Neither did I," he said.

The next morning I stood out in front of my battalion for the last parade for Lieutenant General Rube Jenkins. As he reviewed the troops, standing in his jeep, he passed only about twenty feet from the spot where I stood at parade rest. Rube, unconventional as always, looked at me, smiled broadly, and waved. By regulations I could do nothing to respond except grin broadly.

I never saw Rube Jenkins again.

# Bibliography

Astor, Gerald. *Terrible Terry Allen.* New York: Ballantine Books, 2003.

Atkinson, Rick. *An Army at Dawn.* New York: Henry Holt, 2002.

Barlow, Jeffrey G. *The Revolt of the Admirals.* Washington, D.C.: Naval Historical Center, 1994.

Bradley, Omar N. *A Soldier's Story.* New York: Henry Holt, 1951.

Bryant, Arthur. *The Turn of the Tide.* Garden City, N.Y.: Doubleday, 1957.

Chandler, Alfred E., Jr., et al. *The Papers of Dwight D. Eisenhower.* Vol. 1. Baltimore: Johns Hopkins University Press, 1970.

Churchill, Winston S. *The Second World War.* Vol. 2. Boston: Houghton Mifflin, 1950.

Clark, Mark W. *Calculated Risk.* New York: Harper and Brothers, 1950.

Coffman, Edward M. *The Old Army.* New York: Oxford University Press. 1985.

D'Este, Carlo. *World War II in the Mediterranean, 1942–1945.* Chapel Hill: Algonquin Books, 1990.

Eisenhower, Dwight D. *At Ease: Stories I Tell to Friends.* Garden City, N.Y.: Doubleday, 1967.

——. *Crusade in Europe.* Garden City, N.Y.: Doubleday, 1948.

——. *Mandate for Change.* Garden City, N.Y.: Doubleday, 1963.

——. *Waging Peace.* Garden City, N.Y.: Doubleday, 1965.

Eisenhower, John S. D. *Allies.* Garden City, N.Y.: Doubleday, 1982.

——. *The Bitter Woods.* New York: G. P. Putnam's Sons, 1969.

——. *General Ike.* New York: Free Press, 2003.

——. *Intervention.* New York: W. W. Norton, 1993.

——. *Strictly Personal.* Garden City, N.Y.: Doubleday, 1974.

——. *They Fought at Anzio.* Columbia: University of Missouri Press, 2007.

——. *Yanks.* New York: Free Press, 2001.

Fechert, Charles A. *Mencken: A Study of His Thoughts.* New York: Alfred A. Knopf, 1978.

Frank, Richard B. "The MacArthur No One Knew." *World War II Magazine,* September 2007.

Halberstam, David. *The Best and the Brightest.* New York: Random House, 1969.

Jeffers, H. Paul. *In the Rough Rider's Shadow: The Story of a War Hero, Theodore Roosevelt, Jr.* New York: Ballantine Books, 2002.

Keegan, John. *The First World War.* New York: Alfred A. Knopf, 1999.

Knickerbocker, H. R., et al. *Danger Forward: The Story of the First Division in World War II.* Washington, D.C.: Society of the First Division, 1946.

Manchester, William. *American Caesar.* Boston: Little, Brown, 1978.

Marshall, George. *My Services in the World War, 1917–1918.* Boston: Houghton Mifflin, 1976.

Moorman, Frank. Obituary of General Ridgway. *Assembly Magazine,* March 1994.

Neal, Steve. *Harry and Ike: The Partnership That Remade the Postwar World.* New York: Simon and Schuster, 2001.

Nixon, Richard M. *Six Crises.* Garden City, N.Y.: Doubleday, 1962.

Patton, George S., Jr. *The Patton Papers.* Vol. 2, *1940–1945.* Ed. Martin Blumenson. Boston: Houghton Mifflin, 1974.

——. *War as I Knew It.* Ed. Paul D. Harkins. Boston: Houghton Mifflin, 1947.

Pendar, Kenneth. *Adventure in Diplomacy: Our French Dilemma.* New York: Dodd, Mead, 1945.

Pogue, Forrest C. *George C. Marshall.* Vol. 3, *Organizer of Victory, 1943–1945.* New York: Viking Press, 1973.

Reynolds, Quentin. *The Curtain Rises.* New York: Random House, 1944.

Ridgway, Matthew B. *Soldier: The Memoirs of Matthew B. Ridgway.* As told to Harold H. Martin. New York: Harper and Brothers, 1956.

Ryan, Cornelius. *A Bridge Too Far.* New York: Simon and Schuster, 1974.

——. *The Longest Day: June 6, 1944.* New York: Simon and Schuster, 1959.

Shawcross, William. *Sideshow: Kissinger, Nixon, and the Destruction of Cambodia.* New York: Simon and Schuster, 1979.

Slim, Field Marshal Sir William. *Defeat into Victory.* London, Landsbury Publications. First published by Cassell, 1956.

Truscott, Lucian K., Jr. *Command Missions.* New York: E. P. Dutton, 1954.

*The West Point 1915 HOWITZER.* Yearbook.

Wheeler, James Scott. *The Big Red One.* Lawrence: University Press of Kansas, 2007.

# Index